THE AMERICAN NATION
A HISTORY

FROM ORIGINAL SOURCES BY ASSOCIATED SCHOLARS

EDITED BY

ALBERT BUSHNELL HART, LL.D.
PROFESSOR OF HISTORY IN HARVARD UNIVERSITY

ADVISED BY
VARIOUS HISTORICAL SOCIETIES

THE AMERICAN NATION
A HISTORY

LIST OF AUTHORS AND TITLES

GROUP I
FOUNDATIONS OF THE NATION

GROUP II
TRANSFORMATION INTO A NATION

GROUP V

NATIONAL EXPANSION

COMMITTEES ORIGINALLY APPOINTED TO ADVISE AND CONSULT WITH THE EDITOR

THE MASSACHUSETTS HISTORICAL SOCIETY

Charles Francis Adams, LL.D., President
Samuel A. Green, M.D., Vice-President
James Ford Rhodes, LL.D., 2d Vice-President
Edward Channing, Ph.D., Prof. History Harvard University
Worthington C. Ford, Chief of Division of MSS., Library of Congress

THE WISCONSIN HISTORICAL SOCIETY

Reuben G. Thwaites, LL.D., Secretary and Superintendent
Frederick J. Turner, Ph.D., Prof. of American History, Wisconsin University
James D. Butler, LL.D., formerly Prof. Wisconsin University
William W. Wight, President
Henry E. Legler, Curator

THE VIRGINIA HISTORICAL SOCIETY

William Gordon McCabe, Litt D., President
Lyon G. Tyler, LL.D., Pres. of William and Mary College
Judge David C. Richardson
J. A. C. Chandler, Professor Richmond College
Edward Wilson James

THE TEXAS HISTORICAL SOCIETY

Judge John Henninger Reagan, President
George P. Garrison, Ph.D., Prof. of History, University of Texas
Judge C. W. Raines
Judge Zachary T. Fullmore

Woodrow Wilson

THE AMERICAN NATION: A HISTORY

VOLUME 27

NATIONAL PROGRESS

1907–1917

BY

FREDERIC AUSTIN OGG, Ph.D.

PROFESSOR OF POLITICAL SCIENCE
UNIVERSITY OF WISCONSIN

WITH MAPS

NEW YORK AND LONDON
HARPER & BROTHERS PUBLISHERS

TO
MY WIFE.

CONTENTS

CONTENTS

MAPS

EDITOR'S INTRODUCTION

TO write a critical and balanced narrative of recent times is always a difficult task. In the first place, the materials for judging the character and motives of men are imperfect; for reputations of political leaders wax and wane rapidly in their own lifetimes; and the intimate personal documents and letters, which are the breath of life to the historical writer, commonly appear only after the person to whom they refer has passed off the stage. In the second place, the significance of events undergoes a change; many debates, controversies, discussions, investigations and laws, which absorb the attention for the time being, may a few decades later shrink into forgetfulness. It is a hard matter to seize upon events and issues as they pass and be sure that they are vital things in which later generations will be interested. In the third place, it is hard for a writer to fix on the live point of view which will bring into focus what the people of to-day are really contributing to their own upbuilding.

These difficulties have been faced and so far as possible vanquished, in Professor Ogg's *National Progress*. He has made use of a wealth of material, the extent of which is revealed by the foot-notes and also by the

Critical Essay on Authorities at the end of the volume, which is a convenient brief selection of the books and official material which are most helpful upon the history of the last decade.   The few autobiographies and critical biographies have been used so far as they go; but the main material is newspapers, periodicals, government reports and a large number of special works on limited fields.   Part of the author's results are stated in the useful maps.

The topics chosen for discussion are assembled in the table of contents.   The decade since 1907 has been one of very active political and public life; hence a chapter is devoted to each of the three presidential elections in the period, and several other chapters to the changes in political methods and in the machinery of government.   Outside of these, the main theme of the first part of the volume is the effort of State governments and especially of the National Government to settle the great economic and industrial questions such as the tariff, corporations, railroads, banks, conservation, labor, and immigration.   The principal subject of the latter half of the book is the foreign relations of the United States, in other parts of the two Americas, in Asia, and then in the Great War.   Chapters XVIII, XIX, and XXI make up a concise history of the relations of the United States to that struggle, from its beginning to the declaration of war by Congress.

The point of view selected by Professor Ogg throughout is the necessity of an understanding between the great money power of the United States and the great democracy; and the continuous effort of the Federal

Government to solve this problem in peace and justice. With this is closely connected the growing consciousness that the nation must stand forth as a world power with world responsibilities.

The narrative is careful and full, the arrangement such as to aid the reader. The book furnishes to the reader accurate and well-selected knowledge, and at the same time brings the complicated issues of the period into a judicious whole.

Government to solve this problem in peace and wartime. With this is closely connected the growing conscious- ness that the nation must stand forth as a world power with world responsibilities.

The narrative is careful and full, the arrangements such as to aid the reader. The book furnishes to the reader accurate and well-selected knowledge, and at the same time brings the complicated issues of the period into a judicious whole.

AUTHOR'S PREFACE

WRITTEN in days when war clouds lowered ever more darkly upon the nation's horizon, this book deals with the most significant and critical period in American history since the Civil War; and yet, had there been no war in Europe, or had that conflict met early expectation by coming to an end within six months or a year, or had the United States been able honorably to keep from going into the struggle, the decade (1907–1917) whose events are here chronicled would still have stood out in high relief. For it was a time of national restlessness and awakening, of sharp reaction against the old order in business, politics, and government which was fastened upon the preoccupied and unsuspecting nation in the great epoch of material prosperity from the late seventies to 1890.

The predominating characteristics of that old order were the rise of powerful industrial and commercial corporations; control of government by these corporations rather than by the people; shaping public policies and decisions of public questions under the impetus of business considerations, with only now and then a touch of idealism; prevalence of and indif-

I

ference to corruption; smug materialism **which saw**
little to be aimed at or hoped for save immediate well-
being, measurable in dollars and cents. The reaction
set in slowly in the first Roosevelt administration; in
the second it gathered momentum and achieved important results; under Taft it lagged, at least within
government circles; under Wilson it swept on irresistibly, forcing vested interests under rigorous control, pouring light into darkened corners, and opening
the way for more direct and effective popular rule.
Incident to the movement was the temporary collapse
of the governing party, the rise of the largest third
party since the Civil War, and the elevation to power
of a party which since the days of Buchanan had been
in a position to manage the nation's affairs during
only two brief periods. It is the transformation in
the mutual attitudes of business and government, and
therefore in the factors which determine public policy
—together with the swift changes in party fortunes—
that forms the principal theme of this book.

A second main fact of the decade is the steady extension of the nation's foreign interests and the tendency to take a bolder part in world politics in both
of the hemispheres. The influences of the Spanish
war and of other world events in the same period in
this direction have been sufficiently brought out in a
preceding volume, Professor Latané's *America as a
World Power*. It was with reluctance, and only after
all other expedients had been exhausted, that Congress, by resolution of April 4–6, 1917, declared a
state of war with the Imperial German **Government.**

In doing so, however, it not merely took an imperative step in defense of the national honor; it gave the nation a position in world affairs to which the events of a score of years had been inevitably leading. The logical move was made. What shall come after lies in the lap of the gods.

As the editor of the series has pointed out, the writing of contemporary history is beset with difficulties. Many important materials, especially official and private correspondence, are not available; bewildering masses of detail lie awaiting sifting and interpretation; perspective upon permanent lines is impossible of attainment; and despite one's best efforts to assume a detached view-point, judgments of events and persons are likely to be open to a suspicion of partisanship. Still, the attempt is worth while. The sifting and digesting process must begin some time, and there are reasons why its beginning should not be long postponed. Furthermore, organized information about the times in which one has lived, such as is very properly desired by intelligent men and women, cannot readily be had from newspapers, magazines, and other fleeting sources.

Hence it becomes the function of a book of the present type to perform for the reader and student the task of bringing together facts which are widely scattered, winnowing them, and building them into a compact record of the significant actions and achievements of the period covered. It should seek to serve the future historian by putting the crude materials of the hour to the first necessary tests of authenticity,

sequence, and causal relation. It may even venture
a certain amount of definitive interpretation.

In the search for materials and the verification of
data I have been aided by numerous officials of the
State, Treasury, and Interior Departments, the Interstate Commerce Commission, the Civil Service Commission, the Pan-American Union, and the Bureau of
Railway Economics. I desire, further, to express appreciation of courtesies extended me by the authorities and attendants of the Library of Congress, the
New York Public Library, the Columbia University
Library, and the Library of the State Historical Society of Wisconsin.

FREDERIC AUSTIN OGG.

NATIONAL PROGRESS

NATIONAL PROGRESS

CHAPTER I

THE ELECTION OF 1908

(1907–1908)

UNDER the American system of balanced government, national elections fall at fixed intervals, regardless of the condition of public affairs or the state of public feeling. It follows that electoral contests are often forced, devoid of real issues, and barren of significant results. The campaigns of 1896 and 1900 turned on important questions and led to weighty decisions. But the contest of 1904 was a drab affair; and so was that of 1908, except that it became the starting-point of a new and tempestuous epoch in the country's political life.

The chief concern of the people as the second Roosevelt administration passed into its final year was not elections, but recovery from the business depression produced by the panic of the closing weeks of 1907. Opinion as to the causes of that disaster was divided, but not clearly on party lines. Outside of Wall Street

fair-minded men were ready to admit that the Administration could not be held responsible; no great campaign issue could therefore be got out of it. Vast
national questions loomed on the horizon: tariff revision, currency reform, railroad and trust regulation,
readjustment of the legal status of organized labor,
extension of the principles of direct government. But
the two great parties were not ready to push them.
Their conscious differences were as yet upon matters
of emphasis and detail; on the big issues their minds
were not made up. Only the inborn American love
of politics keeps an electoral campaign under these
conditions from falling utterly flat.

The first phase of the contest to excite public interest was the attitude of Roosevelt toward a third
term. On the night following his election in November, 1904, the President issued a statement to the
effect that he considered himself then to be serving
his first term; that "the wise custom which limits the
President to two terms regards the substance and not
the form"; and that "under no circumstances" would
he be "a candidate for or accept another nomination."[1]
Until the second administration was far advanced, the
country took this declaration to be conclusive.

With the approach of election year many observers
became convinced that the Republican convention
would be stampeded for the President, and that he
would be nominated and re-elected in spite of himself.
The financial world, and certain railroad and industrial
interests, felt bitterly toward him; but among the

[1] *Review of Reviews*, XXX., 646.

masses his popularity was still extraordinary and knew
no bounds of party. There was no Republican name
like his to conjure with, and it seemed doubtful whether
any other man could be depended on to defeat the
probable Democratic candidate, William J. Bryan.
State and local leaders felt that the President's name
at the head of their ticket would be a mighty asset;
and in several states plans were laid to call early conventions which should choose delegates pledged to his
renomination.   The third-term movement was fast
advancing when, December 11, 1907, a statement was
given out from the White House calling attention
to the announcement of 1904, and asserting crisply that
the President had not changed, and would not change,
the determination voiced therein.[1]   The decision
was at last accepted as final, and interest shifted to the
claims of other actual or possible candidates.

At all stages of the pre-convention campaign the
most prominent of these candidates was the Secretary
of War, William H. Taft of Ohio. After serving two
years on the supreme bench of his state, and three
years as Solicitor-General of the United States, Mr.
Taft, in 1892, was made a United States circuit judge.
In 1900 President McKinley appointed him chairman
of the Second Philippine Commission; and on July
4, 1901, he was inaugurated first civil governor of the
Philippines. To an enviable reputation as lawyer and
judge was now added renown as a sympathetic and far-
seeing administrator. Called home early in 1904 to
succeed Elihu Root as Secretary of War, he became

[1] *Review of Reviews*, XXXVII., 4.

one of the most stalwart supporters of the second
Roosevelt administration.[1] From an early date it was
known that the President looked on him with favor
as a successor; and in the early months of 1908 it
was charged that the White House was using undue
influence, mainly through federal office-holders, to
bring about the Secretary's nomination. Roosevelt
entered vigorous denial, but criticism was not silenced.
Other men suggested for the nomination were Governor
Hughes of New York, Governor Cummins of Iowa,
Vice-President Fairbanks, Speaker Cannon, Senator
Knox of Pennsylvania, and Senator La Follette of
Wisconsin. No one of them rose above the level of
a "favorite son."

On the Democratic side the nomination of William
J. Bryan, candidate of the party in 1896 and 1900, was
foreordained. The fiasco of 1904, when the candidate
was an eastern conservative barely known to his own
state, made it clear that the nominee in 1908 must be
a western and well-known radical. More closely than
any one else, Bryan fitted this description. His campaign for the nominaton in 1908 began as soon as
Parker was nominated in 1904. He card-indexed the
country; lectured before Chautuaqua assemblies on
every circuit; sent his newspaper, the *Commoner*, over
all the rural routes; kept informed through correspondents with the politics of every neighborhood.
The honors received on a trip around the world in
1905–1906 were duly "played up" by a friendly press,

[1] Wellman, "Taft Trained to be President," *Review of Reviews*,
XXXVII., 675-682.

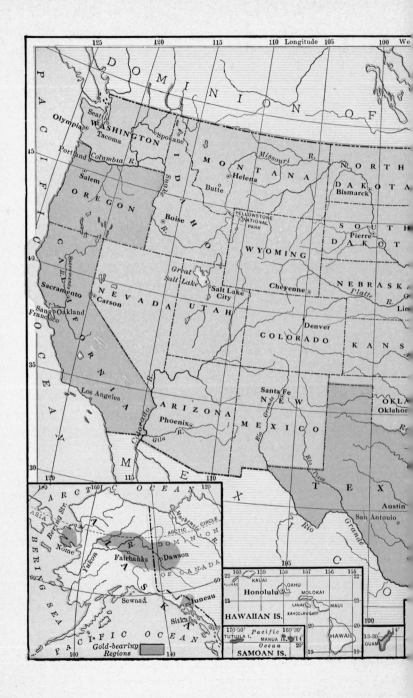

UNITED STATES
1917

Original States
States Admitted 1791-1860
States Admitted 1861-1917
Organized Territories 1917
Unorganized Territories 1917

C A N A D A

L. SUPERIOR

WISCONSIN

St. Paul

Milwaukee

Madison

Chicago

I O W A

Moines

L. MICHIGAN

Grand Rapids

Lansing

Detroit

L. HURON

L. ONTARIO

L. ERIE

Part of Massachusetts until 1820

MAINE

Augusta

Portland

Montpelier

VT.

N.H.

Concord

Rochester

Syracuse

Buffalo

Albany

NEW YORK

Boston

MASS.

Worcester

Hartford

CONN.

Providence

R.I.

New Haven

Bridgeport

Newark

New York

Toledo

Cleveland

PENNSYLVANIA

Harrisburg

Reading

Scranton

NEW JERSEY

Trenton

Philadelphia

Camden

ILLINOIS

Fort Wayne

OHIO

Pittsburgh

Columbus

Dayton

Cincinnati

INDIANA

Springfield

Indianapolis

Baltimore

MD.

Annapolis

Dover

Delaware B.

WASHINGTON

W. VA. Part of Va. until 1863

Charleston

then a separate State

ILLINOIS

St. Louis

Jefferson

MISSOURI

Frankfort

Louisville

KENTUCKY

Part of Virginia from 1776 to 1792

Nashville

TENNESSEE

Chattanooga

Memphis

Ohio R.

Cumberland R.

Tennessee R.

VIRGINIA

Richmond

Norfolk

Raleigh

NORTH CAROLINA

Wilmington

ARKANSAS

Little Rock

Birmingham

ALABAMA

Montgomery

Mobile

Jackson

LOUISIANA

Baton Rouge

New Orleans

MISSISSIPPI

Atlanta

GEORGIA

Savannah

SOUTH CAROLINA

Columbia

Charleston

Savannah R.

Pensacola

Tallahassee

FLORIDA

Galveston

GULF OF MEXICO

ATLANTIC OCEAN

15

40

35

30

25

PANAMA CANAL AND CANAL ZONE

REPUBLIC OF

Panama

Colon

Canal

CANAL ZONE

LIMIT OF CANAL ZONE

PANAMA

Caribbean Sea

Pacific Ocean

90

80

NICARAGUA

Caribbean Sea

LITTLE CORN I.

GREAT CORN I.

PHILIPPINE IS.

116 120 124

South China Sea

LUZON

Manila

MINDORO

Pacific Ocean

16

12

PALAWAN

PANAY

SAMAR

Sulu Sea

MINDANAO

BORNEO

Celebes Sea

8

116 120 124

Atlantic Ocean

San Juan

PORTO RICO

ST. THOMAS

ST. JOHN

VIRGIN IS.

Charlotte Amalie

ST. CROIX

Caribbean Sea

66

18

and the dramatic possibilities of the home-coming were
not overlooked. By 1908 the candidate's hold on his
party was absolute, both in the sense that the party
machinery in most of the states was obedient to his
will and in the sense that he had a vast, idolizing personal following whose votes could be transferred to
no other person. Two classes of Democrats supported him—those who wanted him and those who
accepted him because they had to. The former chiefly
dwelt in the Mississippi Valley and on the plains of the
Great West; the latter were to be found mainly east
of the Alleghanies.

Other Democrats mentioned for the nomination
were Governor John A. Johnson of Minnesota, Judge
George Gray of Delaware, and Judson Harmon of
Ohio. Johnson was a moderate; Gray and Harmon
were decided conservatives. William R. Hearst,
founder and sponsor of the Independence League,
caused some anxiety by setting up the standard of
revolt. But the nomination of Bryan, to meet the
expected nomination of Taft by the Republicans, was
never really in doubt. In an article written for the
New York *Times* a few days before his death (June
24), ex-President Cleveland declared that in a contest
between Taft and Bryan Taft would win. But the
party was not convinced.

The Republican national convention assembled at
Chicago June 16. Flags waved; spectators thronged
the streets and packed the galleries; frock-coated
statesmen harangued the assemblage in true convention style. But the proceedings were as spiritless as

in 1904; for again the guiding influences flowed from the Administration and the real work was done in advance. For several months Arthur Vorys of Ohio and Frank H. Hitchcock, formerly First Assistant Postmaster-General, had carried on a vigorous campaign for the election of Taft delegates, and before the convention opened the Secretary's nomination was a certainty.

In making up the temporary roll, the National Committee passed upon contests involving 223 seats, claimed mainly by rival delegations from southern states. The decisions did not affect the outcome, but they became a precedent in 1912. The total number of delegates was 980; the number of votes required to nominate was 491; and Taft received on the first ballot ʋ2, the remainder being scattered among a half-dozen favorite sons.[1] Among persons mentioned for the vice-presidency were Governor Hughes (who refused to permit his name to be used), Governor Curtis Guild of Massachusetts, ex-Governor Franklin Murphy of New Jersey, Senator Dolliver of Iowa, and Vice-President Fairbanks. For strategic reasons, the second place on the ticket was put at the disposal of the delegation from New York, whose choice fell on James S. Sherman, member of Congress for upwards of twenty years from the Utica district.

Party platforms may generally be ignored as having little effect on public policy. The Chicago platform of 1908, however, derives interest from its unconscious

[1] Fourteenth Republican National Convention, *Official Report of Proceedings*, 182.

prophecy of the coming nation-wide controversy in
Republican ranks.[1] Fully approved in advance by
President Roosevelt and Secretary Taft, the instrument lauded the Administration and pledged the party
to the continuance *en bloc* of present policies. There
it might have stopped. For the question before the
voters was simply whether they wanted four years
more of the kind of administrative control under which
they were living. Several subjects, however, were
taken up in the customary detail.

Protectionist doctrine was reaffirmed, but the party
was pledged to a revision of the existing tariff schedules "by a special session of Congress immediately
following the inauguration of the next President." [2]
Somewhat indefinite promise was made of a currency
system "responding to our greater needs and possess-
ing increased elasticity and adaptability." The Sherman anti-trust law was to be amended so as to give
the government more control over corporations having
"power and opportunity to effect monopolies"; the
interstate commerce law was to be strengthened to
give control over issues of railroad stocks and bonds.
In the proposal that "no injunction or temporary restraining order should be issued without notice, except
where irremediable injury would result from delay,"
labor leaders who had been seeking relief from the
power of the courts to issue injunctions in labor disputes found cold comfort.

[1] Fourteenth Republican National Convention, *Official Report of
Proceedings*, 115–125; *Republican Campaign Text-Book*, 1908, pp. 461–
467.

[2] *Republican Campaign Text-Book*, 1908, p. 462.

The Democratic convention met at Denver, July
7-10. The spectator would hardly have surmised
that it was the gathering of a party that had been
out of power for fifteen years. The physical sur-
roundings lent the occasion particular buoyancy, and
neither delegates nor spectators gave any evidence of
depression of spirit. Bands met arriving delegations
and gave "travelling concerts" on the street-cars at
night. Cowboys, cowgirls, and Indians specially cos-
tumed staged fancy exhibitions of "bronco-busting."
Tons of snow were brought down from the mountains
and heaped in the streets for the delectation of the
city's guests. Vari-colored lights by night and acres
of bunting by day kept the down-town districts aglow.

The work of the convention seemed more spontaneous
than that of the Chicago gathering, but in fact it, too,
was prearranged. The nomination of Bryan was assured; control by Bryan and his aides was complete;
the platform showed at every point the Bryan impress; even the unprecedented "demonstrations" for
the Nebraskan, lasting on two occasions more than an
hour, bore appearance of having been carefully calculated. The total number of delegates was 1,008,
and the number of votes necessary to nominate, under
the two-thirds rule, was 672. On the first ballot Bryan
received 892½ votes, the remainder being divided between Governor Johnson and Judge Gray.[1] Many
persons, among them Governor Folk of Missouri, were
considered for the vice-presidency. In the end, the

[1] Democratic National Convention of 1908, *Official Report of Proceedings*, 248.

nomination went to an Indiana lawyer, John W. Kern, who was Bryan's preference. The nominee lacked distinction, but the vote of his state was considered indispensable.

The Denver platform was packed with vote-catching clauses.[1] It was the platform, furthermore, of a party long out of power, ready to denounce freely and to promise lavishly, because it had lost the habit of accountability. The tariff plank was explicit in asserting that "articles entering into competition with trust-controlled products should be placed upon the free list and material reductions should be made in the tariff upon the necessities of life, especially upon articles competing with such American manufactures as are sold abroad more cheaply than at home; and gradual reductions should be made in such other schedules as may be necessary to restore the tariff to a revenue basis." [2]

The currency was handled more cautiously; but the party pledged itself to compel national banks to establish a guaranty fund for the protection of their depositors. The planks on trusts and railways, embodying peculiarly the ideas of Bryan, displayed a curious mixture of Jeffersonian individualism, state's rights, and federal paternalism. "A private monopoly," it was asserted, "is indefensible and intolerable. We, therefore, favor the vigorous reform of the criminal law against guilty trust magnates and officials,

[1] Democratic National Convention of 1908, *Official Report of Proceedings*, pp. 159–174; *Democratic Campaign Text-Book*, 1908, pp. 220–227.
[2] *Democratic Campaign Text-Book*, 1908, p. 222.

and demand the enactment of such additional legislation as may be necessary to make it impossible for
a private monopoly to exist in the United States." [1]
Three specific remedies were advocated: (1) a law preventing the duplication of directors among competing
corporations; (2) a federal license system; (3) a law
compelling licensed corporations to sell to all purchasers in all parts of the country on the same terms. [2]

At Denver, as at Chicago, the only really perplexing
problem of the platform-makers was injunctions. In
the hope of satisfying labor without at the same time
confirming people of conservative cast in the belief
that Bryan was a visionary and a firebrand, the resolutions committee toiled through two days; and the
resulting plank was a model of guarded language.
Only after proclaiming the courts to be "the bulwarks
of our liberties" and declaring that the Democratic
party yielded to none in the purpose to maintain their
dignity, was the opinion ventured that "injunctions
should not be issued in any cases in which the injunctions would not issue if no industrial dispute were
involved." [3] Jury trial in cases of indirect contempt
was advocated, and the party pledged itself to an eight-
hour day on all government work, a general employers'
liability act, and the establishment of a "department of
labor, represented separately in the President's cabinet."

Of the five minor parties that put tickets in the field,
four had participated in earlier campaigns. The

---

[1] *Democratic Campaign Text-Book*, 1908, p. 224.
[2] *Ibid.*, pp. 222–223.
[3] *Ibid.*, p. 224.

Populists, with vitality fast oozing, nominated Thomas
E. Watson of Georgia. The Socialists named a can-
didate of other days, Eugene V. Debs of Indiana.
The Socialist Labor group put up August Gillhaus of
New York. The Prohibitionists nominated Eugene
W. Chafin of Illinois. The newcomer was Hearst's
Independence Party, sprung from the Independence
League, which in late years had been active in the
politics of Massachusetts, New York, California, and
some other states.[1] In convention at Chicago, it refused to give Bryan its support and nominated Thomas
L. Hisgen of Massachusetts. Its sole reason for
existence was to protest against the conservatism of
the dominant elements in the major parties. Yet its
platform contained little that did not appear in the
program of one or the other of these parties.[2]

After his nomination, Taft retired from the War
Department, being succeeded by Luke E. Wright of
Tennessee; and throughout the summer he remained
in Cincinnati, receiving political visitors at the home
of his brother Charles. On'y near the end of September did he take the stump, first in the Middle West
and later in the East and in the northern tier of southern states; and the Republican campaign, as planned
by the chairman, Frank H. Hitchcock, was concentrated in the last four weeks preceding the election.[3]
Democratic activities were directed by Chairman

<hr/>

[1] *Review of Reviews*, XXXVII., 582–585.

[2] The platforms of the minor parties are printed in the *World Almanac*,
1908, pp. 161–167. Cf. *Review of Reviews*, XXXVIII., 293–309.

[3] Wellman, "Management of the Taft Campaign," *Review of Reviews*,
XXXVIII., 432–438.

2

Norman E. Mack of Buffalo.   From the outset it was
generally admitted that Bryan must carry New York
to be elected.   Yet the Middle West was felt to be the
principal battle-ground; and for the first time in the
party's history, central headquarters were established
in Chicago.   The Democratic campaign was under
way earlier than the Republican, and was carried on
with greater energy than that of 1904.

Still, the contest failed to stir the country.   The
politicians were active and the orators did their best
to pump up a steady flow of eloquence, but the people
did not respond.   Business interests were pressing; no
towering issues appeared; even the tariff failed to
take hold.   Neither candidate inspired a great uprising of followers.   Taft was not the sort of leader for
whom the populace tosses its hat in the air.   Bryan's
style of campaigning had lost its novelty.

Some interest was aroused, none the less, by a new
question—publicity of campaign contributions and expenditures.   For years sentiment had been steadily
rising against the lavish use of money by party organizations, and remedial legislation had been enacted
in several states.   The only federal statute on the subject (approved January 26, 1907) forbade corporations
to make contributions in federal elections.[1]   The Democratic platform of 1908 demanded publicity "above a
reasonable minimum," and at Bryan's request the
National Committee announced that no contributions
would be received from corporations; that no sum
in excess of $10,000 would be received from any indi-

[1] *U. S. Statutes at Large.* XXXV., pt. i., p. 1103.

vidual; and that all contributions exceeding $100 would be published a few days in advance of the election.

The Republican platform made no mention of the subject. Challenged by his principal opponent, Taft announced, however, that his managers would regard themselves as bound by the law of the state of New York requiring the filing of statements of campaign receipts and expenditures after the election. By this move the Republicans relieved themselves of the force of a large part of the charges against them; although their adversaries made the most of the connections of the Republican treasurer, George R. Sheldon, with Wall Street, and argued that publicity after rather than before the election missed the real point. As a matter of fact, neither party in this campaign had a large national fund; and neither pined for publicity. Subsequent congressional investigation showed that the corporations found ways to make contributions, especially to the Republican war-chest. When, shortly before the election, the Democratic managers announced contributions aggregating $248,367, they neglected to take account of offerings to state and local party agencies, although obviously such contributions might have the same effect as funds given directly to the National Committee. The most sensational feature of the campaign was the publication by Hearst of a series of letters disclosing dubious relations between the Standard Oil Company and the Democratic treasurer, Governor Haskell of Oklahoma, who was forced to give way to another man.

Until early autumn the contest seemed substantially even, and as late as the closing week of September the East was swept by a "Bryan scare." Prominent eastern Democrats—Richard Olney, Judge Gray, Judge Parker, and others—came out for the party ticket, as did influential newspapers, notably the New York *World*, which had bitterly opposed the Nebraskan's nomination. Characterizing the Republican injunction plank as "a flimsy, tricky evasion of the issue," and the Democratic plank as "good all the way through," Samuel Gompers, president of the American Federation of Labor, ignored the rule of his organization forbidding political activity, pledged the Democratic candidate his individual support, and promised to deliver, so far as possible, the two million votes of organized labor; and efforts were made to redeem the promise.[1] The action of Roosevelt, in 1907, in disbanding negro regiments under suspicion of a murderous riot at Brownsville was made the ground for an appeal to the negro vote, amounting also to about two millions.

On the other hand, it was clear that even if Bryan should win, the Senate would remain Republican and the House of Representatives would probably be almost evenly divided. Such a situation would be unfavorable to tariff revision and to other legislation which the country wanted. Furthermore, the election came too late to permit the Democrats to capitalize

[1] Hoxie, "President Gompers and the Labor Vote," *Jour. Polit. Econ.*, XVI., 693–700; Dyer, "Can Labor Boycott a Political Party," *World's Work*, XVI., 10831–10834.

the financial panic and business depression of 1907–
1908. By November, currency was again abundant,
the prices of most securities were normal, confidence
was restored, prosperity was general. The fundamental advantage of the Republicans lay, however, in
two facts. (1) They could point to a large program
of constructive legislation and administration in which
the country was deeply interested, and which it was
proposed, under a fresh lease of power, to push toward
completion. (2) While the sincerity and probity of
Bryan were recognized, the average citizen considered
Taft to be not only equally honest and far more experienced, but generally safer. The attempt of the
labor leaders to make it appear that Bryan and the
Democrats stood for workingman's rights failed, notwithstanding the attitude of the Republican candidate, who minimized the dangers of the abuse of injunctions and freely denounced the "secondary boycott" and the Democratic demand for jury trial in
prosecutions for contempt.

"The campaign closes," said the New York *Nation*,
October 29, "with the issues yet undefined and with
many thoughtful men still dubious as to the proper
way to vote." The election of Taft, however, was
virtually assured when the Vermont election of September 1 yielded a normal Republican majority. The
total number of votes cast (November 3) was 14,887,-
133, which exceeded the number cast in 1904 by the
heavy margin of 1,364,025. The vote was distributed
as follows: Taft, 7,679,006; Bryan, 6,409,106; Debs,
420,820; Chafin, 252,683; Hisgen, 83,562; Watson,

28,131; Gillhaus, 13,825.[1] The plurality of Taft over
Bryan was 1,269,900; the majority of Taft over all
other candidates was 470,879. Bryan's vote exceeded
Parker's in 1904 by 1,324,615, but he received a smaller
proportion of the total vote than in either 1896 or
1900. To the states carried by Parker—those of the
South except Missouri—Bryan added Nebraska, Colorado, and Nevada. It is to be observed, however, that
since the election of 1904 Oklahoma had been admitted
to the Union; also that the electoral vote of Maryland
in 1908 was divided between Bryan and Taft, in the
proportion of 6 to 2. The electoral vote stood: Taft,
321; Bryan, 162. Elections to the Sixty-first Congress
resulted in the choice of 219 Republicans and 172
Democrats.

The Democratic party went into the contest of 1908
with a record of fifteen years of unbroken defeat.
Never for an equal period had it been so completely
in eclipse. From the election of Lincoln to the Republican *débâcle* of 1874 was but fourteen years; and
even in that era of darkness there were years, such as
1862 and 1870, when a return of sunshine for the party
seemed imminent.

The outcome in 1908 bore the appearance of a sweeping Republican victory, and on the surface there was
little to cheer the losers. In reality, however, it was
the harbinger of a great shift of party power. Bryan
was badly beaten, but his party was not; in all parts of
the country Democratic candidates for state and local

[1] McLaughlin and Hart, *Cyclopædia of American Government*, III.,
44-45.

offices achieved great successes. Five Democratic governors were elected in states which gave Taft substantial majorities: Harmon in Ohio, Johnson in Minnesota, Marshall in Indiana, Burke in North Dakota,
and Norris in Montana. In Massachusetts the Republican governor-elect's plurality was but half as
large as Taft's, in Connecticut but one-third, in Illinois
but one-sixth. In New York Governor Hughes emerged
from the most significant state contest of the year with
a plurality of but 69,000, as compared with Taft's
200,000.

This meant an exceptional amount of independent
thinking and voting. For a decade national party lines
had been growing dimmer and the power of personality
in politics had been steadily increasing. Platforms,
acceptance speeches, and other official expressions
rapidly merged in the personality of the candidates.
The effect upon Democratic fortunes was disastrous
so long as the party's infatuation with Bryan lasted;
for the personal popularity of this leader never over-
came popular distrust in the East. In 1908 the party
still had no other leader who sounded the bugle-note.
Plainly, however, the rank and file were gathering strength, and only new leadership and a great
moral issue were needed to break the long chain of
defeats.

The election of Taft and a Republican Congress was
due not alone to the weakness of Bryan as a candidate.
Speaking broadly, the people were satisfied with the
record of the Roosevelt administration, and they saw
no reason why the Republicans should not be given

opportunity to prove the merit of the measures that
they had passed and to push their program toward
completion. Roosevelt's confidence in his chosen successor availed more than anything else to reassure the
hesitant.

CHAPTER II

CURRENCY AND TARIFF

(1907-1909)

FEW of the twenty-six successors of Washington
have brought to their high office qualifications
superior to those of Taft.   He had the training of the
lawyer, the judge, the diplomat, and the administrator.
He had deep knowledge of the American people, the
mechanism of government, and the pull and haul of
world politics.   He combined those qualities of industry, endurance, fortitude, and resilience required by
what Theodore Roosevelt has called "the hardest job
on earth."   His personality was adapted to win confidence and to conciliate opposition.   He was buoyant,
optimistic, courteous.   His good nature was prover-
bial.   In his official dealings he was imperturbable,
tactful, and patient.   His sense of justice was keen,
and his years of labor in the Philippines left him sin-
gularly free from race and class prejudices.   Less agile
physically and intellectually than Roosevelt, less likely
to fire the hearts of the people, and by no means so
good a politician, he was still capable of powerful and
sustained effort, and of astute management of men.
At the call of public duty he had sacrificed his chosen
judicial career to administrative work for which he had

no penchant; twice he had refused to abandon his
post in the Philippines to accept a long-coveted appointment to the federal supreme bench.[1]

The new Administration was installed under circumstances of unusual promise. The country expected
Taft to prove a happy medium between McKinley and
Roosevelt, with most of the strength and few of the
weaknesses of both; and it assumed that while he would
maintain the policies of the preceding administration,
the new régime would show less of the novel, the
aggressive, and the spectacular. The new occupant of
the White House could be depended upon not to get
on the nerves of sensitive people. Everybody realized
that the first great task—the revision of the tariff—
would put the majority party to a severe test; but the
outcome was viewed with a fair degree of confidence.
In his inaugural address Taft took pains specially to
approve the measures of his predecessor to curb "the
lawlessness and abuses of power of the great combinations of capital," and he promised further action to
render these reforms lasting, while avoiding alarm on
the part of persons "pursuing proper and progressive
business methods." He likewise forcefully advocated
currency legislation and tariff revision.

Contrary to general expectation, Taft chose to sur-
round himself with a group of advisers of his own
choosing. Only two of Roosevelt's heads of departments were carried over—James Wilson, the veteran

[1] Abbott, "William H. Taft," *Outlook*, LXXXVIII., 773-777; Wellman, "Taft Trained to be President," *Review of Reviews*, XXXVII.,
675-682.

Secretary of Agriculture, and George von L. Meyer, who was transferred from the Post-Office to the Navy Department. Philander C. Knox, Attorney-General of the United States in 1901–1904, and later United States senator from Pennsylvania, became Secretary of State. The remaining appointees were drawn from private life, and were not widely known. Franklin MacVeagh, a wealthy business man of Chicago, was made Secretary of the Treasury; Jacob M. Dickinson of Tennessee, Secretary of War; Frank H. Hitchcock of Washington, Postmaster-General; Richard A. Ballinger of the state of Washington, Secretary of the Interior; Charles Nagel of Missouri, Secretary of Commerce and Labor; and George W. Wickersham of New York, Attorney-General. Two of the group—MacVeagh and Dickinson—had been Democrats of the Cleveland school; and all except the two hold-overs were taken from the President's profession of law.

The work which stretched out ahead was mainly the regulation of economic interests and activities. Certain tasks were inherited directly from the Roosevelt era. They included railroad regulation, trust control, labor legislation, public land protection, conservation of natural resources, reclamation, and immigration restriction; and most of them were carried forward under plans already developed. Two others, which had little interested Roosevelt and his group, pressed for attention: the reform of the currency and banking system, and the revision of the tariff. To both, Taft and his party stood committed beyond the possibility of drawing back. In handling them the

Administration wrote the first chapter of its history, and at the same time sealed its fate.

Currency reform had been under discussion from the day when the question of monetary standards was finally settled by the act of 1900. The main difficulty was lack of elasticity, arising from the rigidity of the note issues of the national banks. For some years Secretary Shaw saved the country from stringency by an ingenious plan of hoarding money at certain seasons and releasing it in the crop-moving months.[1] In 1907 Congress legalized this procedure and made it possible for the Treasury Department to bring to the relief of the money market funds derived from any source.[2] But the expedient could hardly be justified as a permanent part of a nation's monetary system.

In November, 1907, the country was overtaken by a financial crisis almost as severe as the panics of 1873 and 1893. The blow fell with little warning Most banks were in excellent condition; business of every kind was prosperous; industries were flourishing; labor was fully employed; wages were generally satisfactory; and optimism ruled. Yet, uneasiness at some points developed suspicion; and suspicion grew by what it fed on, until certain New York banks, fearing "runs," suddenly refused to pay out money to their depositors or to make loans on any sort of security. Confidence was at once impaired, and unusual demands were made

[1] Patton, "Secretary Shaw and Precedents as to Treasury Control over the Money Market," *Jour. Polit. Econ.*, XV., 65–87.

[2] *U. S. Statutes at Large*, XXXIV., pt. i., p. 1290.

upon banks everywhere, leading to almost universal suspension of cash payments.

The consequences were ruinous. Business was paralyzed, and several great establishments, including the Westinghouse Manufacturing Company, temporarily collapsed; factories were shut down; thousands of people were thrown out of employment; wages were depressed; dividends were reduced; the Seaboard Air Line, the Chicago Great Western, and several other railroads were thrown into the hands of receivers; thirteen banks failed in New York City alone.[1]

To afford relief, pay-roll checks and other extralegal forms of currency were put into circulation, gold was imported from Europe, and the federal treasury poured its surplus into banks of deposit throughout the country. By the middle of January, 1908, confidence was restored and money circulated freely. Bank depositors suffered few direct losses. The recovery of business was, however, gradual; and it is the opinion of able students of American finance that the shrinkage in the value of property and securities, together with losses arising from paralysis or suspension of business, amounted to thousands of millions of dollars.[2]

One cause of the calamity was mismanagement and unscrupulous manipulation at the country's money center, New York; and the crisis left a sickening trail of indictments and suicides in high financial circles. Another cause was the placing of an undue proportion

[1] Johnson, "The Crisis and Panic of 1907," *Polit. Sci. Quart.*, XXIII., 454-467.
[2] Aldrich, *The Work of the National Monetary Commission*, 3.

of the people's money, in recent prosperous years, in fixed investments. Economists were agreed, however, that the fault lay fundamentally with the national currency and banking system. At all stages of the crisis there was an abundance of money in the vaults of the banks. Each bank, however, had to stand substantially alone; and since only by heroic measures could a bank hope to meet unaided the demands made upon it in time of fright among its depositors, the policy inevitably adopted upon the first sound of alarm was to hoard cash reserves, regardless of the interests of all other parties.

The experience of 1907 brought home to the country the inability of the national banks, which were the sole banks of issue, to expand their circulation in times of need; also the inadequacy of the device of supporting the banks by deposits of government money. Several plans of reform were put forward: (1) the issue of emergency notes by the banks for brief periods, subject to a federal tax designed to insure early retirement of the notes and to provide a fund which would justify the government in guaranteeing the issues; (2) a central bank of the sort maintained in European countries, with sole power to issue notes; (3) protection of the solvency of the banks and the security of depositors by government guarantee of deposits.

Early in 1908 some measures relating to currency and banking were introduced in Congress, and on May 30 the Aldrich-Vreeland bill became law.[1] This act authorized national banks to increase their circulation

---

[1] *U. S. Statutes at Large*, XXXV., pt. i., pp. 546–553.

by the issue of emergency notes properly secured, the issues being guaranteed by the government and taxed on a graduated scale up to a maximum of ten per cent. in order to insure retirement as soon as urgent need of them should cease. Full power to determine when such increases were necessary, to fix their time and amount, and to pass upon the security offered, was delegated conjointly to the Comptroller of the Currency, the Treasurer of the United States, and the Secretary of the Treasury. The privilege might be secured either by single banks or by "national currency associations," consisting of not fewer than ten banks in contiguous territory. The act was to expire June 30, 1914.[1]

These arrangements were looked upon as a palliative. The full need could be met by nothing short of a complete reconstruction of the currency and banking system; and this was a task to be undertaken only after careful study by experts. Hence, the Aldrich-Vreeland Act made provision for a National Monetary Commission, composed of nine senators and nine members of the House of Representatives; and under the chairmanship of Senator Aldrich, this group at once began an investigation of currency and banking in the United States and the principal European countries.

While the Commission was at work Taft became President, and the country was given to understand that currency and banking reform would not be long

[1] Laughlin, "The Aldrich-Vreeland Act," *Jour. Polit. Econ.*, XVI., 489-513.

delayed. But the administration was half over before
there were signs of action. In January, 1911, Aldrich
reported a tentative scheme for a National Reserve
Association, to be based on fifteen district reserve associations, each in turn to be based on local associations
of ten or more banks.[1] The object was to secure co-
operation among banks without fully adopting the
principle of a central bank. The proposal appealed
strongly to financial interests, and was supported by
the American Bankers Association. But in Congress
and among the people it was viewed with suspicion.
After remodelling the project the Commission dis-
banded, March 31, 1912. By that time a national
campaign was impending and no great reform could
be carried out.

The Administration, therefore, had to go before the
country with the admission that it had been unable to
speed up the Monetary Commission or to get action
from Congress, and that it had no solution of the currency question to offer. The best it could do was to
pass on the problem to its successor, with nothing to
show for the four years except the results of the Commission's investigation; and the credit for even this
belonged to the Roosevelt régime. The subject was
mentioned in the platforms of the principal parties in

---

[1] *Am. Year Book*, 1911, p. 304; Scott, "The Aldrich Banking Plan,"
Am. Econ. Rev., 4th Series, No. 3, pp. 251–261; Sprague, "The Aldrich
Plan for Monetary Legislation," *ibid.*, 262–271, and "Proposals for
Strengthening the National Banking System," *Quart. Jour. Econ.*,
XXIV., 201–242, 634–659, XXV., 593–633; Kemmerer, "Some Public
Aspects of the Aldrich Plan of Banking Reform," *Jour. Polit. Econ.*,
XIX., 819–830.

1912, but yielded in the campaign to more thrilling issues.

During the Civil War, and for some time thereafter, the Republican party looked upon the high tariffs which it imposed as emergency measures which would be abandoned as fast as the condition of the national treasury would permit. The vast and growing industries which profited by high duties were able to postpone the promised reductions; and under the play of a multitude of interests protectionism gradually took on the character of a settled national policy, upheld consistently by the Republican party and opposed but half-heartedly by the Democrats. If the question had been put directly, perhaps not more than a third of the people would at any time have voted for a higher scale of duties than would yield sufficient revenue, enable "infant" industries to get on their feet, and insure home production of munitions of war.

But tariff-making from 1860 to 1908 was never the people's work. It was carried on by small groups of members of the two houses of Congress, acting under the spur of scores of insatiable special interests, corporate or sectional; and tariff schedules have ramified until not even congressmen, however conscientious, can possibly assure themselves of the merits of one-tenth of the provisions upon which they are expected to vote. Under these circumstances it was easy for the protected interests to capitalize the ignorance and helplessness of the "ultimate consumer," to trade off influence for votes, to obtain multiplied favors, and to perpetuate the system under which they acquired

3

wealth and power. The history of every important piece of tariff legislation of later decades—the mongrel law of 1883, the McKinley Act of 1890, the Wilson Act of 1894, and the Dingley Act of 1897—is a record of the triumph of protectionist forces over disunited and hesitant opposition.

Tariff-making has become a jungle which a party enters at its peril. For while the people have usually failed to obtain from their lawmakers the tariff legislation they desired, they know in a general way when they have been thwarted, and are not slow to visit retribution. The Republicans drew up a new tariff in 1890, and in 1892 the Democrats swept the country. The Democrats framed a tariff in 1894, and within two months of its taking effect the Republicans recovered control of Congress. It therefore was by every token unpromising for the peace of mind and security of tenure of the Taft Administration that it stood pledged to a general tariff revision; and it is not surprising that the Payne-Aldrich Tariff Act of 1909 should have become the most momentous legislation of the period and a prime cause of political upheaval.

The last general tariff revision prior to 1909 was made in the Dingley Act of July 24, 1897. The scale of duties set up was very high; but the President was empowered to negotiate reciprocity treaties with foreign countries, arranging reductions.[1] Despite this feature, the law was never popular; and when the Senate refused to ratify reciprocity conventions, dissatisfaction deepened. After 1905 demands for re-

[1] *U. S. Statutes at Large*, XXX., pt. i., pp. 204–205.

vision appeared in many Republican state platforms, and in some influential party newspapers; while the Democrats, chastened by defeats on other issues, sought again to force the fighting upon this time-honored question. The growth of trusts and the difficulty of regulating them added fuel to the flames, because it was widely believed that the Dingley tariff, if not actually the "mother of the trusts," was one of their main supports. Shortage of revenue, arising partly from increased expenditures and partly from the crisis of 1907, supplied further impetus. In his message of December 3, 1907, President Roosevelt recommended the repeal of the duties on wood-pulp and alluded to the growing feeling among the people that the whole system of revenue legislation must soon be overhauled.[1]

The question pushed its way prominently into the campaign of 1908. In the Denver platform the Democrats demanded that articles competing with trust-controlled products be placed on the free list; that duties on the necessities of life be materially reduced; and that the entire tariff be gradually restored to a revenue basis. The Republican platform reiterated the doctrine of protection; affirmed the "true principle of protection" to be "best maintained by the imposition of such duties as will equal the difference between the cost of production at home and abroad, together with a reasonable profit to American industries"; declared for a system of maximum and minimum rates; and pledged the party to a "revision of the tariff" at a

[1] *Senate Jour.*, 60 Cong., 1 Sess., 8, 13.

special session of Congress immediately following the inauguration of the next President.[1]

After the results of the election were known, the Ways and Means Committee, under the chairmanship of Sereno E. Payne, resumed investigations which it had begun in the preceding May; and on November 10, following custom, it began a series of public hearings. Much testimony was presented by Andrew Carnegie and other well-informed persons to the effect that the industrial development of the decade had so reduced the cost of production that the Dingley rates were more than sufficient to cover the differences of cost in the United States and abroad.[2] The idea that the measure of the tariff should be this difference of cost was now widely held in Republican circles, and the President-elect had given it his assent; although it was evident that nobody possessed the information requisite to measure the costs that were involved in the computation. The supporters of the existing tariff and the advocates of extreme protection were organized and ably represented in Congress, while the advocates of lower rates were, as usual, unprepared to pull together. The steel people, the lumber people, the hosiery people, were vocal, and even eloquent; the "ultimate consumer" was unheard. Consequently, in preparing its bill the Committee was free to indulge its natural inclination to stand by thoroughgoing protection.

[1] Willis, "The Impending Tariff Struggle," *Jour. Polit. Econ.*, XVII. 1-18.

[2] *House Docs.*, 60 Cong., 2 Sess., No. 1505.

The Sixty-first Congress was convened in special session March 15, 1909. Joseph G. Cannon was promptly re-elected Speaker; and though a smouldering controversy concerning the rules of the House flared up, organization was completed with only minor changes intended to reduce the autocratic power of the Speaker and to expedite procedure.[1] Without delay Payne introduced the Ways and Means Committee's tariff measure, in which interest centered. It placed on the free list iron-ore, hides, flax, and wood-pulp; reduced by about one-half the duties on iron and steel manufactures and on lumber; reduced in varying amounts the duties on barley, chemicals, refined sugar, and many other articles; increased the rates on gloves, hosiery, tropical fruits, and sundry commodities adjudged to be inadequately protected; and, with a view solely to revenue, removed from the free list tea, cocoa, and certain other products. The bill provided, further, for free trade between the United States and the Philippines, although limits were placed on the amount of Philippine sugar, tobacco, and cigars that might be brought into the United States free of duty. For revenue purposes, a progressive tax was laid on inheritances.

The House debate on the Payne bill was brief and perfunctory. Interest was lax, and the rules as administered by the Speaker gave no opportunity for spontaneous discussion. Again it was made plain that the tariff was essentially a sectional issue, and that under the crude methods employed tariff legisla-

[1] See p. 172.

tion proceeded in accordance with no clear-cut principle, but by bargaining and log-rolling, and largely
at the dictates of the beneficiaries. Slightly amended,
the bill passed the House, April 9, by a vote of 217 to
161.[1] Four Louisiana Democrats supported it, and a
Tennessee Republican opposed it; otherwise the vote
followed party lines.

It has been remarked by a leading economist that
"in most of the tariff acts of the last generation, the
influence of the Senate on legislation has been greater
than that of the House, and has been exercised in favor
of higher duties." [2] The tariff of 1909 bears out the
observation. On April 12, after the Payne bill had
been referred to the Finance Committee of the upper
chamber, Senator Aldrich reported for the committee
a substitute measure which proposed: (1) to put iron-ore
and flax again on the dutiable list; (2) to restore to their
previous level the duties on various agricultural products and on hosiery; (3) to institute changes of classification whereby the rates on iron, steel, and lead goods
would be increased; (4) to alter the suggested workings
of the maximum and minimum rates. The inheritance
tax was dropped, on the ground that the higher duties
made it unnecessary.

Senator Aldrich's connection with these reactionary
proposals was more than nominal. He was, indeed,
their chief sponsor. His entrance into the Senate in
1881 brought to the protectionist cause its first able
congressional leader, and in the framing of subse-

---

[1] *House Jour.*, 61 Cong., 1 Sess., 148.
[2] Taussig, *Tariff History of the United States* (6th ed.), 373.

quent tariff measures no hand was more influential than his. Alert, astute, somewhat cynical, silent except when questions were to be answered, he was known to be exceptionally familiar with all branches of the country's industries, and to be armed *cap-à-pie* against attack from every quarter. As events proved, he was now making his last great fight for protectionism; and he was again successful.

The Senate debate lasted eleven weeks. Much of it was directed, not to the schedules under consideration, but to the broader question of the equitable distribution of the burden of taxation between rich and poor. Party lines were maintained with difficulty, and gradually a group of western Republicans, including Cummins and Dolliver of Iowa, La Follette of Wisconsin, and Beveridge of Indiana, came to the point of opposing the essentials of the Aldrich bill. These men dared to question the further dominance of the industrial and financial interests that were accustomed to make the tariffs. They pronounced many of the Aldrich schedules outrageous; and to obviate the necessity of high tariffs for revenue purposes, Senator Cummins introduced a bill for a federal tax on incomes. For the Democrats, who long had looked for an opportunity to revive their project of 1894, Senator Bailey of Texas introduced a similar bill; and with no great difficulty the two elements came together in support of a single measure on the subject.

Meanwhile, June 16, President Taft gave the situation a new turn by recommending: (1) that the taxation of incomes be not attempted until the federal

Constitution should have been amended in such manner as clearly to confer the requisite power; (2) that the inheritance tax provided for in the Payne bill be replaced by a tax of two per cent. on the net earnings of corporations.   July 2, the Senate, by a vote of 59 to 11, approved the proposed corporation tax;[1] and three days later it passed unanimously a resolution submitting an income-tax amendment to the states.[2] July 8, the amended Aldrich bill was passed by a vote of 45 to 34.[3]

A conference committee worked out compromises, and on July 31 the resulting measure—now called the Payne-Aldrich bill—was passed by the lower house by a vote of 195 to 183.[4]   Twenty Republicans joined the Democrats in the negative.   August 5, it was passed by the Senate by a vote of 47 to 31, with seven Republicans voting in the negative,[5] and was signed by the President, taking effect immediately.[6]

Beyond securing free trade with the Philippines and reminding his party that it was pledged to "revision downward" and would be answerable to the country, the President kept clear of the tariff discussion until the conference stage was reached.   Thereafter he intervened to compose differences and to encourage reduction of rates.   Yet his only clear achievement was the removal of duties from raw hides.   Woolen, cotton,

[1] *Senate Jour.*, 61 Cong., 1 Sess., 131.
[2] *Ibid.*, 135.
[3] *Ibid.*, 144.
[4] *House Jour.*, 61 Cong., 1 Sess., 301.
[5] *Senate Jour.*, 61 Cong., 1 Sess., 184.
[6] *U. S. Statutes at Large*, XXXVI., pt. i., pp. 11–118.

and other interests whose demands he was disposed to
question proved too powerful for him; and if he felt
moral indignation at the low-plane bargaining and
tinkering by which the whole measure was whipped
into shape, he gave no sign. The circumstances were
strikingly similar to those surrounding the passage
of the Wilson tariff of 1894.[1] But, unlike Cleveland, Taft chose to sign the bill laid before him,
thereby confirming his joint responsibility for the
outcome.

The main features of the Payne-Aldrich Act can be
stated briefly. Minimum and maximum duties were
provided—the former to comprise the normal tariff,
the latter to be imposed on imports from countries
which, in the judgment of the President, discriminated
against the trade of the United States. Expressed
in percentages, the minimum and maximum rates
were identical; but whenever the maximum scale was
in effect, the amount of duty paid was to be increased
by adding twenty-five per cent. to the value of the
articles imported. March 10, 1910, was fixed as the
date at which the maximum scale should be applied
to imports from all countries not specifically excepted
by presidential proclamation.

The act made a general reclassification of commodities, with extensive alterations in the rates of duty.
As for "revision downward," the Senate Committee
on Finance computed that the net effect would be an
actual increase of 1.1 per cent. in the average rate
on all dutiable goods over the average under the Ding·

[1] Dewey, *National Problems* (*Am. Nation*, XXIV.), chap. xvii.

ley law.[1] In the important schedules containing wool
and woolens, sugar and its products, tobacco, hemp,
flax, jute, spirits and wines, and agricultural products,
changes were slight. In many other schedules, as
those relating to iron and steel, earthenware, cottons,
and chemicals, reductions were offset largely or wholly
by increases.[2] The only important commodities newly
placed on the free list were petroleum, raw hides, and
mechanically ground wood-pulp.[3]

To facilitate the work of administration, provision
was made for a Court of Customs Appeals, composed of
five judges, to hear and decide all appeals from the
Board of General Appraisers; and the President was
authorized to appoint a Tariff Board—not, as many
had desired, to undertake inquiries as a basis of future
tariff legislation, but only to assist in the exercise of
executive discretion in the application of the maximum
and minimum rates. Finally, the act provided for
an excise tax of one per cent. on the net incomes of
business corporations in excess of five thousand dollars.
Neither the inheritance tax nor the general income tax
found a place; but on July 12 the House of Representatives adopted the Senate's resolution for the submission of an income tax amendment. Though in its
origin a mere by-product of the Payne-Aldrich tariff

[1] *Review of Reviews*, XL., 341.
[2] Copeland, "Duties on Cotton Goods," *Quart. Jour. Econ.*, XXIV.,
422–428.
[3] Fisk, "The Payne-Aldrich Tariff," *Polit. Sci. Quart.*, XXV., 35–
68; Taussig, "The Tariff Debate of 1909 and the New Tariff Act,"
Quart. Jour. Econ., XXV., 1–38; Willis, "The Tariff of 1909," *Jour.
Polit. Econ.*, XVII., 589–619; XVIII., 1–33, 173–196.

debates, this amendment became one of the most important features of the national revenue system; and four years later its Democratic supporters found it of great assistance in carrying out tariff reform after their own ideas.[1]

At no time did it seem probable that the schedules would be revised on radical lines, and throughout the discussion the country remained, on the whole, apathetic. There was no evidence that it realized the great moral issues involved. Some substantial reductions of duty were, none the less, expected; and when it was disclosed that the new act was one of the most thoroughgoing protectionist measures ever adopted in the United States or in any other land, disappointment was keen. The interests were satisfied, but the people were indignant. The rising cost of living was pressing hard, and it was disappointing to the consumer to find that there would be no saving on food, and that his clothing bill would probably be heavier than before. Fervid protest centered especially around the wool and woolens schedule, which, notwithstanding the fact that the woolen manufacturing companies were declaring dividends up to fifty per cent., showed only insignificant changes. For two decades this "Schedule K" had been the most important in the tariff, both doctrinally and politically; and in succeeding years it drew the fiercest attacks that were leveled against the new legislation. President Taft branded it as unreasonable and unjust, but at the same time

[1] Seligman, "The Income Tax Amendment," *Polit. Sci. Quart.*, XXV., 193–219.

insisted that without it no bill at all could have been passed.

At the close of the special session the President set out on a speech-making tour to the Pacific coast; and on September 17 he delivered at Winona, Minnesota, an address in which he defended the new law with a fervor not displayed by even its immediate sponsors. Still admitting that the wool schedule was "too high," he none the less pronounced the measure "the best tariff law the Republicans ever made, and therefore the best the country ever had." The people were taken by surprise; for the President had not been much criticized for signing the bill, and there appeared no reason why he should so ardently defend it. The explanation naïvely offered at the time was that the speech was written hurriedly on a train, without thought of its possible effect. This would lay the President open to a charge of inexcusable blundering. Besides, in later speeches in all parts of the country the views expressed at Winona were reasserted. Whatever the facts, the Winona speech was widely construed by the press as an attempt to read out of the Republican party the middle western senators who had voted with the Democrats in opposition to the new act. This was probably not the President's intention. But the effect was to accentuate the tendency to division already at work in his party, and to strengthen the hold of the senatorial "insurgents" with their constituents in upwards of a dozen important states.

The aftermath of the Payne-Aldrich law was not

wholly unhappy. The measure could hardly fail to yield revenue abundantly. The corporation tax produced in its first year the twenty-five millions expected of it,[1] and the customs receipts during the fiscal year ending June 30, 1910 ($333,043,800), exceeded by a million dollars the sum collected in the most productive earlier year, 1907. Troublesome treasury deficits disappeared. Furthermore, the President was able to make the gratifying announcement, April 1, 1910, that no nation was unduly discriminating against the United States, and that there was no occasion for putting into operation the maximum scale of duties. Finally, Congress in 1910 recognized the need of further tariff investigations and by a liberal appropriation made it possible for the President to use the Tariff Board for purposes not contemplated in the Payne-Aldrich law.

This, however, tells but a part of the story. Congress had missed a great opportunity. The President had failed to rise to the level of statesmanship expected of him. The Republican party had proved recreant to a solemn trust. No display of treasury balances could obscure these uncomfortable facts; no reasonable excuses could be found. Resentment that flows naturally from abuse of confidence rankled in the public mind, producing a situation unfavorable alike to the furtherance of the Administration's general program and to the continuance of the Republican party in power.

[1] Robinson, "The Federal Corporation Tax," *Am. Econ. Rev.*, I., 501-723.

CHAPTER III

AFTER a period of depression following the panic
of 1893, the United States entered about 1897 on
a long epoch of prosperity. Agriculture yielded fast
increasing returns; manufactures multiplied; foreign
trade pushed into every corner of the world; wealth
and economic power grew amazingly. The day of "big
business" had dawned: capital flowed together in great
masses; huge industrial corporations sprang into being
over night; "trusts" flourished as bay trees; railroads
fell into vast systems, covering many states.

Good times as well as bad bring difficulties. In this
new era the arrogance of corporations grew fast. Consumers had to pay extortionate prices; small producers
were crowded out of markets; weaker competitors were
driven to the wall; the privilege of the strong became
the law of the business world. Competition under the
simple rules of supply and demand broke down; government regulation seemed to offer the only safeguard
of the public well-being.

The foremost problem was presented by the railroads. By 1900 the country was reasonably supplied
with trunk lines and "feeders"; the total single-track

40

mileage was 192,556. The next decade saw some new construction, especially in the far West; but in the main, it was a time of eager rivalry, spectacular fights for rail power, consolidation of local lines into great systems, and the linking up of railroad management with powerful industrial and banking interests.

The typical railway-empire builders of the period were James J. Hill and Edward H. Harriman. To Hill railroad growth meant construction; and his Northern Pacific system, with its tributaries, became one of the great agencies in opening up the Northwest and laying the foundations for a substantial trans-Pacific trade. To Harriman, railroad growth meant rather railroad efficiency. He saw more clearly than most men the transportation possibilities of the newer West and South, and devoted his tremendous powers of strategy to building up a controlling system in those sections. He took hold of the Union Pacific when it was tottering, financed it lavishly, made it the equal in efficiency of the best-managed eastern roads, and used it as a lever with which to move the railway and financial world.

In a spectacular conflict for control of the Northern Pacific in 1901 he was beaten by the combined strength of Hill and J. P. Morgan. But the fight brought him into the center of the railway stage, where he remained until his death in 1909. He made heavy purchases of stock in many roads, voted his stock in eastern lines so as to throw traffic to the Union Pacific, and made the "U. P.," with its dependent roads, banks, and business interests, the railroad and financial

giant of the time. At his death, Harriman controlled
the Southern Pacific (which had absorbed the Union
Pacific), the Illinois Central, and the Georgia Central,
with their tributaries, aggregating twenty-five thousand
miles; he had large influence over other roads aggregating fifty thousand miles; he controlled several
steamboat lines and banks; he had the handling of
more money than any other man in the United States.

Thus, within a decade the railway net of the country
was gathered into a few great systems, controlled by
powerful individuals or banking groups, mainly in New
York City. An investigation in 1905 showed that
majorities of the boards of directors of all important
roads east of the Mississippi River could be selected
from a group of thirty-five persons.

Notwithstanding growth of mileage and improvement of service, the railroad system as a whole failed
to keep pace with the needs of the country. Equipment
was insufficient and antiquated; management was
often poor. Freight was sometimes refused for weeks
together because of lack of cars to transport it; congestion of terminals caused further delays; crops were
moved with difficulty and loss; wrecks and other accidents showed a lack of responsibility for patrons and
employees. In 1906, Hill declared that if the railroads
expected to handle properly the traffic already urged
upon them, they would have to spend five billion five
hundred million dollars in five years for double tracks,
rolling stock, larger terminals, and other improvements.

It was not poor service alone that caused complaint.
Freight rates were pushed to levels which shippers con-

sidered excessive; rebating and other forms of discrimination were common;[1] and in many parts of the country the political activities of the railroad interests were highly obnoxious. As the public viewed it, railroad management had become a titanic and ruthless game of "high finance"; the magnates of Wall Street aimed, not to meet the country's needs, but to concentrate control and enrich still further the men who had amassed fortunes from the business; the small investor and the small shipper were ignored; the inability of the companies to raise funds for improvements was the natural result of their over-capitalization, stock-watering, and other reckless handling of securities. An investigation of the Harriman lines in 1907 greatly weakened public confidence in the honesty of railroad management by disclosing a concentration of irresponsible power and a prevalence of sharp practices until then unknown outside the inner circle of railroad magnates.

Under these conditions, the regulation of common carriers once more became a leading public question. Long before, the country had arrived at the concept, duly affirmed by the Supreme Court, that railroad regulation is a public function, to be exercised by the states over traffic within their boundaries and by the federal government over traffic from state to state. Certain instrumentalities of regulation also had been set up. All states had passed railroad laws; beginning with Massachusetts in 1869, many had created special commissions to enforce these laws; in the Interstate

4   [1] Roosevelt, *Autobiography*, 473.

Commerce Act of 1887 the nation had framed a regulative statute; in the Interstate Commerce Commission it possessed a special agent for investigation
and control.

Much of this regulative machinery was not strong
enough to bear the strain of the changes in the railway world after 1898. Some of it had broken down
before the new conditions appeared; and in this plight
was the Interstate Commerce Commission itself.
Great good had been expected from this body. But
three things worked together to rob it of its necessary
powers. First, appeals from its orders were handled
very slowly by the courts; cases were known to hang
six or eight years. Second, the courts persisted in
treating such appeals as original proceedings, and
based their decisions on evidence freshly taken and
often differing from that which had determined the
Commission's action. Third, the courts refused to
uphold the Commission's most essential power, namely, rate-making.

Though disclaiming the power to make rates on its
own initiative, the Commission from the outset freely
modified rates on complaint. For a time its actions
went unquestioned. Then the courts began to suggest doubts; and finally, in the Maximum Freight Rate
decision of 1896, the Supreme Court held that power
to prescribe a tariff of rates for a common carrier was
of legislative character; that such power could not be
possessed unless conferred; and that "under the Interstate Commerce Act the Commission has no power to
prescribe the tariff of rates which shall control in the

future." [1] This was followed by a decision in the
Alabama Midland Case, in 1897, which nullified the
"long and short haul" clause of the act by denying
the right of the Commission to establish the reasonableness of rates relatively as between competing
places.[2]

The result was to strip the law of all vigor. Up to
that time the Commission, after deciding (on complaint) that a rate was unreasonable, proceeded to
prescribe a new and proper rate, in the belief that this
rate would be enforced by the courts. Thenceforth it
could go no farther than to declare a present or past
rate unreasonable; it could not even fix a maximum
rate. Decisions concerning rates became almost value-
less, and the number of formal complaints filed, never
large, dwindled to twenty or thirty a year. By 1900
the Commission was moribund.

Years were required to bring about a revival of
substantial federal control. But an important step
to that end was taken in 1903 in the Elkins Act, amending the statute of 1887.[3] The carriers had been feeling
the losses arising from rebating and excessive rate-
cutting, and Paul Morton, president of the Santa Fé
system, volunteered to aid the government in putting
an end to these unlawful practices. [4] President Roosevelt seized the opportunity by stirring to action the
Interstate Commerce Commission and the Department

[1] 167 U. S., 479; Ripley, *Railroads: Rates and Regulation*, 469-473,
and *Railway Problems*, 155-197.

[2] 168 U. S., 144.

[3] *U. S. Statutes at Large*, XXXII., pt. i., pp. 847-848.

[4] Roosevelt, *Autobiography*, 473-474.

of Justice, and by securing from Congress the needed legislation. The Elkins amendments were passed practically without opposition, and dealt solely with inequalities of rates. They forbade variations from any published tariff (whether or not involving discrimination), made liable to punishment not only the railway corporation itself, but its officers and agents, and also shippers knowingly accepting favors; abolished the penalty of imprisonment provided for by an amendment of 1889; and specially authorized injunction proceedings to restrain carriers from violating the law.

Consolidation was checked, and the power of the government to deal with all great corporations was vindicated, by a decision handed down by the Supreme Court in the Northern Securities Case, March 14, 1904, wherein it was held that a merger of two or more competing roads was contrary to the Sherman anti-trust law of 1890.[1] This was a great triumph; and the Administration, hitherto deterred by lack of power, threw itself unreservedly into the work of railway and trust regulation. The "big stick" began to be brandished, the "square deal" to be preached.

The chief railroad problem that remained was rate-making. In his annual message of December 6, 1904, the President urged that the Interstate Commerce Commission be given power to fix exact rates;[2] and on February 8, 1906, the House passed, by a vote of

---

[1] 193 U. S., 197; Latané, *America as a World Power* (*Am. Nation,* XXV.), 304–307; Ripley, *Railway Problems,* 553–566; Meyer, *History of the Northern Securities Case,* chaps. viii–ix.

[2] *Senate Jour.*, 58 Cong., 3 Sess., 6.

346 to 7, a comprehensive measure introduced by
Chairman Hepburn of the Interstate and Foreign
Commerce Committee.[1]   The Senate wavered, and the
debates were long and brilliant.   But under executive
pressure, and in the teeth of the most powerful railroad
lobby in the history of the country, it at length fell
into line, with only three dissenting votes.[2]   June 29,
1906, the bill became law.[3]

The Hepburn Act was in form an amendment of the
act of 1887; but it marked a wholly new departure.
It raised the number of members of the Interstate
Commerce Commission from five to seven, lengthened
the term of members from five to seven years, and
brought up their salary from $7,500 to $10,000.   It
extended the interstate commerce laws, and the jurisdiction of the Commission, to interstate pipe lines,
express companies, sleeping-car companies, and all incidental services at terminals.   It authorized the Commission to fix the form of accounts and records used by
the carriers, and to require all accounts to be submitted
for inspection.   It restored the penalty of imprisonment for failure to observe published tariffs, and prescribed a fine of three times the amount of the rebate
for shippers or other parties knowingly accepting or
profiting by unlawful favors. A new and drastic
"commodity clause," intended to divorce transportation from other business, forbade interstate or foreign
transportation, after May 1, 1908, of any commodity

---

[1] *House Jour.*, 59 Cong., 1 Sess., 432.
[2] *Senate Jour.*, 59 Cong., 1 Sess., 507.
[3] *U. S. Statutes at Large*, XXXIV., pt. i., pp. 584–595.

(other than timber) produced or mined by the carrier, except articles required for the carrier's own use.[1]

Of largest importance was the section giving the Commission its first express grant of rate-making power. The grant stopped short of the desires of the radicals. It did not include authority to make interstate rates generally; but it authorized the Commission, on complaint and after a hearing, to determine and prescribe just and reasonable maximum rates, regulations, and practices. Carriers were given the right to bring suit in any circuit court to annul such actions, with appeal to the Supreme Court.[2]

The gains for regulation were: broader jurisdiction, separation of transportation from other business, suppression of passes, uniformity and publicity of accounts, and the express grant of administrative rate-making power. Concessions to the railroads included broad and indefinite court review and the restriction of rate-making to maximum rates. The railroads came off better than they had hoped. The Commission, moreover, took up its added duties in a spirit of moderation. Many early decisions were in the carriers' favor, and for a few years the operators seemed to have accepted the situation with good grace.

It was to be expected that the new legislation would

[1] Jones, "The Commodity Clause Legislation and the Anthracite Railroads," *Quart. Jour. Econ.*, XXVII., 579–615.

[2] Ripley, *Railroads: Rates and Regulation*, 494–556; Dixon, "The Interstate Commerce Act as Amended," *Quart. Jour. Econ.*, XXI., 22–51; Smalley, "Rate Control Act," Am. Acad. Polit. and Soc. Sci., *Annals*, XXIX., 292–309.

be reviewed by the courts. The "commodities" and rebating clauses were tested speedily. September 10, 1908, the Circuit Court of Appeals at Philadelphia rendered a decision in the Delaware and Hudson Case pronouncing the commodities clause unconstitutional. The case was appealed, and on May 3, 1909, the Supreme Court reversed the judgment,[1] but construed the prohibition laid upon carriers not to be applicable to commodities manufactured, mined, or owned by corporations in which the carriers were stockholders. This emasculated the clause; practically all of the anthracite coal roads were exempted, although it was mainly to reach them that the clause had been adopted. On the other hand, in reaffirming, in the same year, a verdict imposing a fine on the New York Central Railroad for giving rebates to the American Sugar Refining Company, the Supreme Court unanimously pronounced the anti-rebating features of the law constitutional.[2]

Under the vigorous direction of President Roosevelt many rebating suits were brought. In 1907 the Standard Oil Company of Indiana, a subsidiary of the Standard Oil Company of New Jersey, was indicted for receiving rebates on petroleum shipped over the Chicago and Alton Railroad from Whiting, Indiana, to East St. Louis. In a decision handed down August 3, 1907, by Judge Kenesaw M. Landis, of the United States District Court at Chicago, the defendant was found guilty on 1,462 counts and was fined to the

[1] 213 U. S., 366.
[2] 212 U. S., 481, 500, 509.

maximum on each count, aggregating $29,240,000.[1] The case was appealed, and on November 10, 1909, Judge Grosscup delivered an opinion of the Circuit Court of Appeals reversing the trial court's action, on the grounds that the fine imposed was confiscatory, that intent to violate the law had not been proved, and that the number of offenses, if any, should have been determined, not by the car-loads shipped, but by the freight bills made out.[2] In March, 1909, the case was brought up for retrial at Chicago before Judge Anderson. After hearing the government's evidence and argument, he dismissed the suit; and thus the matter ended. A good case was lost through judicial blundering; but other actions were more successful.

Meanwhile, railroad regulation had been taken up earnestly in the states. At best, the jurisdiction of the national government was limited; and the country was in no mood to be satisfied with the remedy of abuses in commerce at great distances. The thing that troubled the mass of shippers and consumers was discriminations, excessive rates, and inadequate service in local traffic. A renewed appeal to state authority was stimulated by the Hepburn law; and in the early months of 1907, when the legislatures of thirty-nine states were in session, legislation was passed touching every phase of railroad organization and management. The movement was reminiscent of the grangerism of 1870–1877. But whereas the granger laws appeared

---

[1] 155 *Fed. Rep.*, 305.
[2] 164 *Fed. Rep.*, 376.

in only a few western states, the present legislation
was nation-wide. In all, more than three hundred
railroad measures were enacted—one hundred and
seventy-seven in ten states alone.

Ignoring acts of minor importance, these laws fell
into four principal classes, according as they regulated
hours of labor, increased employers' liability for accidents, created or strengthened railroad commissions,
and fixed rates. Rate regulation became a passion.
In twenty states maximum passenger rates were reduced, in some instances to two and one-half cents a
mile, in some to two and one-fourth cents, and in
many to two cents. Generally there was no attempt
to determine by investigation what rates would be
properly remunerative. In Wisconsin the railroad commission declared two and one-half cents to be a reasonable rate; whereupon the legislature boldly enacted a
two-cent law.[1]

In their zeal the states clearly overshot the mark.
Losses resulted; business was depressed; railroad investments and extensions were discouraged at a time
when they were specially needed. The railroads rightly
regarded a large part of the new legislation as enacted
in ignorance and with a view to retaliation. Some became vindictive, and tense situations resulted. Several stringent measures, on being tested in the courts,
were set aside as confiscatory or otherwise unconstitutional.

In 1908 the railroads, suffering from the financial
crisis of 1907 as well as from ill-advised regulation,

[1] *Wis. Statutes*, 1915, chap. lxxxvii., sec. 1798a.

were hard pressed; twenty-four lines, aggregating eight thousand miles, were forced into the hands of receivers, while others were saved only by rigid economy. Few legislatures were in session during the year, and little railroad legislation was enacted. By 1909 the clamor had somewhat subsided; the forty-one legislatures in session passed a total of six hundred and sixty-four railroad laws; but these measures were less harsh than those of 1907. Thereafter railroad legislation by the states seldom produced serious controversies. The principle of regulation was incontrovertibly established; and difficulties over rate-making were largely avoided by assigning that important function to a body of experts forming a state railroad commission, or, in lieu of such an agency, to the public utilities or corporations commission. In 1917 but two states were without a commission exercising powers of this kind.

Railroad regulation was little discussed in the national campaign of 1908. But President Taft felt that public sentiment demanded further action; besides, he was under pledge to follow up the policies of his predecessor. In its annual report for 1908 the Interstate Commerce Commission asked for fresh grants of power, including authority to make physical valuations, to bring proceedings without complaint, and to control issues of railway stocks and bonds. January 7, 1910, the President laid before Congress the Administration's program, in a tentative bill drawn by Attorney-General Wickersham.[1]

The measure was introduced in the Senate by Stephen

[1] *House Jour.*, 61 Cong., 2 Sess., 126–128.

B. Elkins, chairman of the Committee on Interstate
Commerce, and in the House by James R. Mann,
chairman of the Committee on Interstate and Foreign
Commerce. It failed to arouse either the public or the
railroads, but it was debated at length in both houses
and amended out of all semblance to its original form.
May 10, the House passed it by a vote of 201 to 126.[1]
and on June 3 the Senate adopted it, in somewhat different form, by a vote of 50 to 12.[2] A conference
committee worked out a basis of agreement, and the
measure became law June 18.[3]

While under consideration in Congress the Hepburn Act was much weakened by amendment. The
Mann-Elkins Act, on the other hand, was strengthened;
so that, although a product of compromise, it turned
out to be a very important piece of legislation. Its
provisions were directed mainly to two ends: expediting
appeals from the Interstate Commerce Commission,
and increasing the Commission's powers. The congestion and delay in appeal proceedings called for
remedy. At the President's suggestion, the law provided a new tribunal, composed of five circuit judges
selected by the Chief Justice, and known as the Commerce Court. This court was to sit continuously at
Washington for the purpose of hearing appeals from
the rules and acts of the Commission. Appeals from
its judgments might be carried to the Supreme Court,
with precedence over all save criminal cases.

---

[1] *House Jour.*, 61 Cong., 2 Sess., 666.
[2] *Senate Jour.*, 61 Cong., 2 Sess., 408.
[3] *U. S. Statutes at Large*, XXXVI., pt. i., p. 539.

The powers of the Commission were increased in several ways. (1) Jurisdiction was extended to interstate and foreign telegraph (including wireless), telephone, and cable companies, and the term "railroad" was broadened to include appurtenant bridges and ferries. (2) The Commission was authorized to suspend newly announced tariffs for a period of from four to ten months, pending investigation. (3) It was empowered to proceed against a carrier at any time, and on its own initiative. (4) The "long and short haul" clause was revived in full vigor. The original bill forbade issues of railway stocks and bonds unless approved by the Commission. In the Senate this was stricken out, and the measure as passed merely authorized the President to appoint a commission to investigate the subject and report upon it.[1]

Under the terms of the new law the Commerce Court was organized in December, 1910, with Martin A. Knapp, former chairman of the Interstate Commerce Commission, as presiding judge. The tribunal never gained popular confidence, and in 1912 Congress in effect abolished it by cutting off its appropriation. This action was perhaps influenced by the impeachment and removal, in 1912, of a member of the court, Robert W. Archbald, on the charge of using his position to enhance his personal fortunes. The remaining members of the court were continued as ordinary circuit judges; and appeals from the acts and rulings of the Commission were thereafter lodged with the federal circuit courts of appeal throughout the country, as

[1] Dixon, "The Mann-Elkins Act," *Quart. Jour. Econ.*, XXV., 593–633.

before 1910. The promising idea of a central court
of review was thus abandoned.[1]

Physical valuation as a basis for rate-making had
long been growing in favor. Beginning with Texas in
1893, more than a dozen states passed laws on the subject; and while in most cases the main object was
taxation, the effect on rate-making was always kept
in mind. When the Hepburn bill was before Congress,
Senator La Follette urged nation-wide valuation; and
a valuation clause narrowly escaped insertion in the
Mann-Elkins law. The Interstate Commerce Commission favored the plan, and the special Securities Commission, in a report of November 1, 1911, supplied
fresh impetus. A valuation act was signed by President Taft March 1, 1913, making it the duty of the
Interstate Commerce Commission to "investigate, ascertain, and report in detail," within five years, the
original cost to date, the cost of reproduction new, and
the cost of reproduction less depreciation, of every
piece of property owned or used by common carriers
subject to the Interstate Commerce Act.[2] The Commission organized a Division of Valuation, and appointed a staff of engineers to take charge of the inventory in each of five great sections of the country;
the railroads set up a bureau to co-operate; appraisals
began in 1914; and the first tentative reports appeared
in 1916.[3]

[1] Dunn, "The Commerce Court Question," *Am. Econ. Rev.*, III.,
20–42.

[2] *U. S. Statutes at Large*, XXXVII., pt. i., p. 701.

[3] *Am. Econ. Rev.*, VII., 181–187; Ripley, "Physical Valuation of
Railroads," *Polit. Sci. Quart.*, XXIX., 569–599.

Judicial decisions after the passage of the Hepburn Act tended to exalt the regulative power of the federal government and of its agent, the Interstate Commerce Commission. In the Minnesota Rate Cases, decided June 9, 1913, the Supreme Court took new ground in asserting that state regulation of interstate rates was exclusive only until Congress acted, and that Congress might regulate such rates as against state control whenever it wished, for the reason that intrastate rates indirectly determined interstate rates.[1] In the Texas-Shreveport Case, decided June 8, 1914, the court held not only that the federal government could regulate intrastate rates, but that the Interstate Commerce Commission already had the necessary authority.[2] The Minnesota cases were primarily a test of the rate-making powers of the states; and the court ruled that the states had full power to fix rates on railroad traffic within their borders, except where the use of such power would interfere directly with the regulation of commerce beyond their borders, or amount to confiscation. This was a disappointment to the railroads, which within ten years had developed a preference for federal, as against state, rate-making control; yet there was promise of relief in the new reaches of the federal authority.

Other decisions specially fortified the Interstate Commerce Commission. In *Interstate Commerce Commission vs. Illinois Central Railroad*, decided January

---

[1] 230 U. S., 352; Ripley, *Railway Problems*, 642–715; Bauer, "The Minnesota Rate Cases," *Polit. Sci. Quart.*, XXIX., 57–83.
[2] 234 U. S., 342.

10, 1910, the Supreme Court fully discussed judicial review and made clear its purpose to hold the acts of the Commission subject to judicial authority.[1]   But it announced that review on grounds of reasonableness would be applied only when the Commission's acts were regarded as so unreasonable as to violate a constitutional provision, or to be confiscatory "beyond any just or fair doubt."   The court asserted that it would not pronounce illegal an order or a statute merely because it considered such order or statute unwise or inexpedient; in short, it disclaimed intent to encroach upon the Commission's administrative functions.   Furthermore, in *United States and Interstate Commerce Commission vs. Kansas City Southern Railway*, decided December 1, 1913, the Supreme Court affirmed in sweeping language the power of the Commission to regulate not only rates, but the internal administration of railroad companies.[2]

[1] 215 U. S., 452.

[2] 231 U. S., 423.   On railway labor disputes see p. 85; on the Adamson railroad law of 1916, pp. 353–363.

CHAPTER IV

CORPORATIONS AND TRUSTS

(1901–1912)

THE most striking aspects of American industry and commerce are the organization of capital in vast aggregates and the concentration of management in few hands. Both have come about mainly since 1885. The oldest of the so-called "trusts" is the Standard Oil Company. Yet the beginnings of this corporation as a trust are traceable only to 1882, when oil interests comprising forty concerns in Philadelphia, Pittsburgh, Cleveland, and other centers placed the management of their business in the hands of a single board of trustees. Similar steps were soon taken in other important industries; and presently a system of interlocking interests sprang up which looked toward a general consolidation of staple manufactures, as well as of transportation and trade, under the control of a few rich individuals and powerful corporations. From 1895 to 1905 this concentration went on with astonishing rapidity.

The methods of concentration were many. One was the building up of great individual businesses and aggregates of securities. A second was the establish-

58

ment of pools or agreements, with sometimes common selling agents, by groups of friendly corporations. A third was the transfer of the stock of companies whose combination was aimed at to a small group of persons, who thereafter held the stock "in trust" (whence comes the term *trust* as applied in a more general sense to industrial and commercial combinations) and exercised full control over the business of all of the affiliated companies. This device, employed first by the Standard Oil concerns, was early made use of also by the sugar, whiskey, and cotton-seed oil interests. A fourth mode was the setting up of holding companies, which were corporations formed simply to own, or "hold," the stocks and bonds of subsidiary companies, or such portions of them as would insure control in unison. The holding company first appeared in 1897, and it became for a time the dominant form of consolidation.

A fifth method was the purchase by a corporation of the property and securities of competing corporations, which thereupon lost their identity completely.[1] This plan of complete merger gave rise to several of the combinations of greatest size, chiefly after 1904. Thus it was by the purchase of the stock of eleven large companies controlling three-fourths of the steel industry of the country that the United States Steel Corporation, organized by J. Pierpont Morgan in 1899 and chartered in New Jersey in 1901, eventually brought together capital aggregating $1,100,000,000, and became the most gigantic industrial combination

5   [1] Van Hise, *Concentration and Control*, 60–72.

that the world had ever seen.[1]   The principle of the merger was used also in the organization of the American Tobacco Company and the Bethlehem Steel Corporation in 1904, the American Ice Securities Company and the United Shoe Machinery Company in 1905, and the Corn Products Refining Company and the North American Portland Cement Company in 1906.

So general after 1900 was the tendency to concentration that of a total of 322 groups of industries, 142 showed in 1905 an actual decrease of establishments during the five-year period; more than 300 sugar-refineries, about 300 shoe-factories, and more than 200 woolen-mills were discontinued. Prior to January 1, 1898, eighty-two combinations were formed with an aggregate capitalization of slightly over a billion; between that date and January 1, 1904, 236 combinations were established, with a capitalization of more than six billions.[2]   Combinations gained steadily, too, in compactness and strength.   Pools became trusts; trusts became holding companies; holding companies gave way to complete consolidations. The whole development arose in part from the speculative activities of capitalists and promoters, the effects of the protective tariff, the operation of the patent system, manipulations of railway rates, and the sheer growth of the country's business interests; but the main cause was the plain economic advantages of combination over

[1] U. S. Commissioner of Corporations, *Report on the Steel Industry* (1911).

[2] Moody, *Truth about the Trusts*, 486.

cut-throat competition. The objects chiefly aimed at were economy in production, regulation of output, division of markets, and maintenance of prices.[1]

Under the American form of government, control of economic organization and activity is difficult. The states create corporations and regulate their inter-state operations. The federal government possesses merely the power to regulate such operations as pertain to interstate and foreign commerce, without being able to say whether or not the corporations shall exist, or how, in most important respects, their business shall be conducted. The states were slow to take up the work of regulation; prior to 1890 only four—Maine, Michigan, Tennessee, and Kansas—passed anti-trust acts.[2] The federal government also took action late. The Interstate Commerce Act of 1887 sought to impose restrictions on one class of industrial organizations whose activities came peculiarly close to the public; but the first federal statute to deal with the general conditions of industrial competition was the Sherman Anti-Trust Act of 1890, which declared illegal "every contract, combination in the form of trust or otherwise, or conspiracy, in restraint of trade or commerce among the several states or with foreign nations."[3]

Like the Interstate Commerce Act, the Sherman law long remained ineffective. Few measure have received so much earnest and discriminating attention from

[1] U. S. Industrial Commission, *Report*, I., 1325 *et seq.*; XIII., 1013 *et seq.*; XIX., 594–724.
[2] U. S. Bureau of Corporations, *Trust Laws and Unfair Competition*, 9.
[3] *U. S. Statutes at Large*, XXVI., pt. i., p. 209.

Congress; none have been more consistently upheld
by the courts. But for a long time the executive
branch failed to supply the needed push. Presidents
Harrison, Cleveland, and McKinley were not fitted by
training or conviction to wage contest with the powerful corporate interests opposed to the enforcement of
the law; and the interests of their attorney-general did
not run in this direction.[1] Under Harrison there were
only three indictments, and under Cleveland two;
under McKinley there were none. Action was discouraged by belief that the law was too severe, and
by failures in certain early prosecutions, notably the
case of *United States vs. E. C. Knight Company* (1895),
in which the Supreme Court ruled that the terms of
the law were applicable only to monopoly in restraint
of trade, and not to monopoly in manufacture.[2] In a
period of eleven years only eighteen public suits were
brought under the act, of which eight were unsuccessful. Corporations that feared prosecution reorganized,
actually or fictitiously, and gained immunity; "under-
standings" that could not be overthrown by the courts
took the place of contractual agreements; combination
went on without restraint.

Though mentioned in the party platforms, the
"trust" question was not made an issue in 1900. But
the alarming spread of industrial combination in 1901–
1902, coupled with Roosevelt's accession to the presidency, forced the problem into the foreground. In his

[1] Seager, "The Recent Trust Decisions," *Polit. Sci. Quart.*, **XXVI.**,
584.
[2] 156 U. S., 1; Dewey, *National Problems* (*Am. Nation*, **XXIV.**),
202.

first message to Congress, December 3, 1901, the new
President devoted much space to railroad and trust
questions, taking a position which he consistently maintained throughout his seven and a half years in office.
Large fortunes, he insisted, had arisen inevitably under
the working of natural economic forces. Industrial
concentration could not be prevented. If properly regulated, it was highly desirable. State control, once
adequate, was no longer so; therefore federal control
must be increased. The true remedies would be found
in publicity, the elimination of over-capitalization and
related abuses, and the turning of effort to the regulation, not the suppression, of combination.[1]

Under the President's spur, Congress in 1903 took
two important steps to strengthen trust-regulating machinery. One was the adoption of the Elkins amendments to the Interstate Commerce Act, seeking to cut
off favors hitherto extended by the railroads to the
great corporations.[2] The other was the passage of an
act, approved February 14, creating a Department of
Commerce and Labor, to include a Bureau of Corporations, presided over by a Commissioner, and authorized
to "make . . . diligent investigation into the organization, conduct, and management of corporations (other
than common carriers) engaged in interstate and foreign commerce" and to "gather, compile, publish, and
supply useful information" concerning them.[3] The
Bureau's function was, not to prosecute offenders, but

---

[1] *Senate Jour.*, 57 Cong., 1 Sess., 5-7.   [2] See p. 45.
[3] *U. S. Statutes at Large*, XXXII., pt. i., p. 825.   Cf. Department of
Commerce and Labor, *Organization and Law* (1904).

to provide data for the use of the Department of Justice and of Congress.

Employing to the utmost its new equipment, and supported by a rapidly developing public sentiment, the Roosevelt Administration started a campaign of investigations and prosecutions. In 1903 action was brought to dissolve the Northern Securities Company, and in the favorable verdict handed down by the Supreme Court in 1904 the government won a great moral victory. The General Paper Company was indicted in 1904 and dissolved in 1906. The so-called Beef Trust was investigated by Commissioner Garfield in 1904 and indicted in 1905.[1] Under a ruling of Judge Humphreys of the United States District Court at Chicago, the defendants were discharged because they had supplied needed information tending to incriminate them, and hence were entitled to immunity. But the publicity given the packing business led to a comprehensive statute, approved March 4, 1907, which supplemented the pure-food law of 1906 and required inspection of all meats carried in interstate and foreign commerce.[2] At the end of 1907 the Department of Justice reported that since the accession of President Roosevelt sixteen civil suits had been brought, of which eight had resulted in injunctions and eight were pending; also eighteen criminal suits, of which nine had resulted in convictions and seven were pending.

Progress was slow, and the country was far from satisfied. Cases were thought to be too frequently

[1] U. S. Commissioner of Corporations, *Report on the Beef Industry* (1905).

[2] *U. S. Statutes at Large*, XXXIV., pt. i., pp. 1260–1265.

dismissed on technicalities; convictions seemed too difficult to obtain and court orders too easily evaded. But neither popular demand nor pressure from the White House moved Congress to action. In 1908 the Democrats seized the advantage accruing from a radical position on the subject and urged "reform of the criminal law against guilty trust magnates and officials," together with legislation shaped to make it impossible for a private monopoly to exist in the country. The Republicans pronounced the Sherman law "a wholesome instrument for good," but admitted that it needed to be strengthened. The drift of campaign argument indicated that the country no longer accepted Blaine's aphorism: "trusts are state issues; they have no place in national campaigns."

The first task of the Taft administration was the revision of the tariff, accomplished in the Payne-Aldrich Act of 1909. The Democrats had long contended that the protective tariff was "the mother of the trusts"; and few men in any party were so bold as to deny that the two things were vitally related. But no serious attempt was made in 1909 to ascertain the effects of tariff rates, present and proposed, on corporation growth and practices, and it remained for the Taft Administration to take up the task of trust control where its predecessor had left off—to work for the amendment of the Sherman law, and in the meantime to prosecute offenders as best it could under that measure and cognate statutes.

The President and his advisers decided to make the revision of the interstate commerce and anti-trust laws

the principal task of Congress during the regular
session of 1909–1910. To this end they mapped out
a program of legislation, and also of administrative
readjustment to secure better working relations among
the Department of Justice, the Interstate Commerce
Commission, and the Bureau of Corporations; and in
a special message of January 7, 1910, the proposals
were put before the two houses.[1] The first half of
the suggested measure dealt with railroads; and after
five months it bore fruit in the Mann-Elkins Act of
June 18, 1910.[2] The second part dealt with corporations and trusts.

Like Roosevelt, Taft urged that large aggregations
of capital are necessary under modern economic conditions, and that it was not the intent of the Sherman
law to interfere with any great industrial concern
which abstained from taking advantage of its size to
stifle competition "by methods akin to duress." The
present difficulty, he said, lay in the lack of means of
distinguishing innocent corporations from guilty ones.
Wholesale and continuous prosecutions of all suspected
concerns involved continual disturbance of business
and unnecessary anxiety to investors. The Sherman
law should stand; but it should be supplemented by
a system of voluntary federal incorporation involving
a moderate amount of regulation, with a full measure
of publicity. This recommendation was based on the
belief that concerns which knew their policies and
methods to be wholly within the law would seek the
advantage of incorporation by federal authority; while

[1] *House Jour.*, 61 Cong., 2 Sess., 126–130.   [2] See p. 53.

concerns that feared prosecution because their acts
were illegal would hesitate, or refuse, to avail themselves of the privilege. Corporations which thus placed
themselves under suspicion could be watched or proceeded against without disturbing legitimate business
interests. The plan seemed good; but support of it
by John D. Rockefeller and other trust magnates
cooled public interest.

A bill was introduced, under the President's direction, allowing voluntary federal incorporation of concerns with a capital stock of one hundred thousand
dollars and upwards, with discretion in the Commissioner of Corporations to approve the charters and
in Congress to revoke them. The railroad question,
however, took precedence; and the session closed without action on this promising plan. Subsequently Taft
gave up his project and urged that effort be concentrated upon enforcement of the laws already on the
statute-book;[1] and his administration brought no trust
legislation except such as was included in the Mann-
Elkins Act.

This failure to secure legislation was somewhat compensated by judicial victories, especially by two weighty
decisions handed down by the Supreme Court in May,
1911, dissolving the Standard Oil Company and the
American Tobacco Company, and advancing fresh
doctrine on the interpretation and enforcement of the
existing anti-trust laws. Both of these cases had been
in the courts more than four years, and both enlisted
high legal talent and aroused wide public interest.

[1] *Senate Jour.*, 61 Cong., 3 Sess., 22.

The suit against the Standard Oil Company, seventy subsidiary corporations, and seven individuals (including John D. Rockefeller, William Rockefeller, and John D. Archbold) was brought to dissolve the combination as in violation of the Sherman law. It was begun in the Circuit Court for the Eastern District of Missouri, at St. Louis, November 15, 1906. The first stage ended November 20, 1909, when a bench of four judges held unanimously that the combination was illegal, not only as in restraint of trade, but as a monopoly; they ordered its dissolution and issued a broad injunction against all of the defendants except thirty-three of the subsidiary corporations. On December 17, 1909, an appeal was filed, alleging sixty-five errors. The case was argued before the Supreme Court in March, 1910, and a second time in the spring of 1911.

The counsel for the defendants contended that while the Standard Oil interests were organized in numerous companies, these companies were products of the natural growth of a single business, and, having never been separate and competing organizations, could not be regarded as having combined in restraint of trade; that the concern was a private business enterprise, not a public service corporation; and that as such it was, and must be, free to buy and sell as it chose and to do anything that any of its competitors might do. Attorney-General Wickersham and his spokesmen, on the other hand, contended that from an early date Rockefeller and his associates had sought to build up a monopoly; that they had used price discriminations, railroad rebating, bribery, and other means calculated to crush their competitors; and that their organization was clearly in contravention of law.

The decision, written and delivered by Chief Justice White, was handed down May 15, 1911.[1] In the main, it confirmed the decree of the Circuit Court, and the defendants were given six months in which to readjust their affairs in such a way as to conform to law. Within this period the parent organization, the Standard Oil Company of New Jersey, relinquished its control over the subsidiary corporations, and the stocks of these organizations hitherto held by the New Jersey company were apportioned as individual possessions among the stockholders of that company. Thus the combination was resolved into its elements, each of the subsidiary companies becoming a full-fledged and independent corporation. In theory, these corporations, thirty-eight in number, straightway became competitors. In fact, however, a controlling interest in most of them was retained by a group of ten or twelve men; the offices of seven important ones remained in the quarters which the parent company had occupied; and cooperation rather than competition continued to prevail. The rise in the value of the stock of the offending corporation after the decision was sufficient proof that the vitality of the trust was not greatly impaired.

The importance of the Standard Oil decision lay not so much in its effect on one of the country's largest business concerns, as in the revolutionary principles laid down by the court on the applications of the Sher-

[1] 221 U. S., 1.

man law. In the Trans-Missouri Case, decided in
1897, the court, by a bare majority, had in effect declared that all combinations in restraint of trade,
whether reasonable or unreasonable, were forbidden
by the law; [1] and in several other decisions the question
of reasonableness or unreasonableness was affirmed, by
a similarly divided court, to have no bearing. Justice
White was one of the dissentients; and in the Standard
Oil decision of 1911 he, now sitting as Chief Justice,
had the satisfaction of affirming, with the assent of
all his colleagues save one, that the Sherman Act must
not be construed to prohibit in a blind and arbitrary
manner all contracts and agreements that might seem
to restrain trade, but only such as in their nature were
unreasonable and contrary to individual rights or the
general welfare. For the first time the court read
together the first section of the Sherman Act, which pronounced illegal every combination in restraint of trade,
and the second section, which made it a misdemeanor
to monopolize or attempt to monopolize interstate or
foreign trade; whence it arrived at the conclusion that
only that restraint of trade which monopolizes or attempts to monopolize is "undue," unreasonable, and
interdicted by the law. In dissenting from this portion of the decision, Justice Harlan contended that the
law recognized no such distinctions, and that the "rule
of reason" was but one more illustration of the unfortunate propensity of American courts to make new
laws by reading into old ones unwarranted interpre-

---

[1] *U. S. vs. Trans-Missouri Freight Association*, 166 U. S., 327. Cf.
U. S. vs. Joint Traffic Association, 171 U. S., 566.

tations drawn from sources outside the Constitution
and the statutes.

The business public, which felt the burden of a law
bearing alike upon reasonable and unreasonable restraint, welcomed the new doctrine. So, likewise, did
administrators who, like President Taft, desired some
basis for discrimination between good trusts and bad
trusts. It was recalled, however, that proposals in
Congress to amend the Sherman Act by making it
applicable solely to "unreasonable" combinations had
been repeatedly opposed on the ground that the change
would increase the law's indefiniteness, and hence the
difficulty of its enforcement; and the final feeling was
one of doubt whether the court had not both altered
and weakened the law. At all events, persons who
hoped for a plain and simple doctrine which could be
infallibly applied in advance were disappointed. Even
more than before, every case must be handled on its
individual merits.

In the decision handed down in the case against the
American Tobacco Company, May 29, 1911,[1] the rule
of reason was reaffirmed (Justice Harlan again dissenting); and the opinion was expressed that under this
principle the law would be enforced more effectively.
Since its original incorporation in 1890, the American
Tobacco Company had grown, through combinations,
consolidations, and acquisitions of shares of plants,
stocks, and other properties, to amazing proportions.[2]

[1] 221 U. S., 106.
[2] U. S. Commissioner of Corporations, *Report on the Tobacco Industry:*
pt. i., *Position of the Tobacco Combination in the Industry* (1909);
pt. ii., *Capitalization, Investments, and Earnings* (1911).

On July 10, 1907, suit was brought in the Circuit Court for the Southern District of New York against twenty-nine individuals and seventy-one companies (sixty-nine American and two English), alleged to comprise the "trust"; and on November 7, 1908, the defendants were declared to constitute a combination in restraint of trade and were enjoined from engaging in interstate commerce until competition should have been restored among them. On appeal, a stay in the execution of the injunction was granted, and the case was carried to the Supreme Court.

This tribunal reaffirmed the decree of the Circuit Court; ordered the dissolution of the central company; and suggested a program for the reorganization of the company's interests on lawful lines. The task of readjustment was more difficult than that imposed by the Standard Oil decision; for, unlike the Standard Oil Company, the American Tobacco Company was not a mere holding corporation; it was also a manufacturing concern. But under judicial supervision the reorganization was carried out. The fourteen resulting companies were enjoined from co-operation in any form and from having, within a period of five years, common offices, directors, or sales agents; no one of them might hold stock in another.[1] The dissolution was, accordingly, more thorough than that of the Standard Oil Company.

President Taft expressed satisfaction with these two

[1] Raymond, "The Standard Oil and Tobacco Cases," *Harvard Law Rev.*, XXV., 31–58; Seager, "The Recent Trust Decisions," *Polit. Sci. Quart.*, XXVI., 581–614 (cf. *Quart. Jour. Econ.*, XXIX., 848–851); Taft, *The Anti-Trust Act and the Supreme Court*, chap. vi.

great decisions, and affirmed that the meaning of the
anti-trust law was now sufficiently clear to enable
business to organize and reorganize without creating
excessive disturbance; although he advocated supplementary legislation to define yet more precisely the
methods and practices held to be objectionable. Attorney-General Wickersham was similarly optimistic.
But students of trust problems were inclined to doubt
whether real competition would exist among the sep-
arated concerns, and the general public refused to take
the decisions seriously.

Three main solutions of the trust problem have been
suggested: (1) *laissez-faire*, or non-action; (2) extermination; (3) regulation. The great number of combinations, pools, and agreements that have gone to
pieces of themselves prove that "hands off" is not
without virtue; but by 1900 it ceased to meet general
favor. The plan of extermination, put forward enthusiastically by Bryan and by Senator Cummins,
once made wide appeal, but to most people appears
impracticable. The policy of regulation is based on
the fact that concentration is the law of the modern
industrial world, and is an indispensable means of
steadying prices, reducing waste, promoting regularity
of employment, and correcting abuses of unrestricted
competition. Regulation looks to perpetuation of the
economies flowing from monopoly, with suppression of
monopoly's evils; it means that the power of the government is to be used to compel business concerns to
share with the public the gains which they derive from
operating on a grand scale.

After 1900 regulation steadily gained in favor. The great service of Roosevelt in dealing with corporations was not the galvanizing of the Sherman law into life, nor yet the securing of new legislation, but the bringing of the people to the view, hitherto but imperfectly conceived, that capitalistic combination is not an evil *per se*, and that any proper system of restraint must be continually readapted to changing economic conditions. The frank announcement of the "rule of reason" in the Supreme Court decisions of 1909 marked a long-delayed conversion of the highest tribunal of the land to the essentials of this doctrine.

At the close of the last century an American economist wrote: "If there is any serious student of our economic life who believes that anything substantial has been gained by all the laws passed against trusts, by all the newspaper editorials which have thus far been penned, by all the sermons which have been preached against them, this authority has yet to be heard from. Forms and names have been changed in many instances, but the dreaded work of vast aggregation of capital has gone on practically as heretofore."[1] Perhaps after eighteen years, and in view of some of the great trust dissolutions that have been mentioned, judgment would be less severe. Yet the fact is patent that the Sherman law totally failed to accomplish its primary purpose—namely, to prevent monopoly and restraint of trade. In periods of vigorous enforcement it caused corporations to walk more circumspectly, and the public profited. It brought

[1] Ely, *Monopolies and Trusts*, 243.

about some desirable reorganizations. It eliminated some unfair practices. By and large, the effect of its operation was, however, to drive great combinations successively from one intrenchment to another, rather than to sweep them wholly from the field.[1]

The fundamental defects of the law arose from the attempt to do too much. In so far as its framers sought the complete elimination of monopoly from industry and trade, they were aiming at the impossible; for there are parts of the economic world in which monopoly is inevitable. Telephone service affords a good illustration. Furthermore, apart from monopoly, big business is not necessarily bad business. Concentration may serve the interest of the consumer no less than that of the producer and transporter. What was needed was a more tolerant attitude toward industrial combination, more encouragement of mutually beneficial co-operation, and a great administrative agency capable of keeping close watch on the situation and asserting intelligent control. The first fruitful effort to supply these conditions was delayed until 1913.[2]

[1] Van Hise, *Concentration and Control*, 191.   [2] See chap. xiii.

6

CHAPTER V

INDUSTRY AND LABOR

(1905–1914)

LABOR, the world over, takes its cue from capital. In branches of industry in which the organization of capital plays small part there is usually little organization of labor; periods of rapid capitalistic concentration become periods of accelerated labor movement; great industrial and commercial corporations tend to be counterbalanced by powerful labor unions and federations. Accordingly, the years after 1900 became in the United States a time of notable activity in the labor field, falling into three main phases: (1) growth of labor organizations; (2) judicial determination of the status and rights of these organizations; (3) increased participation of organized labor in politics.

Chief among the labor organizations of the time was the American Federation of Labor, organized in 1881 as a rival of the Knights of Labor, and modelled on the British Trades Union Congress. The Federation was composed of American branches of various international labor unions, together with national, state, and local societies, of widely differing size, strength, and character. At the beginning of 1916 there were more than a hundred of the national and international associations; and in that year the last important independent international, the Bricklayers' and Masons' Union, was brought in. The number of dues-paying members of the affiliated organizations rose from 1,494,300 in 1905 to 2,071,836 in 1916.

Beginning in 1882, the Federation from year to year re-elected as its president Samuel Gompers, who became the most conspicuous figure in the labor world. Gompers was an English Jew who came to the United States during boyhood and early attained influence in labor circles in New York. His mental horizon took in little except labor problems, and many liberal-minded labor men felt that he was not sufficiently receptive to the newer devices of arbitration as against the older methods of the strike and the boycott. But his hold on the machinery of the Federation was broken only once (1895), and then for but a single year. He was ambitious, energetic, resourceful; his ability as an organizer and strategist was unsurpassed.

Outside of the Federation stood several important labor organizations, notably the American Flint Glass Workers' Union, the Western Federation of Miners, and four great brotherhoods of railway employees. But the bulk of workingmen were not organized for labor purposes at all. Combination was easy only in the relatively compact skilled and semi-skilled trades; farm laborers and most unskilled industrial employees lacked the contact, leadership, and *morale* necessary for unity of purpose and action. When, therefore, organized labor pressed its demands upon employers and upon the public authorities, it was always possible to point out that it spoke for but a small minority of the working population of the country.[1]

Of new labor organizations, the most important that appeared in the earlier years of the century was the Industrial Workers of the World, established at Chicago in June, 1905. This ultra-radical society sprang from an unsuccessful effort, in 1903-1904, to commit the American Federation to the tenets of socialism. It drew mainly from the Trade and Labor Alliance, and from the American Labor Union, formed in 1898 by the Western Federation of Miners upon its withdrawal from the American Federation. The basis of the "I. W. W." was industry in general, not trades or crafts; and existing trade unions were denounced as the pliant tools of labor exploiters. "The working class and the employing class," declared the initial manifesto, "have nothing in common. Between these two classes a struggle must go on until the workers of the world, organized as a class, take possession of the earth and the machinery of production, and abolish the wage system."

In 1906 the new organization lost more than half of its membership through the secession of the Western Federation of Miners;[2] and two years later the re-maining body was cleft asunder by a quarrel which resulted in the ejection of that portion of the member-ship which was identified with the Socialist Labor party. Thereafter the non-political, syndicalist branch

[1] Barnett, "Growth of Labor Organization in the United States, 1897-1914," *Quart. Jour. Econ.*, XXX., 780-795.
[2] *Senate Docs.*, 58 Cong., 3 Sess., Nc. 122.

maintained headquarters at Chicago, while the "conservative" wing carried on its propaganda from Detroit. In 1915, the Detroit branch, desiring to dissociate itself in the public mind from the I. W. W., voted to adopt the name "Workers' International Industrial Union." The importance of the I. W. W. movement lay, not in the number of adherents, but in the introduction into American labor of the principles and methods of "direct action" preached by the syndicalists of France, Italy, and other European countries. In 1917 the nonpolitical branch was still active in instigating and leading strikes, and firm in advocating sabotage; but there were evidences of decline in both membership and influence.[1]

Toward the close of Roosevelt's second administration the attention of the country was directed to two great legal questions pertaining to organized labor: (1) the relation of the Sherman anti-trust law to the boycott; (2) the use of the writ of injunction in labor disputes.[2] Both were brought to the fore by important cases in the courts. In 1903 D. E. Loewe & Co., manufacturers of hats in Danbury, Connecticut, brought suit against the United Hatters of North America to restrain that organization from prosecuting a boycott against the plaintiff's hats, begun because the company had declared an open shop and had discontinued use of the union label. The lower courts dismissed the complaint; but in a decision handed down

---

[1] Hoxie, "The Truth about the I. W. W.," *Jour. Polit. Econ.*, XXI., 785–797.

[2] Groat, "Injunctions in Labor Disputes," *Polit. Sci. Quart.*, XXIII., 408–439.

February 3, 1908, the Supreme Court found unanimously in the plaintiff's favor.[1] A boycott, the highest court declared, obstructs the free flow of commerce among the states; as a combination in restraint of trade, it violates the Sherman law. The company was authorized to bring suit against the United Hatters for damages. This it did; and eventually it got judgment.

In September, 1907, the Bucks Stove and Range Company of St. Louis brought suit in the Supreme Court of the District of Columbia against the American Federation of Labor, and asked both a temporary and a permanent injunction restraining the defendant from continuing a boycott againt the plaintiff. The boycott complained of was instituted in 1906, as a result of a dispute between the company and the Metal Polishers' Union, and consisted in the repeated printing of the plaintiff's name in the "We don't patronize," or "unfair," list appearing in the columns of the *American Federationist*. The case was regarded as a trial of strength between the Federation, led by Gompers, and the National Association of Manufacturers, whose president, J. W. Van Cleave, was also president of the Bucks Company. As in the Hatters' case, the question was whether workingmen might legitimately combine to withhold their patronage from a person or firm and incite others to do so—in other words, whether the boycott could lawfully be used as a weapon in industrial warfare.

A temporary injunction was granted; and, on March

[1] *Loewe vs. Lawlor*, 208 U. S., 274.

23, 1908, a permanent injunction, in line with the Hatters' decision of a few weeks before, restrained the defendants from "publishing or otherwise circulating, whether in writing or orally, any statement or notice of any kind or character" calling attention to a boycott against the plaintiff or advising any one not to purchase the plaintiff's goods. Individuals, said the court, might refuse to patronize a firm; but incitement of others to do so amounted to a conspiracy in restraint of trade, and under the Sherman law was illegal.

In trade-union circles these decisions aroused intense feeling. They tended to cast doubt upon the legality of the unions themselves—as, indeed, upon that of consumers' leagues and many other kinds of organizations whose purposes was to influence the course and character of trade. Speaking for the unions, Gompers argued that the authors of the Sherman law did not intend the measure to be applied to labor; that labor is not a commodity, and that therefore no "trust" in it can be formed; that it is the right of all men to dispose of both their labor and their patronage as they choose; and that the right of an individual in this matter must be equally the right of a group. He pronounced the Bucks decision "the most sweeping invasion of the liberty of the press and of the right of free speech that ever emanated from an American court."

The questions raised by the decisions had long been foreseen by labor leaders, and effort had been made to anticipate them by legislation which would legalize the boycott and restrict the use of the injunction in labor controversies. This effort failed, and it was mainly on that account that the American Federation of Labor, in 1906, for the first time definitely entered the field of politics. Its attempt to prevent the re-election of Speaker Cannon, Charles E. Littlefield of Maine, and other congressmen considered to be hostile to labor interests was unsuccessful. But a new line of defensive activity was clearly marked out.

Failing to obtain legislation in the session of 1907–1908, the labor leaders turned to the national party conventions. From the Republicans they got only an acknowledgement that the rules governing the use of injunctions should be "more accurately defined by statute," and that "no injunction or temporary restraining order should be issued without notice, except where irreparable injury would result from delay, in which case a speedy hearing thereafter should be granted." From the Democrats they obtained a declaration that "injunctions should not be issued in any cases in which injunctions would not issue if no industrial dispute were involved." The Democratic position was obviously the more satisfactory, and in the campaign Gompers strove to swing the support of labor to Bryan.

During the contest Taft freely admitted that the writ of injunction in labor disputes had been abused, and suggested a constitutional amendment against temporary injunctions without notice and hearing. Several times in succeeding years he urged Congress to act, but never with effect; and the whole question went over to the next administration, when the legal status of labor organizations was defined, on lines long advocated by these organizations, in the Clayton Anti-Trust Act of October 15, 1914.[1]   In 1913 a special committee of the American Bar Association reported that out of a total of 730 injunctions granted by federal courts between November, 1902, and January, 1913, only 26 related to labor cases.

Meanwhile, the Danbury Hatters' and other cases involving injunctions came to a point where conclusions could be reached.   The Bucks Stove and Range controversy was finally settled out of court, on terms reasonably satisfactory to the labor interests: the company accepted the principle of the closed shop.   The Hatters' case had a different history.   Under warrant of the Supreme Court decision of February 3, 1908, the Loewe Company brought suit in the Circuit Court of Connecticut against the United Hatters of North America, and in 1910 it won a judgment of $222,000. A fine in this amount was levied on the individual members of the union, and their property was attached to secure payment.   The case was carried to the Circuit Court of Appeals, which upheld the opinion that a boycott affecting the flow of interstate trade is a violation of the anti-trust laws, but took the ground that the individual members of a trade union cannot be made liable in their property for the acts of the union's agents, unless a jury determines that by their express or tacit approval they have incurred such responsibility.[2]   This decision, which in effect denied that by bare membership in a trade union a man becomes

[1]See p. 235.   [2] 187 *Fed. Rep.*, 522.

liable in his property for every act of the authorities
of the organization, was received by labor men with
satisfaction. The litigation, however, was continued,
and on January 5, 1915, the Supreme Court reaffirmed
a judgment of $252,130 against 186 members of the
Hatters' Union.[1] The final echo of the case came in
1917, when the plaintiff collected the amount due,
partly from savings banks deposits under attachment.[2]

The controversy over injunctions and boycotts kept
organized labor in a state of unrest and added to the
ill effects of strikes and lockouts. In the period 1901–
1905, 13,964 strikes and 541 lockouts were recorded;
and during the following decade the number per year
increased, until in 1916 a high-water mark was reached
in 1,947 strikes and 77 lockouts within the space of
seven months. None was so serious as the anthracite
coal strike of 1902;[3] but many attracted nation-wide
attention and deranged the business interests of large
numbers of people. Among the most formidable were
the strike of the miners at Goldfield, Nevada, in 1907;
that of the shirt-waist makers of New York City (the
largest women's strike in the history of the country)
in 1909; that of the New York cloakmakers in 1910;
those of the textile workers of Lawrence, Massachusetts, in 1912, and the silk-workers of Paterson,
New Jersey, in 1913 (both carried on under the leadership of the I. W. W.); that of the coal-miners of

[1]235 U. S., 522.
[2] Merritt, "The Law of the Danbury Hatters' Case," Am. Acad.
Polit. and Soc. Sci., *Annals*, XXVI., 265–276; Schaffner, "Effect of the
Recent Boycott Decisions," *ibid.*, 276–287.
[3] Latané, *America as a World Power* (*Am. Nation*, XXV.), 310–313.

southern Colorado in 1913–1914, which was unusually
violent and required federal intervention; that of the
iron and steel workers of East Youngstown, Ohio, in
1915; and that of employees of the Standard Oil
Company and other oil and chemical plants at Bayonne,
New Jersey, in 1916.   Except during a portion of 1912,
the anthracite industry was kept at peace by means
of successive three-year agreements negotiated by the
same commission that in 1903 worked out the terms of
settlement of the great strike of the preceding year.
The first considerable strike in the United States by
public employees was one unsuccessfully undertaken
by the New York street cleaners in 1911.

These and other disorders did not stay the progress
of industrial peace.   Mediation and arbitration grew
in favor; many threatened strikes were prevented.
Agencies of conciliation were especially active in the
domain of railroad transportation.   As early as 1888
an arbitration act applying to interstate carriers was
put on the federal statute book.   It proved a dead
letter, and in June, 1898, it was superseded by a new
and better measure, known as the Erdman Arbitration
Act.[1]   This law, which was strongly favored by the
railway unions, applied to all employees of interstate
railways who were engaged in train operation and train
service.   It looked to both mediation and arbitration.
It created no special agency of mediation, and it authorized nobody to offer mediation of his own accord.
But it provided that in case of dispute between a carrier and its employees either party might request the

---

[1] *U. S. Statutes at Large*, XXX., pt. i., p. 429.

chairman of the Interstate Commerce Commission and the United States Commissioner of Labor to offer mediation. If both parties to the dispute gave their assent, these two officials were to use their best endeavors to adjust the difficulty. The object chiefly aimed at in the law was, however, voluntary arbitration. On the basis of a written agreement, carriers and employees might submit their case to an arbitral board, consisting of a representative of each side to the controversy and a third person selected by these two; and the award of the board was, in somewhat indefinite terms, made legally binding.

For eight years only one attempt was made to take advantage of the Erdman Act; but between 1907 and 1913 the measure was brought into use no fewer than sixty-one times, and forty cases were settled under it— thirty-six by, or as a result of, mediation by Chairman Knapp and Commissioner Neill; four by arbitration alone. An adjustment of a wage dispute between the Brotherhood of Locomotive Engineers and the fifty-two railroads of the eastern district, instituted under the law (although carried out on somewhat original lines) in 1912, became the most important triumph of industrial arbitration in the United States since the anthracite coal settlement of 1902–1903.

Notwithstanding these proofs of usefulness, the Erdman Act was imperfect. The officials upon whom the task of mediation was imposed were already overburdened; and the objection arose that the representative of the employers was likely to take one side and the representative of the employees the other, leaving the third arbitrator to make the decision single-handed. By 1913 demand for revision was strong; and when, in that year, the law failed to save the eastern district from imminent danger of a ruinous strike on forty-two roads, Congress hastily replaced it with a new measure —the Newlands Act—introduced in the Senate June 10, and approved July 15.[1]

The Newlands Act set up a United States Board of Mediation and Conciliation, consisting of a Commissioner, an Assistant Commissioner, and not more than two other government officials, all appointed by the President with the consent of the Senate. It was made the duty of this board, at times of controversy between an interstate railroad and its employees, to receive appeals from either party and to try to bring about an amicable agreement. The board was given power to take the initiative by proffering its services; and in the event of failure to carry out mediation, it must seek to induce the parties to accept arbitration, through either three-member or six-member boards. The new law contained no more compulsion than did the old one.

In the main, the Newlands Act proved successful. It averted the strike which was impending when it was passed; and to October, 1916, a total of sixty-one controversies were adjusted under it—forty-six by mediation, eleven by arbitration, and four by mediation and arbitration. In twenty-one cases employees made application for the services of the board; in fifteen the railroads applied; in seventeen the parties made joint

---

[1] *U. S. Statutes at Large*, **XXXVIII.**, pt. i., pp. 103–108.

application; in eight the board made a tender of services which was accepted. A number of the cases involved the railway service of a whole section of the country; one in 1914–1915 affected all roads west of the Mississippi River. And it is worthy of note that within the period mentioned no strike occurred in any case actually taken up by the board. Only in 1916, when the four great railroad brotherhoods of the country made a concerted demand upon the operators for an eight-hour basic day, with time-and-a-half for overtime, did the new machinery of conciliation fail. Congress met this emergency by passing an act to settle the questions immediately in dispute, and the Newlands law was left intact, in the hope that it would continue to serve in ordinary controversies.[1]

Steadily the conviction grew that new means of securing industrial peace on broad lines must be found. Experts, however, could not agree on a policy. Some urged compulsory arbitration, such as prevails in New Zealand and Australia; others wanted compulsory investigation by an impartial board, after the principle of the Canadian Trades Disputes Investigation Act of 1907; still others preferred the extension of the principles of the Erdman and Newlands laws to branches of employment outside transportation.

In 1913 an important step was taken by conferring power on the head of the newly created Department of Labor to "act as mediator and to appoint com-

[1] Cf. chap. xix; *Am. Econ. Rev.*, VII., 195–198; Chambers, "American Experiences in Settlement of Disputes," Acad. Polit. Sci., *Proceedings*, VII., 1–9; McCabe, "The Erdman, Newlands, and Adamson Acts," *ibid.*, 94–107.

missioners of conciliation in labor disputes whenever in his judgment the interests of industrial peace may require it to be done." [1]   No mediation bureau or other special administrative machinery was provided; but the first Secretary of Labor, W. B. Wilson, gave much attention to the development of this important function, and requests for his mediation soon became numerous. In the fiscal year 1916, 227 cases, representing almost every important branch of industry, were handled by the Department; and hardly more than a score proved beyond its power to adjust. The Department did not dictate or arbitrate, but negotiated and recommended through commissioners specially named for each case.[2]

If labor unrest continued to produce strikes and other disorders, it also gave rise to much legislation, state and federal, on employer's liability, unemployment, the labor of women and children, wages, hours, and conditions of safety and sanitation. Employer's liability for accidents to workmen found a place in the law of several states before 1900, and by 1917 all except ten or eleven set up insurance systems, in either optional or compulsory form. Compulsory insurance offered constitutional difficulties in some states; but in a series of decisions handed down in 1916 the federal Supreme Court upheld the laws of New York, Iowa, and Washington, and gave presumptive validity to the whole body of such legislation.[3]

[1] *U. S. Statutes at Large*, XXXVII., pt. i., p. 738.
[2] Secretary of Labor, *Annual Report*, 1916, p. 8.
[3] Fisher, "The Scope of Workmen's Compensation in the United States," *Quart. Jour. Econ.*, XXX., 22–63.

The federal government was drawn into law-making of this nature by its relation to labor in the domain of interstate transportation. In June, 1906, at the suggestion of President Roosevelt, Congress passed an employer's liability law, making all interstate commerce carriers liable for injuries suffered by employees during hours of employment.[1] In decisions handed down January 6, 1908, the Supreme Court declared the measure unconstitutional, on the grounds: (1) that the power to control interstate commerce does not involve the power to regulate the relations of employer and employee; (2) that the law did not sufficiently distinguish employees in interstate from those in intrastate commerce.[2] With little delay Congress passed a new law (April 22, 1908), whose provisions were expressly confined to interstate railroads and to common carriers in territories, the District of Columbia, and other portions of the United States subject immediately to the control of Congress.[3] An accompanying measure established the liability of the United States government for occupational injuries suffered, through no misconduct or negligence of their own, by any of its employees engaged as artisans or laborers in arsenals and dock-yards, in work on rivers, harbors, or fortifications, and in hazardous service on the Panama Canal and reclamation projects.[4] Subsequently the terms of this act were extended to other classes of employees,

---

[1] *U. S. Statutes at Large*, XXXIV., pt. i., pp. 232–233.
[2] *Howard vs. Ill. Cent. Railroad Co.* and *Brooks vs. Southern Pacific Railroad Co.*, 207 U. S., 463.
[3] *U. S. Statutes at Large*, XXXV., pt. i., pp. 64–65.
[4] *Ibid.*, 556–558.

and in 1916 a Workmen's Compensation Act brought all of the half-million civil employees of the United States under the system.[1] In its final form the law provided compensation on a scale of two-thirds of the actual wages, not exceeding $66.67 a month, for the total period of disability. The administrative agency is an Employees' Compensation Commission, appointed by the President. In decisions announced January 15, 1912, in a group of cases hinging on the constitutionality of features of the federal Employer's Liability Act of 1908, as amended in 1910, the Supreme Court took the ground that the power to regulate interstate commerce includes the power to compel interstate carriers, and all persons or corporations engaged in interstate commerce, to assume liability for accidents to employees; and it held that any act of Congress on the subject would prevail as against state statutes in conflict therewith.[2]

The early years of the century brought to the fore the difficult problem of child labor in factories, mines, and miscellaneous trades. A National Child Labor Committee, established in 1904, started a campaign for reform; exhibits were set up, conferences were held, literature was circulated, and legislatures were flooded with petitions. After 1905 state legislation on the subject steadily grew, reaching a maximum in 1913, when child labor laws were passed in thirty-one states. Age limits were raised; hours were shortened; night

[1] *U. S. Statutes at Large*, XXXIX., pt. I., pp. 742–750.
[2] *Mondou vs. New York, New Haven, and Hartford Railroad Co.*, 223 U. S., I.

7

work was restricted; dangerous trades were closed to children; messenger and other street trades were regulated; better opportunities for school attendance were required.

State regulation was subject to many delays and difficulties, and some of the laws enacted were of little value. Leaders of the cause therefore turned to the federal government. The obvious appeal was to the power of Congress to regulate interstate commerce, and in December, 1906, Senator Beveridge of Indiana introduced as an amendment to a District of Columbia child labor bill a measure forbidding any interstate carrier to transport, or accept for transportation, the products of any factory or mine in which children under fourteen years of age were employed or permitted to work.[1] The main bill failed; and despite a powerful three-days' speech by its author, the amending measure did not come to a vote. Most lawyers considered it unconstitutional.

In 1908 Congress passed a very satisfactory child labor law for the District of Columbia.[2] For some years the larger proposal was not pushed farther, because it seemed expedient to pave the way for a federal statute by advanced legislation in an impressive proportion of the states. A bill passed in 1912 created in the Department of Commerce and Labor a Children's Bureau, charged with the duty of investigating "all matters pertaining to the welfare of children and child life."[3] This bureau was given no administra-

[1] *Cong. Record*, 59 Cong., 2 Sess., pt. ii., p. 1552.
[2] *U. S. Statutes at Large*, XXXV., pt. i., pp. 420-423.
[3] *Ibid.*, XXXVII., pt. i., pp. 79-80.

tive powers, and the investigations to which it first turned, *e.g.*, infant mortality, were but remotely related to child labor. Child labor reformers, however, welcomed the new agency as a valuable ally.

By 1916 the position of state child-labor regulation and of public sentiment upon the subject was wholly favorable to the long-delayed federal legislation. All of the leading parties demanded it in their national platforms, and when Congress showed a disposition to postpone action President Wilson intervened with complete success to turn the scale. The Keating-Owen child labor law, passed by large majorities in both houses, was approved September 1, 1916, to take effect one year later.[1] Following the general lines of the Beveridge bill of 1906, it forbade shipment in interstate commerce of products of any factory, shop, or cannery employing children under fourteen years of age; products of any mine or quarry employing children under sixteen years of age; and products of any of these establishments employing children under sixteen years of age more than eight hours a day or in night work. It was estimated that the measure would directly affect 150,000 working children; though the National Child Labor Committee considered that its chief value would be its tendency to raise and standardize the laws and administration in the states, to the relief of the 1,850,-000 child laborers who were beyond the direct reach of the federal government.

No more sweeping use of the power of Congress to regulate commerce was ever made. Years before, Wil-

[1] *U. S. Statutes at Large*, XXXIX., pt. i., pp. 675–676.

son had pronounced the Beveridge bill "obviously absurd." Now he was willing to use the spur on Congress in behalf of a measure that was decidedly more drastic. In his change of attitude was reflected something of the centralizing tendency which in a decade had led the whole country to a new way of thinking.[1]

In still other directions the interests of labor were served by the federal government. An act of 1912 placed a prohibitive tax on the manufacture of white phosphorus matches, as being ruinous to the health of the workers. A clause of the Post-Office Appropriation Act of 1912 definitely legalized organizations of federal employees, provided that the employees' associations should not be affiliated with any outside organization "imposing an obligation or duty upon the employees to engage in any strike, or proposing to assist them in any strike, against the United States.[2] Largely as a result of a proposal in Congress to increase the working day for government clerks from seven to eight hours, a union of civil service employees with over five thousand members was established in Washington in 1916 and brought into relation with the American Federation of Labor. A measure which took effect March 4, 1913, established an eight-hour day in contract work performed for the United States, with minor exceptions, and for letter-carriers and post-office

[1] McKelway, "Another Emancipation Proclamation," *Review of Reviews*, LIV., 423–426; Hull and Parkinson, "The Federal Child-Labor Law; the Question of its Constitutionality," *Polit. Sci. Quart.*, XXXI., 519–540.

[2] *U. S. Statutes at Large*, XXXVII., pt. i., p. 555; U. S. Civil Service Commission, *Annual Report*, 1913, pp. 54–55.

clerks in the larger cities. Labor in the same year
was awarded separate representation in the President's
cabinet. Finally may be mentioned the La Follette
Seaman's Act of March 4, 1915, intended to improve
the living and working conditions of employees on
ocean-going vessels and on lake and river craft.[1]

[1] *U. S. Statutes at Large*, XXXVIII., pt. i., pp. 1164–1185; Parvin,
"The Working of the Seaman's Act," Acad. Polit. Sci., *Proceedings*, VI.,
113–125; Farnam, "The Seaman's Act of 1915," *Am. Labor Legis. Rev.*,
VI., 41–60.

CHAPTER VI

CONSERVATION AND RECLAMATION

(1905–1916)

THE capital fact in the economic development of the United States is the spread of a fast-growing population over a continental area of cheap and productive land. Almost all of the land west of the Alleghanies was at one time publicly owned, and has passed into private hands by purchase from the government, or in other ways which the government liberally threw open. The country's public land policy has included five main features: (1) Retention of parcels needed for the common defense and the general welfare; lands have thus been withheld for military posts, Indian reservations, forest reservations, and several other purposes. (2) Grants to individuals, corporations, or states in aid of railroads, canals, and other improvements, or in the furtherance of education and philanthropy. (3) Grants of inferior lands—swamp lands under acts of 1850 and 1860 and desert lands under the Carey Act of 1894—in large areas, to be irrigated, reclaimed, and disposed of under direction of the states. (4) Grants to soldiers and sailors in lieu of, or supplementary to, money pensions. (5) Disposal, by sale or otherwise, to individuals under regulations made by Congress to secure titles to *bona fide* purchasers or settlers. Despite prolonged and generous alienation, the public domain on June 1, 1907, included 774,385,069 acres, of which less than one-third had been surveyed. Approximately one-half was in Alaska. The remainder was largely in Montana, Utah, Wyoming, Nevada, Arizona, and New Mexico, although portions lay in not fewer than twenty-five states and territories.[1]

The detection of widespread land frauds during President Roosevelt's second administration raised serious questions concerning the whole public land policy. For a hundred years the country had been prodigal. The land supply seemed inexhaustible; the demand, especially after the Civil War, was steady; and agricultural land and land that was rich in timber, minerals, and water-power were alike sold on easy terms or bestowed gratis.

Foresters, physiographers, geologists, and other experts had long criticized the system. They pointed out that the remaining lands were much less extensive than was popularly supposed, and they especially deplored the waste or perversion of forest, mineral, and water-power resources which loose land administration made possible. At the present rate of consumption, the United States, they said, had timber for less than thirty years, anthracite coal for only fifty years, and bituminous coal for about a hundred years; while supplies of iron ore, mineral oil, and natural gas were

[1] Secretary of the Interior, *Annual Report*, 1907, I., 69-260.

being rapidly depleted, and many great fields were already exhausted. The entire people, urged the scientists, should be aroused to greater care in the use of resources, whether publicly or privately owned. From France, Spain, Italy, North Africa, and especially China, were drawn powerful arguments on the effects of unchecked waste of forest, mineral, and other natural wealth.

After 1900 several conditions made it easier to drive these arguments home. One was the discovery that, through fraud, great areas in the most attractive regions were falling into the hands of speculators and exploiters. Another was the squabbling of private irrigation companies in the western states and territories. A third was the increasing cost of lumber and other natural products. A fourth was the leadership of President Roosevelt.

The demand for a more frugal land system and for the protection of the bounties of nature for the public good fell in aptly with the Rooseveltian ideas and policies. It aimed at the detection and punishment of fraud; it centered in the well-being of the great West; it looked to the extension of national, as opposed to state, control of economic interests and business activities; it raised the same deep issue as the railroads and trusts—should the people or the vested interests rule? Quickly discerning the movement's significance, the President threw to it his full support and eventually gave it a leading place in his program.[1] He pushed the prosecution of violators of the land laws, established

[1] Roosevelt, *Autobiography*, 429–431.

forest reserves, pressed for remedial legislation, and, finally, as a means of preventing the acquisition for alleged agricultural purposes of lands which were chiefly valuable for their coal or oil deposits or as water-power sites, he withdrew from entry extensive tracts, until they could be classified in accordance with their true values. By a single stroke, in December, 1906, he thus extended protection to sixty-four million acres of mineral lands, in nine states.

The conservation movement first became broadly national during the last half of Roosevelt's second administration. On March 14, 1907, an Inland Waterways Commission was created to make a study of the interlocking problems of waterways and forest preservation.[1] On May 13, 1908, at the suggestion of this commission and by invitation of the President, a largely attended meeting of officials was held at the White House for the discussion of questions of every character pertaining to conservation. At the close of its deliberations this conference adopted a Declaration of Principles affirming that "the conservation of our natural resources is a subject of transcendent importance, which should engage unremittingly the attention of the nation, the states, and the people in earnest co-operation." Specific recommendations included: (1) protection of source waters of navigable streams through purchase or control by the nation of the necessary lands; (2) adoption, by both nation and states, of more adequate means of preventing forest fires; (3) regulation of timber-cutting on both public

[1] See p. 114.

and private lands, where demanded by public interest; (4) extension of practical forestry; (5) granting of titles separately to the surface of public lands and to the minerals beneath; (6) retention by the federal government of title to all public lands containing phosphate rock, coal, oil, or natural gas, and arrangement for the extraction of these deposits by carefully regulated private enterprise; (7) preparation by the Inland Waterways Commission of a comprehensive plan of waterway development; (8) appointment by each state of a commission on the conservation of natural resources, to co-operate one with another and with the federal authorities.[1]

The adjournment of the White House conference was followed shortly by the appointment of a National Conservation Commission, consisting of one member from each state and territory, under the chairmanship of Gifford Pinchot; and within eighteen months were created forty-one state conservation commissions and fifty-one conservation commissions representing unofficial national organizations. The national commission took as its principal task the listing of the country's resources, and for this purpose it was divided into four sections, having to do with minerals, forests, waters, and soils. Though handicapped by lack of funds, it succeeded in making an inventory such as had never before been attempted; and its voluminous report, transmitted to the President January 11, 1909,

[1] *House Docs.*, 60 Cong., 2 Sess., No. 1425. The Declaration of Principles is reprinted in Van Hise, *Conservation of Natural Resources in the United States*, 381-389.

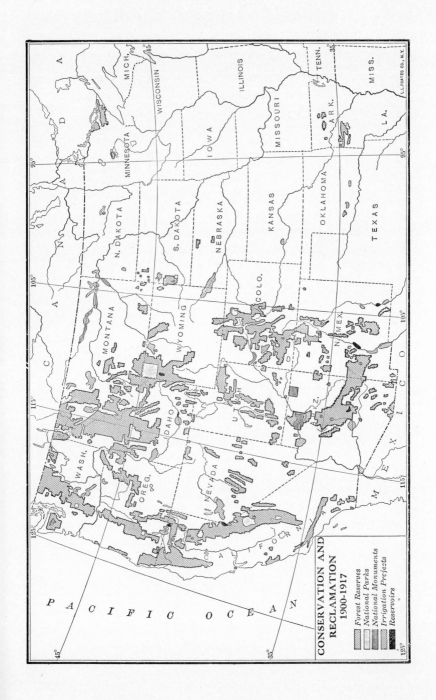

CONSERVATION AND
RECLAMATION
1900-1917

Forest Reserves
National Parks
National Monuments
Irrigation Projects
Reservoirs

L.L.POATES CO., N.Y.

remains the principal source of information upon all
matters with which it deals.[1]

The most obvious task of conservation was to preserve the forests; and, aside from President Roosevelt,
the most prominent leader of the conservation movement was the Chief Forester, Gifford Pinchot.[2] The
first measure of Congress authorizing the President to
set apart public forest land as reserves was passed
in 1891, and the first national forest reserve was proclaimed by President Harrison in that year. In 1897
a Division of Forestry was established in the Department of Agriculture, and in 1898 Pinchot was made its
chief. For seven years the only work of the division
was scientific investigation; the management of such
national forests as existed was vested in the Department of the Interior. "Forests and foresters," as
Roosevelt observes, "had nothing whatever to do with
each other."[3] In 1905, however, the two functions
were consolidated in a Bureau of Forestry in the Department of Agriculture, and from that date, under
Pinchot's able and enthusiastic direction, the service
ramified until it became the principal agent in conservation.[4]

Withdrawal of public land for incorporation in forest
reserves proceeded rapidly. During Harrison's administration thirteen million acres were set apart;
during Cleveland's, twenty-five million acres; and dur-

[1] *Senate Docs.*, 60 Cong., 2 Sess., No. 676.
[2] Roosevelt, *Autobiography*, 429.
[3] *Ibid.*, 430.
[4] *Ibid.*, 435–443; Graves, "The Advance of Forestry in the U. S.,"
Review of Reviews, XLI., 461–466.

ing McKinley's, seven million acres. Under Roosevelt's direction one hundred and forty-eight million acres were withdrawn, and the national forest area—149 tracts, in twenty-two states and territories—was raised to upwards of two hundred million acres. By 1909 the larger part of the great forests remaining on public lands in the Pacific and Rocky Mountain states had been set apart to be held and used perpetually in the interest of the whole nation. In his last annual message, December 8, 1908, Roosevelt warmly urged the continuance of forest preservation, not alone to keep up a lumber supply adequate to meet increasing needs at reasonable prices, but to prevent the erosion of soil and diminution of rainfall which would follow the denuding of mountain areas.[1] Advocates of forest conservation labored with some success to induce the states to establish and enlarge reserves and to discourage timber waste by imposing taxes on timber values only at the time when the trees were cut. It was suggested that the federal government should increase its reserves, both by setting apart fresh portions of the public domain in the West and by purchasing eastern forest land—notably in the White Mountains and the southern Appalachians—which had passed into private hands.

Thus, at the close of the Roosevelt administration the conservation movement was on the upward swing. Two main obstacles appeared. One was the coolness of the people of the farther West. This attitude is not difficult to understand. The populations of the

[1] *Senate Jour.*, 60 Cong., 2 Sess., 10–11.

older sections of the country had, in their day, ex-
ploited the lands, the minerals, and the water-power
which lay about them, and there had been no one
to say them nay.   The westerner was now to be held
in check: he must keep out of great areas of land; he
must leave rich mineral deposits untouched; he must
not turn the rivers to his use as the thrifty New Englanders had turned the Merrimac and the Penobscot to
theirs.   And the men who said he must not do these
things were easterners—many of them persons who
owed their wealth and standing to unrestrained exploitation of the riches of nature.   Apostles of conservation were, therefore, never popular in the West;
Roosevelt kept his hold there in spite of, not because
of, his interest in the subject.

A second obstacle was congressional apathy.   Fresh
evidence of it was supplied in an amendment to the
Sundry Civil Bill of March 4, 1909, cutting off the
Conservation Commission from further activity.[1]   Two
new organizations, however, took up the propaganda
during the year.   One was an unofficial Joint Committee on Conservation, established at the second governors' conference, in 1909.   The other was the National
Conservation Association, whose first president, ex-
President Charles W. Eliot of Harvard University,
was succeeded in 1910 by Gifford Pinchot.   Both organizations sought to bring national, state, and local
conservation agencies into relation, to stimulate public interest in the subject, and to obtain legislation.

Protection of the public lands and of their resources

[1] Roosevelt, *Autobiography*, 455.

appealed strongly to Roosevelt's successor. The right
to withdraw land from entry by simple executive
order, however, was questioned, and Taft obtained
from Congress an act (June 25, 1910) directly conferring the desired authority.[1] Thus equipped, he
withdrew from entry large quantities of land, including most of the areas withdrawn by Roosevelt, although portions were re-opened after surveys proved
that they contained no coal, oil, or other mineral wealth.
Special pains were taken to withdraw lands known to
contain water-power possibilities, pending legislation
to prevent power-sites from being acquired by persons
or corporations with a view to monopolizing them or
otherwise controlling them in a manner contrary to
the public interest. Prosecution of violators of the
land laws was continued, and during 1909 one hundred
and fifteen persons were convicted.

In the early part of the Taft administration opportunities seemed ripe for a general and much needed
revision of the land laws. In his first annual report
(December, 1909), the Secretary of the Interior,
Richard A. Ballinger, opened out an ambitious program of legislation.[2] He urged a thorough overhauling
of the existing land statutes, pointing out that they
were adapted only to the prairie country of the Middle
West, and not to the timber and mineral lands, or the
arid and semi-arid areas, of the farther West. He
objected to the current classification of lands (in five
categories, designated as agricultural, desert, min-

[1] *U. S. Statutes at Large*, XXXVI., pt. i., pp. 847–848.
[2] Secretary of the Interior, *Annual Report*, 1909, I., 5–14.

eral, timber, and coal), and called attention to the fact
that it was based principally on the inexpert reports
of the government surveyors who plotted the land.
He asked for a fresh, more exact, and legally binding
classification, based on scientific surveys of resources,
with provisions for changing tracts from one class to
another as reason for so doing should appear.   He also
recommended the disposal of all timber, and of all
coal-mining rights, on the public lands separately from
the soil.

For a time the outlook for legislation, and for conservation itself, was darkened by an unseemly controversy between Secretary Ballinger and Chief Forester
Pinchot, mainly over alleged coal-land frauds in Alaska.
On January 7, 1910, the trouble culminated in Pinchot's
dismissal from the service.   The impression got abroad
that Taft and his associates were not properly mindful
of conservation interests.   But a week after the removal of Pinchot the President laid before Congress
a definite, practical, and progressive conservation program; and at the same time nine conservation bills,
embodying Ballinger's proposed reforms, were introduced.   Two of the most important of these measures
dealt with coal, phosphate, oil, natural gas, and as-
phalt lands, separating title to the surface from title
to the underlying minerals, and providing for disposal
of the minerals by lease rather than sale.   All received
the unqualified support of the National Conservation
Association, and all became law.

The most notable single triumph of the conservation movement during the Taft administration was the

Appalachian Forest Reserve Act, approved March 1, 1911. It set apart two million dollars a year, until June 30, 1915, for the purchase of lands lying in the vicinity of the headwaters of navigable streams and for the upkeep of these lands as national forests. Although couched in general terms, the measure was passed expressly to meet the demand for forest preservation in the White Mountains and the southern Appalachian system, and the purchases made under it were restricted to those regions. At the expiration of the period of the law's operation it was reported that a total of 1,285,000 acres had been acquired, at an average cost of $5.83 per acre. The Agricultural Appropriation Act of 1916 provided for a further expenditure of a million dollars in 1917 and two millions in 1918. More than seven million acres of desirable White Mountain and Appalachian forest lands were still, in 1916, in private hands..

Meanwhile the management of the public lands was improved at many points. Better methods of surveying were introduced, and a scientific classification, on the lines suggested by Ballinger, was undertaken by the Land Classification Board of the Geological Survey.[1] The transfer of land to purchasers and settlers went forward at the rate of twelve to seventeen million acres a year; and the quantity of public land of all kinds remaining on July 1, 1915, was 657,710,254 acres, of which 378,165,760 were in Alaska. The total cash receipts from the sale of public land in the fiscal

[1] "The Classification of the Public Lands," *Bull. of Geological Survey*, No. 537 (1913).

year ending June 30, 1916, were $3,428,588.[1] The rigor
of the land laws was somewhat eased by a measure
of June 6, 1912, which reduced the period of residence
required of the homesteader from five to three years.[2]

Conservation included the reclaiming of unproduc-
tive areas which could be converted into tillable land.
Some of these areas—in Virginia, Florida, and elsewhere—were swamps requiring drainage; but most of
them, located in the western states, were arid or semi-
arid regions needing irrigation. After liberal deduc-
tions of mountainous territory and of forest and mineral districts, the quantity of western land suitable for
agriculture, provided only that water should be supplied, was estimated in 1900 at four hundred million
acres, although water was not to be had at reasonable cost for more than one-tenth of this great area.
So long as free or cheap land was available in regions
of adequate rainfall, there was little demand for lands
which were less favored. After 1880, however, the
pressure of population began to suggest the reclamation of arid lands, and irrigation became an important
question both of private enterprise and of public policy.

The reclamation of arid lands proceeded on three
bases, according as the initiative was private, state,
or federal. Prior to 1890 irrigation was left almost
entirely to private enterprise. Individuals or syndicates of landowners secured favorable irrigation sites
and constructed works, sometimes to supply water for
use on their own lands, more often to yield profits from

[1] Secretary of the Interior, *Annual Report*, 1916, p. 14.
[2] *U. S. Statutes at Large*, XXXVII., pt. i., p. 123.

8

rights sold to other landowners in the region served. Disputes frequently arose between the water companies and their patrons, and experience showed that the companies which did not own or control both the water supply and the lands irrigated were unlikely to succeed. The water companies, too, were accused of being monopolies, and demand arose that rivers and lakes that could supply irrigation waters should be protected from their rapacity. Altogether, the limits of private irrigation enterprise were soon reached.

Gradually the task was taken over by the states. Reclamation under state auspices was carried on in two principal ways: (1) by the creation of irrigation districts; (2) by a system of contracts and land sales instituted under federal law. Beginning with California in 1887, most of the states containing arid land passed measures in the later years of the nineteenth century providing for the organization, under state supervision, of districts authorized to issue bonds for the construction of irrigation works and to tax the property within the districts so as to produce the necessary interest and sinking funds, and to provide for the maintenance and operation of the works built. Until after 1900 this system gained little headway. But by 1907 large amounts of land were being reclaimed under it; and in 1909 Wyoming, Montana, and New Mexico were added to the list of states employing the irrigation-district plan.

After 1900 state reclamation was aided most by the national Carey Act of August 18, 1894.[1] This meas-

[1] *U. S. Statutes at Large*, XXVIII., pt. i., pp. 422–423.

ure authorized the Secretary of the Interior to enter into contracts with arid states to patent to them public desert land, in amounts such as the state should apply for, to a maximum of one million acres in each state, on condition that the state should forthwith undertake reclamation of the land. Under further provision of the act the state was required to contract with parties for the construction of irrigation works, and to agree to sell the land, at a nominal price, only to persons who should have contracted with the construction company for a water supply at prices fixed in the company's agreement with the state. For some time after 1894 applications from the states were few, and the quantity of land reclaimed was small. But by 1908 the states were availing themselves extensively of their privileges, and in that year it became necessary for Congress to increase the maximum amount patentable, in favor of Colorado and Idaho, to two million acres. At the same time the provisions of the original law were extended to the territories. To June 3, 1910, the total amount applied for by the states and territories was 6,587,508 acres. In some states the lands were sold to private purchasers at a price as small as fifty cents an acre.[1]

To persons of large vision, reclamation by private and state agencies seemed intolerably slow, and soon after the Civil War demand was heard for irrigation by national authority. In 1888 Congress authorized a comprehensive study of the water supply of the arid states and appropriated money to enable the Director

[1] Mead, *Irrigation Institutions*, 24–27.

of the Geological Survey to make a selection of reservoir sites. Several hundred sites were designated. But, aside from the enactment of the Carey law, no further steps of importance were taken until the agitation begun by George H. Maxwell, and carried forward prominently by F. H. Newell and Representative Francis G. Newlands of Nevada, culminated in the Newlands Reclamation Act of June 17, 1902. This measure thereafter served as the basis of all efforts of the federal government to reclaim arid lands by its own direct action.[1]

The main provisions of the Newlands Act were as follows: (1) All receipts from sales of public lands in the sixteen so-called arid and semi-arid states and territories, beginning with the fiscal year ending June 30, 1901, should be set apart in the Treasury as a special reclamation fund, to be employed, under the direction of the Secretary of the Interior, in the construction of irrigation works. (2) The costs of construction should be repaid, in ten equal annual instalments, by the water-users. (3) When payment had been completed for a majority of the lands included in any project, the management of the local irrigation system, and the future cost of maintenance, should devolve upon the owners of the lands served. (4) Moneys paid in by the beneficiaries should be added to the proceeds of land sales, thus creating a revolving fund by which the work could be carried forward perpetually without further legislation and without cost to the nation at large. (5) Lands included

[1] *U. S. Statutes at Large*, XXXII., pt. i., p. 338.

within reclamation projects should be acquired only under the terms of the homestead law. (6) Sales of water-rights to private proprietors should be restricted to owners of tracts of one hundred and sixty acres or less, who were *bona fide* residents thereon.

Without delay the work contemplated in the statute was entrusted by the Secretary of the Interior to a new branch of his department, named the Reclamation Service. The first contract was let in September, 1903, and the first important construction—a section of the Truckee-Carson project, in Nevada—was opened June 17, 1905. To June 30, 1907, the amount paid into the reclamation fund was $41,156,576; at that date twenty-four projects aggregating almost two million acres were in hand, so that federal reclamation was proceeding almost as rapidly as was state reclamation under the Carey Act. In succeeding years one great project after another was undertaken and carried forward by stages; and a few were brought to completion. Among the more notable were the Engle dam on the Rio Grande, the Roosevelt dam on the Salt River in Arizona, the Loguna dam on the Colorado, the Pathfinder dam on the North Platte, and the Shoshone dam (the loftiest structure of its kind in the world) on the Shoshone River in Wyoming.

Serious difficulties appeared. So many costly projects were undertaken that funds became insufficient, and to avert injustice to settlers Congress was obliged, by act of June 25, 1910, to authorize a bond issue in aid of the Service to the amount of twenty million dollars. Embarrassment arose, too, from the slowness of settlers to make entry of the irrigated lands, and from the inability of some to keep up their payments to the government. Early in the administration of President Wilson the conviction that the main need was more intelligent and more intensive farming led to an arrangement whereby each of the fifteen principal projects was provided with an expert agriculturist to advise the settlers and to assist them in growing better crops and finding better markets;[1] and in 1914 the period covered by the payments due from settlers was extended from ten to twenty years. During the crop season of 1914 the service was prepared to furnish water to 1,240,875 acres. Of this area, 761,271 acres were actually irrigated, and 703,424 acres were cropped. To June 30, 1915, the total net expenditure of the Service was $94,613,554; and the outlay approved by Congress for the fiscal year ending June 30, 1916, was $13,530,000.[2]

Another important type of reclamation was the drainage of swamp lands. The report of the National Conservation Commission of 1906 showed that there were in the United States approximately 74,541,000 acres of swamp and overflowed land, so widely distributed that sixteen states contained more than a million acres each.[3] Six-sevenths of this land had been turned over to the states by laws of 1850 and 1860, and a large part of it had passed into the ownership of private individuals and syndicates. Most of

[1] *Am. Year Book*, 1913, p. 278.
[2] Secretary of the Interior, *Annual Report*, 1916, pp. 36–49.
[3] *Statistical Abstract of the U. S.*, 1909, p. 27.

the swamp-land states had drainage laws, and in several cases drainage was proceeding fairly rapidly under private initiative and state enterprise. The awakening of interest in problems of conservation gave rise to a demand that the federal government should increase the meager amount of aid which since 1902 it had given drainage projects; and to promote this end a National Drainage Association was organized at Chicago December 8, 1911. The interstate character of many large drainage projects was urged as a sufficient ground for increased national action. In 1914, and again in 1915, Congress appropriated sums to be used by the Department of Agriculture in carrying on an investigation of the wet-lands problem.[1]

Closely related to the interests of conservation and reclamation was the development of the nation's inland waterways; for that problem involved not only the clearing and deepening of river channels and the linking up of navigable streams by means of canals for purposes of commerce, but also the reconstruction of water-courses and the erection of dykes for flood prevention. The United States contains almost three hundred streams which are used for commercial purposes, aggregating over twenty-six thousand miles of navigable water. More than forty-five hundred miles of canals, also, have been constructed. Since the dawn of the railroad era, however, inland water transportation has failed to develop; and at the opening of the

---

[1] National Conservation Commission, *Report*, III., 361–374; Mitchell, "To Farm America's Swamps," *Review of Reviews*, XXXVII., 433-449; Hill, "Our Wealth in Swamp and Forest," *World's Work*, XIX., 12595–12617.

twentieth century not more than a tenth of the domestic commerce of the country was water-borne.

Railroad competition killed water traffic. Yet the railroads failed to keep pace with the nation's business, and, as has been pointed out, by 1905 insufficiency of transportation facilities had become a nation-wide problem.[1] The result was a revival of interest in the possibilities of water transportation. Rebuilding of river and canal traffic appeared to be one of the surest ways of relieving railway congestion and reducing freight rates. Incidentally, the improvement of streams would lessen flood damage, reduce soil erosion, and aid in the reclamation of wet lands. The railway companies were at first disposed to frown upon every proposal of the kind, but in time they came to the view that their position might be improved rather than injured by the use of waterways in the shipment of heavier and less profitable freight.

In several messages President Roosevelt advocated waterway improvement, and on March 14, 1907, he appointed an Inland Waterways Commission of nine members, with Theodore E. Burton of Ohio as chairman. In a report submitted in 1908 the commission urged that all plans for the development of waterways should take close account of the present and prospective relation of rail lines to the river courses, with a view to rendering the two systems complementary and harmonious in services and rates; and it recommended that Congress be asked to make suitable provision for waterway improvement at a pace commensurate with

[1] See p. 42.

the needs of the nation.[1] In a message accompanying the report the President urged that adequate funds be provided, by the issue of bonds if necessary, to develop the country's waterways "to their full capacity."

Throughout succeeding years the cause of inland waterways development was kept before the country by a number of organizations, and appropriations for river improvement steadily mounted. Log-rolling diverted considerable sums to unimportant projects. Indeed, as Roosevelt has said, "our magnificent river system, with its superb possibilities for public usefulness, was dealt with by the national government not as a unit, but as a disconnected series of pork-barrel problems, whose only real interest was in their effect on the re-election or defeat of a congressman here and there."[2] None the less, a good share of the funds voted were expended on large and necessary enterprises.

[1] Inland Waterways Commission, *Preliminary Report* (1908), 25–27.
[2] Roosevelt, *Autobiography*, 430.

CHAPTER VII

POPULATION AND IMMIGRATION

(1906–1917)

THE United States was the first nation in the world to make provision for periodic censuses; but as late as 1900 the central machinery of control, as well as the staff of local enumerators and supervisors, was set up anew in each decennial year. So long as the range of inquiry was limited, this hand-to-mouth procedure served. But after the Civil War the censuses grew less and less satisfactory. Statisticians urged the need of more numerous, more experienced, and more permanent census officials; and at last Congress was induced to establish (March 6, 1902) a permanent Bureau of the Census, designed to hold in the service persons familiar with census work, and also to make possible the collection of various classes of statistics during the interval between decennial enumerations.[1] Organized originally in the Department of the Interior, the Bureau was transferred in 1903 to the newly created Department of Commerce and Labor; whence, in 1913, it passed to the separate Department of Commerce. The thirteenth census, authorized by Congress July 2, 1909, and taken as of

[1] *U. S. Statutes at Large*, XXXII., pt. i., p. 51.

the date April 15, 1910, was the first complete test of the new facilities. The results were very satisfactory.[1]

The census of 1910 showed the population of the continental United States to be 91,972,266, and of the United States including Alaska, Hawaii, and Porto Rico, 93,402,151. No enumeration was made in the Philippines, Guam, Samoa, or the Panama Canal Zone; but it was computed that the total number of persons living under the American flag was 101,100,000.[2] Only three countries of the world had larger populations: China, India, and Russia. Of the population of the continental United States, 56.1 per cent. was adult, *i. e.*, twenty-one years of age or over; while as a consequence mainly of the heavy preponderance of males among immigrants, the ratio of males to females was 106 to 100.

Speaking broadly, population grows in two ways: by excess of births over deaths, and by excess of immigration over emigration. Increase of both kinds has been exceptionally rapid in the United States. Nevertheless, the rate of growth has gradually declined. During each decade from 1790 to 1860 the population increased, in round terms, one-third; from 1860 to 1890, one-fourth; and from 1890 to 1910, one-fifth. Still, during the decade ending in 1910 the increase was 21 per cent., as compared with 20.7 per cent. in the preceding ten years, and it reached the formidable figure of 15,977,691.

[1] Willcox, "The American Census Office," *Polit. Sci. Quart.*, XXIX., 438-459; Willis, "The Thirteenth Census," *Jour. Polit. Econ.*, XXI., 577-592.
[2] *Abstract of Thirteenth Census*, 1913, p. 21.

More significant than sheer increase is distribution. The capital facts in the populational history of the United States have been the advance from eastern seaboard to western, and the shift from rural localities to towns and cities. At all times population has been mobile. The economic independence of the individual has meant freedom and capacity to move about; ease of transportation has promoted migration from state to state and from section to section. Each census from 1870 to 1910 showed that about one-fifth of the native-born migrated from the states of their nativity to other states. In 1910 this proportion rose to 21.7 per cent.

During the decade 1901-1910 the pull of population was steadily westward. The center of the country's population, which during the preceding ten-year period was borne westward by only 14.4 miles, was advanced 38.9 miles, to a point in the city of Bloomington, Indiana.[1] Increase was smallest in the New England, the South Atlantic, the East South Central, and the West North Central states, and greatest in the Rocky Mountain, Pacific Coast, and Middle Atlantic groups; and all of the eleven states in which a growth of more than fifty per cent. appeared lay west of the Mississippi River. The extraordinary rate of increase in the western portions of the country—rising to seventy-three per cent. in the Pacific Coast states—was caused principally by the migration of native-born Americans; the number of aliens, except in two or three leading cities, was never large. A heavy alien influx in the states on the Atlantic seaboard, however,

[1] *Statistical Atlas of U. S.*, 1914, p. 27.

more than offset there the effects of emigration westward, and of a declining birthrate.

The density of population in 1910 ranged from 3.1
inhabitants per square mile in the Rocky Mountain
states to 193.2 in the Middle Atlantic states. The
average for the country was 30.9. Only ten states—
all east of the Alleghanies except Ohio and Illinois—
had a population density exceeding 100 per square mile.
The population thus did not yet press heavily upon
the country's resources. At census dates between 1911
and 1914 France had 194 people to the square mile;
Germany, 311; Italy, 322; Holland, 495; England and
Wales, 614; Belgium, 654.[1]

The decade saw also a rapid growth of cities. In
every one of the nine geographical divisions set up for
the purposes of the Census Bureau the proportion of
the population living in urban communities (cities and
other incorporated places of 2,500 inhabitants or more,
including New England towns of similar population)
was larger than in 1900, and in 1900 had been larger
than in 1890. Between 1900 and 1910 the proportion
of the entire population classed as rural fell from 59.5
per cent. to 53.7 per cent.; and accordingly the proportion classed as urban rose from 40.5 per cent. to
46.3 per cent.[2] Indeed, if residents of incorporated
places of fewer than 2,500 inhabitants be included, a
total of 55.1 per cent. of the entire population in 1910
dwelt under conditions more or less urban. The rate

---

[1] Ogg, *Economic Development of Modern Europe*, chap. xvi; Levasseur,
La population française, I., 398-464.

[2] *Abstract of Thirteenth Census*, 1913, p. 55.

of urban increase during the decade varied from 21.5 per cent. in New England, where the rural population underwent actual decline, to 101.8 per cent. in the Pacific Coast states, where, despite rural increase at the rate of 46.4 per cent., cities grew amazingly. Rural population fell off, too, in some of the most prosperous agricultural states of the Middle West. The South continued to show the lowest proportion of urban population, which there rose in but few states beyond twenty-five per cent. Almost a tenth of the country's population dwelt in the three cities of New York, Chicago, and Philadelphia; upwards of one-quarter lived in fifty cities which had each 100,000 inhabitants or more.

The population of the United States contained many racial elements, although the proportions of the great stocks changed slowly. The whites, in 1910, numbered 81,731,957, or 88.9 per cent. of the total; the negroes, 9,827,763, or 10.7 per cent.; the Indians, 266,683, or .3 per cent.; and the Chinese, Japanese, and other Asiatics, 146,863, or about .2 per cent. During the decade 1901–1910 the Indians increased slightly; the negroes gained by about one million, or 11.2 per cent.; while the white population, chiefly because of the direct and indirect effects of immigration, increased by almost fifteen millions, or 22.3 per cent. The proportion of whites in the total population, which was approximately four-fifths in 1790, has been found larger at each succeeding census except that of 1810.

This preponderant white population, however, is itself racially complex. The census of 1910 revealed the following groups: (1) natives born of native parentage, 49,488,575, or 53.8 per cent. of the total population; (2) natives born of foreign parentage, 12,916,311, or 14 per cent.; (3) natives born of mixed parentage, 5,981,526, or 6.5 per cent.; (4) foreign born, 13,345,545, or 14.5 per cent. These percentages are almost identical with those yielded by the census of 1900, save that the proportion of the foreign born at that date was 13.4.[1] The foreign-born in 1910, comprising one in every seven of the population, aggregated more than twice the population of the six New England states, and exceeded the entire negro population of the country by three and a half millions.

Furthermore, the foreign-born element is a composite, including people from every geographic division of the world. Approximately 87 per cent. in 1910 was of European origin; most of the remainder came from American countries, principally Canada. Of the European-born inhabitants, 49.9 per cent. were from countries of the north and west, 37.4 per cent. from countries of the south and east. Germany contributed 18.5 per cent., Austria-Hungary 12.4, Russia 11.9, Ireland 10, and Italy 9.9. Illustrative of the changing character of immigration in the decade is the fact that in 1900 persons from northern and western Europe constituted 67.8 per cent. of the foreign-born population, and persons from southern and eastern lands only 17.7 per cent. In 1910 almost three-fourths of the foreign-born population was urban. New York City alone contained one-seventh of the total.

[1] *Abstract of Thirteenth Census*, 1913, p. 77.

Not only was the United States a nation of immigrant origins; the country continued to attract aliens in astonishing numbers, with the double effect of keeping up the exceptional rates of population growth and of adding to the variety of race elements. During the decade 1904–1914 the influx of aliens rose to record proportions. In the fiscal year ending June 30, 1903, it was 857,046, and two years later it was 1,026,499. In 1907 it reached a maximum of 1,285,349. The panic of 1907 and the consequent industrial depression caused it to fall to 782,870 in 1908 and 751,786 in 1909. Thereafter it rose again, until in 1914 it was 1,218,480, notwithstanding a sharp falling-off incident to the war, during the last five months of the year. The war-time figure for 1915 was 326,700, and for 1916, 298,826.[1] In ten years (1904–1914) more than ten million men, women, and children from foreign lands were admitted to the country—a larger number than during the twenty years preceding, and almost one-third of the total number since 1820.

The rise in absolute and proportionate numbers of immigrants from the countries of southern and eastern Europe, which began about 1880, continued unabated. While the movement from Great Britain and Ireland was heavier than during the preceding decade, that from Germany showed little change, and that from the Scandinavian lands slackened. On the other hand, the influx from Italy rose from 100,135 in 1900 to 283,738 in 1914; that from Austria-Hungary, from 114,847 to 278,152; and that from Russia, from 90,787 to 255,660.

[1] Commissioner-General of Immigration, *Annual Report*, 1917, p. 140.

By 1912 only nineteen per cent. of the immigrants admitted to the country came from the northern and western lands.

The pressure was somewhat relieved by the return of many aliens to their old homes, after sojourning briefly in the United States. Until very recently, no record of returning immigrants was kept; in 1906 the Commissioner-General of Immigration wildly guessed the number at 200,000 a year. Statistics on the subject were first collected in 1907, and in the year ending June 30, 1908, when the number of immigrant and non-immigrant arrivals was 924,695, the number of alien departures was reported as 714,828. Business was depressed, and this proportion was unusual. The next year, under more normal conditions, the number of arrivals was 751,786, and the number of departures 400,392. Thereafter departures ran from two-fifths to three-fifths of arrivals. During the eight years ending in 1915 the flow of the tide brought 8,379,000 people, and the ebb took away 4,259,000. The net immigration was thus not quite half of the total number of arrivals.[1]

Population movements on such a scale could not fail to affect the national life profoundly. They brought in great numbers of industrious and worthy liberty-seekers and home-builders, but also many idle, worthless, and dangerous people, whose presence imposed special burdens on public philanthropy and social control. The foreigners clogged the labor marts, depressed wages, and lowered the standard of living

9   [1] Warne, *The Tide of Immigration*, chap. xviii.

among the working classes.   No longer was it possible
for native laborers, hard pressed by alien competition,
to go west, get free or cheap land, and regain economic
well-being.   The unoccupied arable lands were almost
exhausted; the equalizing influences of the pioneer era
were ended; native labor must take its chances in
direct competition with ill-kept, ignorant, unprogressive
toilers from southern Europe.   On an alarming scale
native labor was thus given a downward slant.[1]

Problems of government were likewise intensified.
Population became steadily more heterogeneous. Aliens
of the most diverse traditions and standards of conduct rubbed elbows with one another and with the
native-born, and the enforcement of laws on such
matters as the liquor traffic and Sunday observance,
which were unsupported by a common sentiment, offered increasing difficulties.   Municipal government
was especially affected; for while the foreign-born contributed little directly in taxes, their presence added
heavily to the city's budget for police, sanitation, education, and charities.   From the rising volume of immigrant departures little comfort was to be drawn,
because it merely revealed the large proportion of
immigrants who had no prospect or intention of
assimilation.

These startling aspects of the new immigration led
President Roosevelt to declare that the immigrant
problem was more urgent than any other before the
nation, with the possible exception of the conservation
of natural resources; and during his second adminis-

[1] Commission on Industrial Relations, *Final Report*, 157.

tration the attention of the country was drawn sharply to the subject. Systematic regulation by federal authority began with two statutes of 1882; and from that year to Roosevelt's inauguration in 1905 seven or eight important restrictive acts were passed. The Chinese were excluded; criminals and other undesirables were debarred; the importation of contract laborers was forbidden; the head tax on entering aliens was raised by stages from fifty cents to two dollars; and the work of inspection was fully taken over from the states by the federal government. In February, 1897, both houses of Congress passed by heavy majorities a bill excluding persons over sixteen years of age (except parents or grandparents of admissible or resident aliens) who were unable to read or write English or some other language. This was the first appearance of the long-debated literacy test. Feeling that the proposal looked to "a radical departure from our national policy relating to immigrants," President Cleveland interposed his veto; and the measure failed, although for the lack of only a few votes in the Senate.[1]

Agitation for increased restriction bore fruit in an important statute in the Roosevelt period, approved February 20, 1907.[2] It raised the head tax to four dollars; made fresh additions to the excluded classes; required for the first time the registration of departing aliens; provided for a bureau of information which should assist in directing immigrants to sections of the

[1] Latané, *America as a World Power* (*Am. Nation*, XXV., chap xvii).

[2] *U. S. Statutes at Large*, XXXIV., pt. i., pp. 898–911.

country in which they were most likely to find satisfactory employment; and created a commission composed of three senators, three representatives, and three persons appointed by the President, to undertake an investigation of immigration in all of its aspects. A literacy test, although adopted in the Senate, was finally abandoned.

Under the chairmanship of Senator William P. Dillingham of Vermont, and aided by a corps of experts, the Immigration Commission gathered and sifted evidence, in Europe and America, with a thoroughness never before attempted. After almost four years it presented (December 5, 1910) a comprehensive report, with forty-one portly volumes of testimony and other original materials. The report recommended further restriction, and especially urged that unskilled laborers should be admitted less freely, with a view to remedying the present over-supply in the basic industries. Among methods of restriction proposed were: increase of the head tax; increase of the amount of money required to be in the possession of an incoming alien; exclusion of unskilled laborers unaccompanied by wives or families; limitation of the number of each race admitted each year. All members of the Commission except one favored the reading and writing test as "the most feasible single method of restricting undesirable immigration."[1]

From 1907 discussion centered mainly about the literacy test. On the fundamental proposition that the volume of immigration was outrunning the coun-

[1] Immigration Commission, *Abstracts of Reports*, I., 45-49.

try's capacity for assimilation there was general agreement. The obvious need, therefore, was legislation which would not only safeguard the quality but greatly reduce the quantity of the yearly influx. For such legislation organized labor was especially clamorous.[1] As a means to the desired end, the literacy test had much in its favor. It was simple, direct, and easily enforceable. It would bar that part of the immigrant influx which, by and large, was the least intelligent and the least likely to become good citizens. If it might work against some desirable aliens and let in some undesirables, the same was true of any plan that would meet the main purpose. Furthermore, the test had substantial backing: Presidents McKinley and Roosevelt advocated it; the Immigration Commission urged it; proposals for it passed both houses of Congress; the American Federation of Labor, the railroad brotherhoods, and practically all other labor organizations were on record for it.

These arguments were by no means conclusive. It was both charged and admitted that the proposed policy was one of restriction, not selection. But was any policy justifiable whose main purpose was not selection? Would this form of test accord with the American tradition of hospitality to honest men of every condition? Would it not close the door of hope to the oppressed, especially the Russian Jews? Was it not, at best, an arbitrary method of attaining the purpose in hand?

In April, 1912, the Senate passed an immigration

[1] Samuel Gompers in the *American Federationist*, Jan., 1911.

bill, introduced by W. P. Dillingham, containing the
literacy test; and in the following June the House
passed a bill, introduced by John L. Burnett of Georgia, applying the test in somewhat milder form. A
compromise was reached; but after hearings in which
the literacy clause was warmly supported by the labor
interests, President Taft reluctantly vetoed the bill,
February 14, 1913, on the ground that it violated a
principle "which ought to be upheld in dealing with
our immigration."[1] The Senate re-passed the measure
by a vote of 72 to 18, but by a margin of thirty-three
votes the House failed to raise the necessary two-thirds
majority.

At the first regular session of Congress in Wilson's
administration fresh bills upon the subject made their
appearance, and on February 15, 1914, the House
passed a measure substantially identical with that
vetoed by President Taft. Action in the Senate was
delayed until January 2, 1915, when by a vote of 50
to 7 a bill of similar purport was got through. Again
the proposed legislation was blocked by a veto.[2] Hearings were held, but President Wilson could not be
brought to accept a test based on any principle other
than qualitative selection. Like Cleveland and Taft,
he saw in a clause excluding "those to whom the opportunities of elementary education have been denied,
without regard to their character, their purposes, or
their natural capacity," a radical and unwarranted departure from "the traditional and long-established

[1] *Cong. Record*, 62 Cong., 3 Sess., pt. iv., p. 3156.
[2] *Ibid.*, 63 Cong., 3 Sess., pt. iii., p. 2481.

policy" of the country. The Senate re-passed the bill, but the House lacked four votes of a sufficient majority.

The forces behind the measure refused to be balked, and at last their efforts were crowned with success. A new bill, carried in both houses early in the session of 1916–1917, was vetoed by the President, on grounds similar to those earlier advanced. The House, however, promptly overrode the veto by a vote of 287 to 106, and the Senate by a vote of 62 to 19. At the last it was apparent that the main object in the legislation was to limit the labor supply; and the placing of the law upon the statute book was one of the multiplying evidences of the power of organized labor in the country. There was reason to believe that the views of unbiassed people were represented rather by the President than by Congress.[1]

The new law took effect May 1, 1917.[2] In addition to numerous provisions designed to strengthen existing regulations, it excluded all aliens over sixteen years of age who were unable to read English or some other language; except that any admissible alien, or any American citizen, might bring in his wife, daughter, mother, grandmother, and also father and grandfather if they were over fifty-five years of age, regardless of whether such relatives could read. The trend of the act was apparent from the fact that sixty-eight

[1] Hoyt, "The Relation of the Literacy Test to a Constructive Immigration Policy," *Jour. Polit. Econ.*, XXIV., 445–473; Fairchild, "The Literacy Test and its Making," *Quart. Jour. Econ.*, XXXI., 447–460.
[2] *U. S. Statutes at Large*, XXXIX., pt. i., pp. 874–899.

per cent. of the immigrants from the countries of southern and southeastern Europe were illiterate, as compared with not more than three per cent. of those from Great Britain and Ireland, Germany, and the Scandinavian lands. The effect was therefore certain to be a sharp curtailment of the hitherto preponderating influx from Italy, Austria-Hungary, Russia, the Balkan states, and Syria.[1]

[1] Warne, *Tide of Immigration*, chaps. xxi–xxiv. On the problem of Japanese immigration, see pp. 307–311 below.

CHAPTER VIII

ADMINISTRATIVE EXPANSION AND REORGANIZATION
(1900–1916)

GOVERNMENT in the United States has undergone two principal changes in recent decades. One is the extension of the range of its activities, making necessary a remarkable expansion of the machinery of administration. The other is the introduction of the direct primary, the initiative, the referendum, the recall, and similar devices designed to promote popular control of public affairs and to increase the responsibility of officials to the electorate.[1]

In the federal government the first of these developments led to the creation of three new executive departments in less than a quarter of a century, in addition to a long list of new bureaus and services in the older departments, and of commissions and administrative agencies attached to no department. Until near the close of the first administration of President Cleveland, all of the then existing executive departments—State, Treasury, War, Navy, Post-Office, Interior, and Justice—performed functions which are universally recognized as political in character and essential to the conduct of a government. When,

[1] See chap. ix.

however, an act of February 9, 1889, raised to the status of an executive department a subordinate "department of agriculture" organized in 1862, the nation committed itself as never before to the promotion of social and economic welfare, as distinguished from necessary administrative work. The step was both desirable and inevitable. But as critics at the time pointed out, there was no clear limit beyond which the newer type of governmental activity might not be carried.[1]

Indeed, the recognition of the claim of agriculture raised afresh the demands of the commercial, mining, and industrial elements for attention to their welfare, and especially for representation in the President's cabinet. A bureau of labor created in the Department of the Interior in 1884 was converted, by act of June 13, 1888, into a detached "department of labor," without a status entitling its chief officer to a cabinet seat. By the close of the century the growing complexity of the industrial situation called for better facilities for investigation and control; and, acting on urgent recommendation of President Roosevelt, Congress, in 1903, created a Department of Commerce and Labor, charged with the duty of fostering and promoting "the foreign and domestic commerce, the mining, manufacturing, shipping, and fishery industries, the labor interests, and the transportation facilities of the United States."[2] From the State Department

[1] *Cong. Record*, 50 Cong., 1 Sess., pt. ix., pp. 8778, 8801 *et seq.*
[2] *U. S. Statutes at Large*, XXXII., pt. i., pp. 825–831; Department of Commerce and Labor, *Organization and Law*, 25–34.

was transferred the Bureau of Navigation, the Bureau
of Immigration, the Coast and Geodetic Survey, and
some other services; and two new bureaus—Manufactures and Corporations—were created in the Department. The so-called department of labor became
again a bureau.

Organized labor wanted a separate department, and
on the closing day of his administration President Taft
signed a bill meeting this demand.[1] In doing so, he
expressed the opinion that the number of departments
had become sufficiently large, and that "no new department ought to be created without a reorganization of
all departments in the government and a redistribution
of the bureaus between them." "If there is one thing
that is needed in the present situation," he asserted,
"it is the reorganization of our government on business
principles and with a view to economy in the administration of the regular governmental machinery." The
new department was designed "to foster, promote,
and develop the welfare of the wage-earners of the
United States, to improve their working conditions,
and to advance their opportunities for profitable employment." To it were transferred from the Department of Commerce and Labor (henceforth known as
the Department of Commerce): (1) the Bureau of
Labor, renamed the Bureau of Labor Statistics; (2)
the Children's Bureau, created in 1912; (3) the Bureau
of Immigration and Naturalization, established in 1906,
and now reorganized as two bureaus.

After 1913 most of the great economic interests had

[1] *U. S. Statutes at Large*, XXXVII., pt. i., pp. 736–739.

direct touch with the President's circle of advisers.
None the less, the pressure for new executive departments continued. The fast increasing but scattered
federal services pertaining to public health seemed to
many persons to need consolidation. Departments of
education and public works were suggested; and when
the nation entered the world war, in 1917, proposals
were made for a ministry of munitions, a ministry of
food control, and even a ministry of aeronautics.
Public men inclined, however, to the opinion of Taft
that no more permanent departments should be created
until a general administrative reorganization had shown
that they were needed.

An important but unexpected result of the broaden-
ing of governmental functions—federal, state, and
municipal—was the spread of "government by commission." The main feature of the commission system
was the setting up of special boards of impartially appointed, well-paid experts to apply and enforce a given
law or body of laws. Some commissions were investigative and advisory, but most of them were endowed
with administrative, quasi-legislative, and quasi-judi-
cial powers; so that they tended not only to break up
and decentralize the executive organs, but to abstract
authority from the legislative and judicial branches.
Some states set up scores of such bodies, with jurisdiction over railroads, municipal utilities, taxation, industry, labor, food production, and what not. After
1912 increasing tax burdens led to criticism of the
system as being unduly expensive; but there was little
actual retrenchment.

The oldest federal agencies of the kind were the Civil Service Commission (1883) and the Interstate Commerce Commission (1887). In the first Wilson administration five new national commissions sprang up, with sweeping governmental powers: the Reserve Board, the Trade Commission, the Farm Loan Board, the Shipping Board, and the Employees' Compensation Commission. One other, the Tariff Commission of 1916, was only investigative and advisory. But all except the Farm Loan Board stood outside the ten executive departments, indicating a tendency toward administrative decentralization out of accord with the best teachings of experience and contrary to the advice of experts.

The executive service of the United States includes the entire body of officials, from the President down to the least important letter-carriers and clerks, who have part in the enforcement of the nation's laws and the management of its business interests. In a century and a quarter the service grew from a few hundred persons to a staff numbering (June 30, 1916) 480,327.[1] Obviously, no questions relative to such a service could be more important than the mode and conditions of appointment and removal. The battle for the merit principle was fought and won during the first two decades following the Civil War; and the legal basis of the later merit system was the Pendleton Act of January 16, 1883.[2] The number of officials

---

[1] U. S. Civil Service Commission, *Annual Report*, 1916, p. v.

[2] *U. S. Statutes at Large*, XXII., pt. i., p. 403–407; Dewey, *National Problems* (*Am. Nation*, XXIV.), chap. ii.

placed under the protection of the merit law was at
the outset only 14,000. Gradually the "classified"
service was extended, by executive order or by act of
Congress, so as to include many new groups. In 1897 it
contained 87,108 persons; in 1905, 178,807; and in 1916,
296,926, or more than sixty-one per cent. of the
total.[1]

From the outset effort was made to protect employees
in the classified service from party pressure, and likewise to restrain them from party activity. In 1907 an
order of President Roosevelt prescribed that "all persons . . . in the competitive classified service, while re-
taining the right to vote as they please and to express
privately their opinions on all political subjects, shall
take no active part in political management or in political campaigns.[2] The injunction was construed to
apply to service on party committees, participation in
party caucuses or conventions, publication of partisan newspapers, and even membership in clubs engaging actively in party campaigns; and, as administered
by the Civil Service Commission, it proved to be an
effective remedy.

In an act approved August 23, 1912, many executive rules bearing on removals were made statutory.[3]
No person in the classified service might be removed
"except for such causes as will promote the efficiency
of said service and for reasons given in writing"; and
a person whose removal was sought must be furnished

[1] U. S. Civil Service Commission, *Annual Report*, 1916, p. v.
[2] *Ibid.*, 1908, p. 9.
[3] *U. S. Statutes at Large*, XXXVII., pt. i., pp. 413–414.

with a copy of the charges against him, and must be
allowed "a reasonable time for personally answering
the same in writing."   All papers relating to the trans-
action must be "made a part of the records of the proper
department or office."[1]   Furthermore, the Civil Service Commission was required to install a system of
efficiency ratings for the classified service in Washington, "based upon records kept in each department
and independent establishment with such frequency
as to make them as nearly as possible records of fact."[2]
March 25, 1913, the Commission set up a Division of
Efficiency, charged with receiving, tabulating, and filing
records of diligence, faithfulness, punctuality, and ac-
curacy of employees as transmitted to it by the several
departments; and on February 28, 1916, Congress gave
this division an independent status as the United
States Bureau of Efficiency.[3]

The three branches of administration most affected
by extensions of the merit system after 1900 were the
consular service, the diplomatic service, and the postal
service.   By order of June 20, 1895, President Cleveland provided for the appointment of consuls receiving
salaries of from one thousand to twenty-five hundred
dollars on a basis of competitive examination.   McKinley dropped the practice.   But on June 27, 1906,
President Roosevelt promulgated an order providing:
(1) that all vacancies in the office of consul-general and
consul in the topmost seven of the nine classes estab-

---

[1] U. S. Civil Service Commission, *Annual Report*, 1913, p. 14.
[2] *Ibid.*, 20.
[3] *U. S. Statutes at Large*, XXXIX., pt. i., p. 15.

lished by an act of the preceding April 5,[1] should be filled "by promotion from the lower grades of the consular service, based on ability and efficiency as shown in the service"; (2) that vacancies in classes eight and nine should be filled by promotion on the basis of ability and efficiency or by new appointments of candidates who should have passed a satisfactory examination.[2] An act of February 5, 1915, further prescribed that consuls-general and consuls should be appointed to grades and classes of the service, rather than to definite posts; only after being thus appointed should they be designated by the President to particular stations.

Demand for extension of the merit principle to subordinates in the diplomatic service was met in part by an order of President Roosevelt in 1905, but more fully in an order of President Taft, November 26, 1909, prescribing that "initial appointments from outside the service to secretaryships" should be made "only to inferior positions, and on the basis of competitive examination," and requiring that the higher posts, whether as secretaries or as chiefs of mission, should be filled by promotion.[3]

The last great stronghold of the spoils system was the postal service. In 1915 the number of officers and employees in the Post-Office Department was approximately three hundred thousand, or more than in all other departments combined. Between 1905 and 1914

[1] *U. S. Statutes at Large*, XXXIV., pt. i., pp. 99–102.
[2] *Am. Jour. Internat. Law*, I., Supplement, 314–316; Hunt, *Department of State*, 335–339.
[3] U. S. Civil Service Commission, *Annual Report*, 1909, p. 32.

the bulk of this army of employees was brought into the classified service, the most conspicuous exception being the postmasters of first, second, and third-class post-offices, *i. e.*, offices whose annual receipts amounted to $1,900 or more. During the first Roosevelt administration security of tenure of postmasters was more generally maintained than at any earlier period; and on November 30, 1908, the President issued an order bringing into the classified service all the 15,000 fourth-class postmasters north of the Ohio River and east of the Mississippi. An order of President Taft, September 30, 1910, placed in the classified service all assistant postmasters and clerks in first and second-class post-offices, and this was followed by regulations of February 19, 1912, similarly affecting about forty-two thousand rural free-delivery carriers. Finally, on October 15, 1912, Taft placed in the classified service all remaining fourth-class postmasters. Democratic congressmen charged that the last-mentioned order, issued a few weeks after the President's defeat at the polls, was inspired by political motives. In reply Taft reminded his critics that he had repeatedly asked for statutes conferring power to classify postmasters of all grades.

In 1913 control of the federal government passed from one party to another for the first time in sixteen years, and there was some fear that the merit system would suffer. The victors were pledged to the system by their platform, and the new Chief Executive was, at the time of his election, a vice-president of the National Civil Service Reform League. But the party

10

was office-hungry; Congress was well sprinkled with spoilsmen; and powerful pressure for an increase of patronage was certain. The record achieved by the Wilson Administration was uneven. Notwithstanding strong opposition, the orders of 1906 and 1909 relating to the consular service and the lower grades of the diplomatic service were faithfully carried out. But the efforts of preceding administrations to build up an experienced diplomatic service of the higher grades, based on security of tenure, was abandoned; and within twelve months the "voluntary" resignations of seven of the eleven ambassadors, and of twenty-two of the thirty-five ministers, were accepted. The new appointees were men of character and ability; but with few exceptions they lacked diplomatic experience.

In the postal service the first important action was to require, by executive order of May 7, 1913, that no fourth-class postmaster having a salary of as much as $180 a year should be given a classified status unless he had been, or should be, appointed as a result of a competitive examination.[1] Inasmuch as it had been usual to "cover in" the immediate holders of positions which were brought into the classified service, this order provoked much criticism. But the President won credit by refusing to rescind the Taft order of October 12, 1912, and yet more by an exceptionally important order of March 31, 1917, indirectly extending the competitive system to all of the 9,175 postmasterships of the first, second, and third classes.

[1] U. S. Civil Service Commission, *Annual Report*, 1916, pp. xiv.-xx., 99–100.

The Federal Reserve Act of 1913 ignored the merit principle, although the Reserve Board made up its staff in voluntary consultation with the Civil Service Commission.[1] The Farm Loan Act of 1916 expressly excepted subordinates of the new service from the merit law; and a rider to an emergency deficiency appropriation act of 1913 took out of the classified service all subordinates of United States marshals and of collectors of internal revenue. As a whole, the Administration's record was such as to confirm the impression that the civil service in the United States, far from having attained the stable and scientific basis which had been arrived at in Great Britain, was still in the "reform" stage; in other words, that the merit system, notwithstanding all its notable triumphs, was as yet on trial.[2]

On the intrinsic value of the merit plan opinion still differed. No one of repute was left to defend the spoils system *per se*. But the merit system showed weaknesses, and in the judgment of some people contained possible dangers. The abilities of candidates for many kinds of positions could be ascertained only in a very general way by such examinations as the Civil Service Commission could administer. The safeguards against removal for political or personal reasons were made so strong that removals for the good of the service became more difficult and rare than was desirable. Security of tenure made for the growth of a bureaucratic spirit in the departments and in the staffs of the independent

[1] U. S. Civil Service Commission, *Annual Report*, 1916, p. 82.
[2] Moses, *Civil Service of Great Britain*, 250.

commissions. Furthermore, the system was not sufficiently flexible to permit mature or established persons
of obvious qualifications to be taken into the classified
service on conditions that were likely to be acceptable
to them. The general judgment was that these disad-
vantages were heavily outweighed by the gains flowing
from the competitive system; yet they seemed likely
to take a larger place in future discussions of the
subject.

The oldest branch of the federal administrative
system, and the one which touches most directly the
everyday life of the citizen, is the postal service. From
1900 much effort was made to readjust postal arrangements more perfectly to the needs of the country. In
the first place, the free delivery of mail, begun in the
largest cities in 1863 and in rural districts in 1896,
was rapidly extended. Between 1901 and 1916 the
number of people served by the free rural delivery
system was raised from four millions to twenty-six
millions; so that it became possible to reduce the
number of post-offices from 76,688 to 56,541.

Of equal importance was the establishment, by act
of June 25, 1910, of a system of postal deposits.[1]
Postal savings-banks have long been operated successfully in European countries, and as early as 1895
economists and officials of the Post-Office Department
warmly advocated such facilities for the United States.
They urged that a postal-savings system would promote thrift; that it would afford banking advantages
for remote and backward communities; that through

[1] *U. S. Statutes at Large*, XXXVI., pt. i., 814–819.

the post-offices money withdrawn from banks in time of panic would be brought back into circulation; and that opportunity to make postal deposits would be especially acceptable to the foreign-born who were accustomed to government savings-banks and distrustful of the ordinary American commercial banks. On the other hand, some people objected that the proposal was "socialistic," and that the investment of the funds placed on deposit would offer serious difficulty; and banking interests insisted that the country had savings-banks enough.

By the terms of the act of 1910, any person ten years of age or over might open an account at a post-office by depositing a minimum of one dollar. The maximum deposit for one person was originally $500; by amendment of 1916 it was raised to $2,000. Interest was paid on deposits up to $500 originally, and up to $1,000 after 1916, at the rate of two per cent.; and deposits might be turned into government bonds, in multiples of twenty dollars, yielding two and one-half per cent. One-twentieth of the deposits must be held as a cash reserve. The remainder was to be placed in state and national banks, which must pay interest thereon at the rate of two and one-half per cent. When, on January 3, 1911, the law went into operation, only one post-office in each state and territory was empowered to receive deposits. But the system was rapidly extended, until on June 30, 1916, there were 8,421 depositories (7,701 post-offices and 720 branches), with 603,000 depositors and $86,000,000 deposits. About fifty-eight per cent. of the depositors were foreign-born, and their deposits formed more than seventy-one per cent. of the total.[1]

Yet another addition to the postal service was a parcels-post system, set up by act of August 24, 1912.[2] Here again European countries led the way; and the popular demand which lay back of the American legislation drew argument chiefly from English, French, and German experience. The demand itself sprang from dissatisfaction with the high rates charged by the ten principal private express companies for the transportation of merchandise and other bulky matter. But an important economic purpose was to bring producers and consumers closer together, enlarging markets for the one and reducing prices for the other. The new arrangements immediately became popular, and by 1915 the Post-Office was handling a billion parcels a year—more than three times the number handled by it before the system was installed.

Steady accumulation of offices and functions made the administrative system of the United States a complicated mechanism. On the whole, it served its purpose well; yet its gaps, overlappings, and other structural defects caused inefficiency and waste. President Taft was the sort of man to be disturbed by the lack of symmetry and order, and he gave administrative reform a prominent place in his public program. He could not bring about much actual change; but in

[1] Post-Office Department, *Annual Report*, 1916, p. 171; Kemmerer, "The United States Postal Savings Bank," *Polit. Sci. Quart.*, XXVI., 462–499, and "Six Years of Postal Savings in the United States," *Am. Econ. Rev.*, VII., 46–90.

[2] *U. S. Statutes at Large*, XXXVII., pt. i., pp. 557–559.

1910 he secured an appropriation of $100,000 for an Efficiency and Economy Commission "to enable the President to inquire into the methods of transacting the public business of the Executive Department and other government establishments, and to recommend to Congress such legislation as may be necessary." The failure of Congress in 1913 to provide further funds obliged the Commission to discontinue its work, but not until a large part of the ground had been covered and several comprehensive reports had been submitted.[1]

The Commission's recommendations included: (1) an annual budget; (2) a permanent co-ordinating and supervising body, a "bureau of central administration," on the analogy of the English Treasury; (3) abandonment of the system of geographical apportionment of candidates for civil service positions; (4) extension of the merit system to include all higher officials in the executive departments except cabinet officers and other officials whose functions have to do with the determination of policy; (5) a system of contributory pensions for government employees, on lines suggested in the report of Roosevelt's Committee on Departmental Methods, popularly known as the Keep Commission, in 1907.[2]

Wilson's energies were absorbed by other matters, and the Taft program was not followed up. Administrative reform became, however, a prime concern in many of the states. In Illinois, Minnesota, New Jersey,

[1] *House Docs.*, 62 Cong., 2 Sess., No. 670; Cleveland, "The Federal Budget," Acad. Polit. Sci., *Proceedings*, III., 117–131.

[2] Forbes-Lindsay, "New Business Standards at Washington—Work of the Keep Commission," *Review of Reviews*, XXXVII., 190–195.

Pennsylvania, Massachusetts, and elsewhere, efficiency and economy commissions made protracted studies and submitted useful reports.[1] In 1917 these state efforts began to bear fruit in long-needed reorganizations; and it was expected that the interest which they aroused, re-enforced by war-time demands, would keep alive the project of reform in the federal field.

[1] *Am. Polit. Sci. Rev.*, X., 96–97; Ill. Efficiency and Economy Committee, *Report*, 871–998; Mathews, *Principles of Am. State Administration*, chap. xix.

CHAPTER IX

DEMOCRACY AND RESPONSIBILITY IN GOVERNMENT
(1900–1916)

IN no period after the Civil War was the American system of government more clearly on trial than in the opening decade of the present century. Beginning with the campaign of 1896, Bryan marshalled the radicals of every school in opposition to what was conceived to be government by plutocrats and bosses; and the reaction spread until it ceased to be a party matter and took on the aspect of a nation-wide movement for political reform. The object mainly sought was increased popular control over the instrumentalities of government; and scarcely an existing political institution or practice escaped attack in the press, on the stump, in academic halls, in party assemblages, in legislative chambers, and in constitutional conventions. How far should popular election of officers be carried? What extensions of the suffrage should be made? How should the people secure effective popular control over the nomination of candidates for public office? How should officials be made more responsible to their constituents? Should the people be empowered to amend constitutions and make laws by direct action, and, if so, through what means and under what limitations?

From the free discussion of these and other weighty
problems sprang in quick succession popular election
of United States senators, the short ballot movement,
the enfranchisement of women in a dozen states, the
primary in its several forms, the recall of administrative officers and of judges, the initiative, the referendum
for statutes, sweeping changes in the organization and
procedure of the national House of Representatives,
home rule for cities, and the commission and commis-
sion-manager types of municipal organization.

Upon the question of appointing rather than electing
executive officials, two conceptions were sharply opposed. One was that real democracy required almost
all offices to be filled by vote of the people; the other
was that the number that could be so filled with discrimination was small, and that government could be
efficient only if the mass of administrative and judicial
officials were appointed by governors, mayors, or other
appropriate authorities. Since the people control
their governments mainly through nominations and
elections, the first theory appeared plausible. But
experience showed that the suffrage may be made to
defeat its own ends. If the voter is summoned to the
polls too frequently, he grows callous to the call. If
the ballot put in his hands is overloaded with names,
he can make no proper choice.[1]

Convinced that frequent elections and "blanket"
ballots were responsible for a large share of the ills of
American state and local government, political re-

---

[1] Beard, "The Ballot's Burden," *Polit. Sci. Quart.*, XXIV., 589–614.
Childs, *Short Ballot Principles*, chap. iii.

formers started a movement to reduce the number of elections and of elective offices; the year 1910 saw the appearance of a National Short Ballot Association. The obstacles were many: the people were skeptical; the bosses were hostile; inertia weighed heavily against change. Substantial progress, however, was made, notably through the spread of the commission form of government in towns and cities.[1] By 1915 the place of the short ballot in the state governments was widely under consideration, and a new constitution drawn up in that year for the state of New York, though rejected by the voters, showed the influence of short-ballot ideas. In states, counties, and even townships, as well as in cities, reduction of the number of elective offices seemed likely to continue.[2]

The short ballot was no novelty: in the national government there had never been any other kind. For a century and a quarter the only officials in the federal system who were voted for directly by the people were the presidential electors and the members of the House of Representatives. In 1913 the Seventeenth Amendment added senators. The movement for direct popular election of senators began as early as 1826, but it won no distinct triumph until 1893, when an amendment on the subject passed the House of Representatives by the requisite two-thirds majority. Many of the ablest senators, as Hoar of Massa-

[1] Childs, "The Short Ballot and the Commission Plan," Am. Acad. Polit. and Soc. Sci., *Annals*, XXXVIII., 816.
[2] Mathews, *Principles of Am. State Administration*, chap. viii.; Thompson, "Are Too Many Executive Officers Elective" *Mich. Law Rev.*, VI., 228–237.

chusetts and Spooner of Wisconsin, opposed the change, on the ground that the upper branch of Congress ought to be constituted on a different basis from the lower. But desire grew to free the elections from the dictation of bosses and the corrupt activities of railroad and other lobbyists; and within a brief period the legislatures of more than three-fourths of the states passed favorable resolutions.

Finally the Senate itself yielded, mainly because of the spread of popular nomination of senators through the agency of the direct primary. As early as 1875 provision was made in the constitution of Nebraska for a popular preferential vote on candidates for senatorial seats. In 1899 Nevada enacted a measure "to secure the election of United States senators in accordance with the will of the people." In 1904 Oregon established what was in effect a system of popular election, comprising: (1) nomination of senatorial candidates in state-wide primaries; (2) voluntary written pledges of candidates for the state legislature to vote for the senatorial candidate most largely supported by the people; (3) determination, by ballot at the regular election, of the "people's choice"; (4) ratification by the legislature, under moral if not legal compulsion, of this popular verdict. By 1912 senators were popularly nominated in twenty-nine of the forty-eight states; and in the majority of cases popular nomination was, in law or in fact, equivalent to election.

In this situation further resistance to uniform popular election was futile. On June 12, 1911, a resolution to submit to the states the long-desired amendment was carried in the Senate by five votes in excess of the necessary two-thirds.[1] Some southern members of the House disliked the proposal to give the federal government the same control over senatorial elections that it possessed over the election of representatives; but opposition finally gave way, and on May 13, 1912, the resolution passed the lower chamber by a vote of 238 to 39.[2] Most of the state legislatures were in session during the ensuing winter, and ratification was easily secured.   The amendment was proclaimed May 31, 1913.[3] The reform was logical and inevitable, but it did not lead to an early change in the personnel or temper of the upper chamber.

Save for certain restrictions imposed by the Fourteenth and Fifteenth Amendments, the state and federal suffrage remained under state control. Some states required payment of a tax; some used educational tests; and some in the South had mixed property and educational requirements, especially devised to exclude the mass of the negro population. The period after 1907 saw no significant changes in these arrangements, except the active revival and widespread gains of woman suffrage.

Demand for the enfranchisement of women was heard before the middle of the nineteenth century; and the subject received increasing attention in the later stages of anti-slavery agitation and in the period of the extension of political privileges to the freedmen, when

---

[1] *Senate Jour.*, 62 Cong., 1 Sess., 95.
[2] *House Jour.*, 62 Cong., 2 Sess., 676.
[3] *U. S. Statutes at Large*, XXXVIII., pt. ii., p. 2049.

every aspect of human rights was under discussion. In the last two decades of the century the cause achieved victories in two principal directions: (1) beginning with Michigan and Minnesota in 1875, a number of states conferred upon women the privilege of voting in school and other special elections; (2) Wyoming, on being admitted to the Union in 1890, continued the suffrage of women, which had been established by the territory in 1869; and in 1893 Colorado, and in 1896 Idaho, admitted women to the suffrage on the same terms as men; while in 1896 Utah, which as a territory had enfranchised women, was admitted as a woman-suffrage state.

Notwithstanding these successes, at the opening of the new century the movement seemed to have run its course. Public interest had waned; agitation encountered only ridicule. In England, likewise, an issue once live had lost its vigor. There, however, the Woman's Social and Political Union (established in 1903) took over leadership in 1905; and within a few years the country was shaken to its depths by the campaign of the militants. Gathering inspiration from these developments, and aided powerfully by the radical, experimenting, reforming political temper of the times, the American protagonists of the cause reorganized their forces and soon began to win fresh triumphs. In 1910 they carried the state of Washington; in 1911 they carried California; in 1912 they procured the introduction of bills for the submission of a woman-suffrage amendment in the legislatures of twenty-two states; and they won in Kansas, Oregon, and Arizona, though losing in Wisconsin, Ohio, and Michigan. In 1912, they gained the platform indorsement of the national Progressive party. In 1913 the new territorial legislature of Alaska conferred the franchise on women, and in Illinois the legislature empowered women to vote for presidential electors and for all state and local officers whose election was not restricted to men by the state constitution; but a suffrage amendment resubmitted in Michigan was decisively rejected. In 1914 the number of equal suffrage states was increased to twelve (counting Illinois) by the accession of Montana and Nevada.

Woman's enfranchisement was now rapidly coming to be a national issue. In 1913 systematic attempts were made to stimulate the cause in the southern states; and in the same year hearings were held by committees of both houses of Congress, resulting in a report by a Senate committee favorable to the establishment of equal suffrage throughout the country by an amendment of the federal Constitution.[1] In 1914 the national movement was definitely indorsed by the Federation of Women's Clubs and by the National Educational Association.

Federal amendment was proposed in two forms. One was the "Susan B. Anthony amendment," first advocated as early as 1869. It provided that "the right of citizens of the United States to vote shall not be denied or abridged by the United States, or by any state, on account of sex." Its effect would be to secure the franchise for women in all states on the same terms

[1] *Senate Docs.*, 63 Cong., 1 Sess., No. 155.

as men. To meet the objections, however, of persons
who believed that each state should be permitted to
settle the question for itself, a "states-rights" amendment was suggested, providing that a woman-suffrage
amendment should be submitted to the people of any
state upon petition by eight per cent. of the voters
thereof, and adopted by a majority of those voting
thereon. The effect of this would be to simplify the
process of getting suffrage amendments before the
voters, without withdrawing from any state the right
to reach its own decision.

From 1913 Congress was beset with demands for
one or the other of these amendments. Under the
guidance of the Democratic caucus, the House of Representatives long refused to take up the subject.
But on March 19, 1914, the Susan B. Anthony amendment was brought to a vote in the Senate. The result
was 35 yeas and 34 nays, with 26 members not voting.
The constitutional two-thirds majority was, therefore,
lacking. Senators from the woman-suffrage states
were practically unanimous for the amendment, senators from other northern and western states were almost equally divided, and senators from the southern
states were generally opposed. When, on January 12,
1915, the amendment was brought up in the House, it
was lost by a vote of 204 to 174 (not two-thirds).[2]
Effort to force the states-rights amendment to a vote
failed in both houses. In the congressional elections
of 1914 the suffragists made their first overt and nation-

---

[1] *Senate Jour.*, 63 Cong., 2 Sess., 183.
[2] *House Jour.*, 63 Cong., 3 Sess., 105–106.

wide attempt to bring about the defeat of members of Congress who were conspicuously opposed to their project.

The net result of the legislative activity of 1914–1915 in the states was: (1) the submission of the question of votes for women to the voters of four states—Massachusetts, New York, Pennsylvania, and New Jersey—in 1915; (2) similar action in three other states—Iowa, South Dakota, and West Virginia—in 1916; (3) contingent provision for the submission of the question at some future time in Tennessee and Arkansas. Interest centered especially in the action of the four great eastern states which voted in 1915. On October 19 the suffrage proposal was defeated in New Jersey, and on November 2 in Massachusetts, New York, and Pennsylvania—in all cases by a vote of about two to one. The effect of this reverse was to stimulate afresh the demand for a national amendment, and strong effort was made to enlist the support of President Wilson. He, however, refused to give a place in the program of his administration to the subject. He expressed sympathy with the end sought, but insisted that the issue was one which should be settled by each state for itself.

As the campaign of 1916 drew on, the suffragists sought from all parties specific indorsement of a federal amendment; and inasmuch as women voters were now in a position to take part in the choice of ninety-one presidential electors—more than one-sixth of the total—the demand was not to be lightly regarded. The platform of every party represented in the presidential

11

contest contained a declaration favorable to the extension of the suffrage to women; every presidential candidate was on record as a suffragist; and the Progressive party declared for the Susan B. Anthony amendment. Both Democrats and Republicans advocated enfranchisement by state rather than federal action.[1]

The National Woman Suffrage Association was grateful for these unprecedented triumphs and was disposed to maintain its non-partisan attitude. The newer Congressional Union, however, was not satisfied. It launched a national Woman's Party, composed of woman voters in suffrage states; and when, shortly after the opening of the campaign, the Republican candidate, Hughes, came out for enfranchisement by federal amendment, the union threw such influence as it possessed into the scale against the Democrats. There is no evidence that its action affected the results: Wilson carried every equal-suffrage state except Illinois and Oregon. Indeed, the suffrage cause drew no clear advantage from the elections. Suffrage proposals were defeated in every one of the three states that voted on them: West Virginia, Iowa, and South Dakota.

In the last two decades of the nineteenth century electoral procedure was revolutionized in most of the states by the introduction of the Australian ballot system. Experience showed that full remedy of electoral abuses required also the bringing of parties and

[1] *Democratic Text-Book*, 1916, p. 21; *Republican Campaign Text-Book*, 1916, p. 59.

party machinery within the pale of the law, and especially the regulation of the processes of nominating candidates for office, so as to secure a greater measure of popular control. These two impulses of regulation and democratization, working together, brought about the widespread adoption of the direct primary.

Prior to 1900 "primaries" were usually caucuses employed to choose delegates to party conventions; and it was by these conventions that all except purely local nominations were made. The convention theoretically represented the mass of the party members. But it was always liable to domination by interests seeking control of the government for private ends; and often it ignored, and even defied, the popular will. It was to restore to the voters the power of choosing their candidates that the direct primary was instituted. The principle of the new device was that the adherents of each party should select at the polls their candidates for the offices to be filled, in the same manner in which all of the voters at a later time chose the public officials from among these candidates. The plan admitted of a variety of arrangements as to the methods of making up the list of persons to be voted on, the imposition of party tests, and other matters; but in any form that it might take it contrasted sharply with the convention system.

The first state-wide primary law was enacted in Wisconsin in 1903. In Oregon a law upon the subject was adopted in 1904; in Washington and the five closely grouped states of Iowa, Missouri, Nebraska, North

Dakota, and South Dakota in 1907; and in Kansas in 1908. In some instances the system was first established in restricted areas and the restrictions were subsequently removed; in other cases it was put in operation at a stroke in substantially its completest form. From the West it spread to the East, being adopted in 1908 in New Hampshire, in 1911 in Massachusetts, Maine, and New Jersey, and in 1913 in New York and Pennsylvania. At the close of 1915 the primary in its state-wide form had been set up in thirty-seven of the forty-eight states; while in five others (all in the South) it was operated under rules of the Democratic party without having been made obligatory upon all parties by statute.

At the end of a decade the results of the change remained uncertain. Some gains were visible in the direction of simplicity and popular control. On the other hand, the power of the boss was not eliminated; methods were different, but the results might be no less pernicious than under the convention system. Furthermore, the idea that the primary would make candidacy for office less costly and burdensome, and thereby give more opportunity to the poor man or to the man who hesitated to enter a pre-convention campaign, was proved a delusion. Frequently the pre-primary campaign was just as heated, just as costly, and just as unlikely to result in the triumph of the best man as a pre-convention campaign could possibly be. At least, the notion was dislodged that the primary was a panacea for all political ills; in practice it displayed all the vices and virtues, all the tendencies to blunder and to go straight, which are characteristic of the American democracy.[1]

Originally the primary laws applied only to state-created offices, and occasionally to seats in Congress. Beginning in Oregon in 1910, they were gradually widened so as to provide for recording the preference of voters among candidates for the presidency. In general, the laws of this type stipulated that delegates to the national convention of parties of recognized legal status should be chosen directly by the party voters, and that at the same time the voters might indicate their preference among the possible presidential nominees of the party. By the summer of 1912, presidential primary legislation had been enacted in thirteen states; in twelve the device, in one form or another, was used in the presidential campaign of that year.

In 1913 presidential preference laws were passed in several more states; and in his annual message of December 2 President Wilson advocated nation-wide establishment of the system.[2] His idea was that the national convention should be so reconstructed as to contain only persons already nominated for seats in the House of Representatives and for vacant seats in the Senate, senators with unexpired terms, the members of the national committee, and the presidential candidate. Its function should be merely to ratify

[1] Munro, *Government of American Cities* (rev. ed.), 132–139; Dunn, "The Direct Primary; Promise and Performance," *Review of Reviews*, XLVI., 439–445; Hart, "The Direct Primary versus the Convention," Acad. Polit. Sci., *Proceedings*, III., 162–171.

[2] *Senate Jour.*, 63 Cong., 2 Sess., 8.

the verdict of the primaries and to formulate the party platform. In 1914 several bills based upon the President's suggestion were introduced. Brief discussion, however, brought out the fact that a system of presidential primaries under federal law would raise many constitutional difficulties, and no action was taken. The President did not renew his proposals, and the country readily fell back upon the plan of leaving the matter to the states.

By 1916 twenty-three states had provided for either the simple presidential preference primary or the election of delegates to national conventions by direct vote, or both; and approximately sixty per cent. of the delegates to the conventions of the major parties in that year were either chosen by direct primary or morally bound by the preference vote for president.[1] The system, none the less, was not fairly tested in that campaign. There was no contest for the Democratic presidential nomination, and the majority party's primaries were perfunctory; while on the Republican side the two principal candidates refused to engage in a primary campaign, and the contestants voted on at the primaries were chiefly "favorite sons." In this situation, public interest in the presidential primary waned.

The popularizing of a great branch of Congress, the doubling of the electorate in a dozen states, and the wresting of the control of nominations in some degree from the bosses did not satisfy the demand for more

[1] *Am. Polit. Sci. Rev.*, X., 116–120; Dickey, "The Presidential Primary in Oregon," *Polit. Sci. Quart.*, XXXI., 81–104.

democratic, responsible, and efficient government. On the contrary, even the representative principle was criticized and challenged, and pressure for change swept on to include the making of constitutions and the enactment of statutes by direct voice of the people. Two special devices which lent themselves to the demands of this extremer democracy were the initiative and the referendum. With the referendum the country had long been familiar. The practice of submitting constitutions and constitutional amendments to a popular vote became almost universal before the middle of the nineteenth century, and in some states ordinary statutes of a special nature were, by law or by custom, sometimes similarly referred.[1] The initiative was, until late, known only in theory. In 1897, when Populism still retained much of its vigor in portions of the West, South Dakota adopted a constitutional amendment providing for both the referendum and initiative for ordinary legislation; and in 1900 Utah did the same. In the one case, the new devices long lay unused, and in the other the purposes of the radicals were frustrated by the refusal of a new legislature to enact the enabling clause necessary to put the amendment into operation; and throughout the country as a whole the two measures were looked upon as sporadic and barren of significance.

In several other western states "direct democracy," however, made strong appeal; and agitation in its behalf spread to all parts of the land. Oregon adopted

[1] Oberholtzer, *The Referendum, Initiative, and Recall in America* (rev. ed.), chaps. IV–XIII.

the initiative and referendum in 1902; Montana in 1906; Oklahoma in 1907; Missouri and Maine in 1908; Arkansas and Colorado in 1910; Arizona and California in 1911; Nebraska, Washington, Idaho, and Ohio in 1912; Michigan in 1913; North Dakota in 1914; and Maryland in 1915. By 1917 there were few states in which proposals on the subject had not been brought to a vote in the legislature or among the people, or both.[1] The proportion of the voters requisite to propose both laws and amendments, and to compel a referendum on measures of different kinds, ran from three to fifteen per cent.; in six states statutes could be popularly initiated, but not constitutional amendments.

Familiarity flowing from years of experience brought the public to a new view of both devices. Both continued to be regarded by some people as dangerous; but in the general mind they established themselves as natural and reasonable features of a democratic political system—not essential, but not revolutionary or contrary to sound government. Their chief fault seemed to lie in the tendency to use them to excess, to overload the ballot with trifling or ill-considered proposals. Thus in Oregon, where trial had been fullest and fairest, six biennial elections (1904 to 1912) brought before the voters forty-one amendments and sixty-one laws.[2] Even with the aid of the booklet of

---

[1] *Am. Polit. Sci. Rev.*, X., 320–327.

[2] Barnett, *Operation of the Initiative, Referendum, and Recall in Oregon*, 78; Haynes, "People's Rule in Oregon, 1910," *Polit. Sci. Quart.*, **XXVI.**, 32–62.

information which was sent to every voter at each election, the people could not act intelligently upon so many measures—in addition, of course, to the task of making selection among scores of candidates for office. In 1914 a total of 286 constitutional and legislative measures were voted on by the people in thirty-one states; in 1916, 111 measures in twenty-three states. In both years, about two-fifths of the proposals were adopted.[1]

The argument which carried the new system triumphantly across the country was that the initiative and the referendum, as applied to statutes, were to be weapons whose possession by the people would tend to keep legislatures mindful of their duties; that they would be brought into actual play only under unusual circumstances. The looseness with which the devices were used in Oregon and other states unquestionably stayed their spread and influenced states about to adopt the system to avert similar abuses by raising the percentage of the voters needed to set the new machinery in motion. At the close of a decade of experiment, the fact was fairly established that the representative type of government could still hold its own as against "direct government" in any of its forms.[2]

From immediate popular control over legislation it

[1] *Nation*, Vol. 104, p. 127.

[2] Croly, *Progressive Democracy*, 267–283; Cushman, "Recent Experience with the Initiative and Referendum," *Am. Polit. Sci. Rev.*, XXIX., 84–110; Thomas, "Direct Legislation in Arkansas," *Polit. Sci. Quart.*, XXIX., 84–110; Shippee, "Direct Legislation in Washington," *ibid.*, XXX., 235–253.

was but a step to like control over administration; and
to attain that end the recall was introduced. The
principle of the recall was that elective officials, being
responsible directly to the people, might, on petition
of a requisite number of voters (commonly twenty-five
per cent.), be compelled before the expiration of their
terms to stand for re-election, or, at their option, to
retire from office. The advantages of the plan were
supposed to be: (1) closer responsiveness of officials
to popular sentiment; (2) the possibility of lengthening
official terms with greater safety; (3) immediate action
on the part of a community to relieve itself of an unworthy public servant. The earliest adoptions of the
scheme were in cities—in Los Angeles in 1903 and in
Seattle in 1906; and in subsequent years it appeared
in the charters of a majority of commission-governed
municipalities.[1] The first state to adopt it was Oregon,
whose constitution was so amended in 1908 as to make
all elective officers subject to recall. California
adopted the system in 1911; Arizona in 1911–1912;
Arkansas, Colorado, Idaho, Nevada, and Washington
in 1912; Michigan in 1913; and Kansas and Louisiana
in 1914.

Like the initiative and the referendum, the recall
assumed many forms and presented many problems.
The most difficult question was the recall of judges—
an issue discussed at much length in 1911–1912, when
Congress had under consideration the proposed constitution of the incoming state of Arizona. As origi-

[1] Oberholtzer, *The Referendum, Initiative, and Recall in America*
(rev. ed.), 455–461.

nally framed, this constitution carried the recall to
remarkable lengths. A resolution of Congress approved the instrument, subject to the condition that
the provisions relating to the recall should be submitted separately to the voters. President Taft vetoed the resolution and sent in a vigorous message
opposing the principle of judicial recall in any
form.[1]

A substitute resolution was thereupon passed, admitting the state on condition that the recall of judges
be wholly stricken from its constitution. The terms
were accepted, and the state was admitted; but in a
few months a popular vote restored the disputed provision. In only four of the ten states in which the
recall was established (Michigan, Louisiana, Idaho, and
Washington) were judicial officers exempt. Furthermore, Colorado in 1912 adopted a constitutional amendment, on lines suggested by ex-President Roosevelt in
a speech before the Ohio constitutional convention of
the same year,[2] providing for the "recall" of judicial
decisions by popular vote.[3]

If the advocates of the initiative and referendum
were surprised by the over-use of their pet expedients,
the friends of the recall were taken aback by popular
indifference to their invention. In very few instances
was the weapon brought to bear against state officers;
and even in counties, municipalities, and other local

---

[1] *Cong. Record,* 62 Cong., 1 Sess., pt. iv., p. 3964.
[2] *Outlook,* Vol. 100, pp. 390, 618.
[3] Lewis and Ashley, "The Recall of Judicial Decisions," Acad. Polit.
Sci., *Proceedings,* III., 37–51.

areas, it was used sparingly.   None the less, it proved
its usefulness as a warning, a threat, or even a punishment.[1]

[1] Munro, *Government of American Cities*, 354; Barnett, *Operation of
the Initiative, Referendum, and Recall in Oregon*, 189–218.

CHAPTER X

POLITICAL UNREST AND PARTY DISINTEGRATION
(1909–1912)

THE opening decade of the twentieth century
brought to the fore the greatest issue in American
politics since the Civil War. This was the question
whether government was to be administered in the
interest of privilege or of the people. The McKinley
era had been a period of amazing industrial and commercial expansion: manufactures multiplied; trade
made new conquests; railroads were consolidated in
vast systems; corporations absorbed their competitors and became trusts; capital poured into all branches
of "big business."

Government in that day set up few obstacles. The
courts had drawn the teeth of the Sherman anti-trust
law; they likewise had much reduced the power of the
Interstate Commerce Commission; and neither Congress nor the executive authorities showed much
regret. On the contrary, the sweep of business growth
was deliberately promoted by the Dingley tariff law of
1897, the gold standard act of 1900, and other economic
legislation.

Dubious results followed. Vested interests grew
accustomed to immunity from governmental inter-

ference; more than that, it came to expect governmental favors, and easily fell into the habit of using influence to secure those favors. Hence the spectacle everywhere appeared of nominating conventions dominated by self-seeking industrial magnates or their representatives, legislatures overrun by corporation lobbyists, officials sensitive to private interest but deaf to public demand. Public sentiment was inarticulate; popular rule was assumed rather than assured; the pressure of privilege was tremendous; government readily fell captive.

The situation was not wholly novel, nor the issue raised by it wholly unforeseen. President Cleveland saw the problem and made some effort to meet it, although lack of support tied his hands; and throughout the great epoch of business expansion the Democratic attitude on the tariff, railroad and trust regulation, and taxation was guided by the purpose to compel the special interests to relax their hold on public affairs. Disagreement on the silver issue disrupted the party, and confusion of the principles of popular rule with this issue caused the entire Democratic program to be rejected.

By 1901 popular discontent was at a point to be powerfully energized by capable leadership. That leadership was supplied by President Roosevelt. The people were prepared to applaud any attempt to rid the government of those who used its machinery and its cunningly drawn laws to further their private ends. Accordingly, they warmly supported the prosecutions of offenders against the land laws, the measures for conservation of natural resources, the suits to dissolve trusts, the new railroad legislation, and the laws passed with a view to social and industrial justice.

The things that were done, however, seemed to touch only the fringes of the problem. Sometimes power was lacking; sometimes Congress was dilatory or reactionary; sometimes the administrative officers were lax. Furthermore, the problem was not wholly national. Indeed, it lay mainly within the several states, and could be solved only by state action.

This condition of affairs suggested alterations in the machinery of government; and the efforts of states and nation from the beginning of the Roosevelt era to curb the influence of privilege by direct action was paralleled by the series of governmental changes described in the preceding chapter. Protection of the public against the menace of privilege seemed to call for a rebuilding of the whole political structure—nominations, elections, legislation, and administration; and for years the reformers kept these changes in the foreground.

The pressure for fuller popular control of government and for advanced social and economic legislation, though for a time scattered and incoherent, fast gathered unity, depth, and force; and eventually it came to be called "the progressive movement." Progressivism, in this broad and proper sense, though strongest in the West, was confined to no single section of the country. Furthermore, it found adherents in all political parties. Its earliest notable victories were achieved under the leadership of a Republican president, and of a group of Republican governors, chiefly La Follette in Wisconsin, Cummins in Iowa, Johnson in California, Pingree in Michigan, and Hughes in New York. But Democrats subscribed widely to its principles; and it remained for a Democrat, President Wilson, to succeed where others had failed in carrying its program into effect.

The retirement of President Roosevelt from office, March 4, 1909, brought the movement to a critical stage. The new President, Taft, was of conservative temper, as were also his chosen advisers; and while both houses of Congress contained able men of progressive inclination, their number was not large. Senator La Follette was the only recognized Republican leader in official life who was committed at every point to the progressive principles. Yet, six or eight years of agitation had prepared the public mind for a great advance on progressive lines; the gains that had been realized were as nothing compared with the achievements which the people wanted and expected. Taft had been accepted as president because he promised to carry on the policies of his predecessor, and because Roosevelt vouched for his progressive-mindedness.

The great fact of the Taft administration was the failure of the President, of the Republican majority in Congress, and of the Republican party at large, to rise to the situation by giving the country the progressive legislation which it demanded. The issue was forced at once by the tariff question. The Republicans had promised "immediate revision." The peo-

ple took this to mean a considerable revision downward. The Payne-Aldrich law of 1909, however,
levelled rates up rather than down, and a group of
"insurgent" Republican senators from the West—principally Cummins and Dolliver of Iowa, La Follette
of Wisconsin, Clapp of Minnesota, Beveridge of Indiana, and Bristow of Kansas—fought it to the end.
The President's characterization of the law as the best
of the kind ever passed cut squarely across the grain
of public opinion, and the whole effect of the episode
was to sharpen hitherto indistinct lines between progressivism and reaction, and to produce a rift in the
Republican party which became a chasm.[1]

Senator Aldrich and other conservatives proposed to
read the insurgents out of the party; and it was widely
believed that this was the intent of Taft in his famous
Winona speech.[2] But the low-tariff members knew
that they had the support of their constituents and refused to be intimidated. On the contrary, they became free lances, acting in most matters with their
Republican colleagues, yet ready upon occasion to co-
operate with the Democratic opposition in making
trouble for the Administration.

If the "stand-pat" forces were best represented at
one end of the Capitol by Aldrich, author of the high-
tariff features of the Payne-Aldrich Act, they were
most ably led at the other end by Joseph G. Cannon,
Speaker of the House of Representatives. Cannon
was a coarse, shrewd, successful country politician, of
a type familiar to every rural community. He had a

12   [1] La Follette, *Autobiography*, 447.   [2] See p. 38.

stock of sound old-fashioned principles, but to attain his ends he was accustomed to rely not so much on principles as on tricks of management. He was from the Middle West. But even had his temperament permitted, he could have had nothing in common with the insurgents; for the Speaker's office, and particularly Cannon's administration of it, had become the chosen target of the progressives.

Through a long course of natural development it had come about that the speaker had not only the power to appoint all committees in the House and to name their chairmen, but also the power, through his membership in and dominance of the Committee on Rules, to fix the limits of debate, to compel or prevent the consideration of any particular measure, and, in general, to govern legislative procedure with such completeness that no member could gain the ear of the House without having first secured the Speaker's express consent. Such authority in the hands of a masterful parliamentarian like Cannon meant complete subordination of the ordinary member. Rumblings of discontent were heard as early as 1907, especially when members who did not support the Cannon régime found themselves left off of the desirable committees. It was recognized that the size of the House required limiting the freedom of members more than in the Senate; but in the judgment of able men of both parties the concentration of control had been carried too far.

When Congress convened in special session in 1909, the dissatisfied Republican members offered no re-

sistance to Cannon's re-election. But they seized on
the usual motion that the new Congress should be
governed by the rules of its predecessor as an opportunity to trim the claws of the speakership; and
thirty-one Republicans united with the Democrats in
defeating the motion.[1] It was then moved by the
Democratic leader, Champ Clark, that the rules of
the preceding Congress should be adopted, with the
important modifications that the Speaker should appoint committees only as instructed by the House,
and that the Committee on Rules should be enlarged
to fifteen members, should be elected by the House,
and should be instructed to report at the next session
upon the entire subject of rules revision.   These proposals seemed too radical, and the only immediate
result was a change of procedure, moved by John J.
Fitzgerald, a Democratic member from New York,
designed to free members somewhat from the necessity of "seeing the Speaker" before offering motions.
Amid the tariff debates of this session, opposition to
"Cannonism" steadily increased; and while most of
the faults of the Payne-Aldrich Act must be laid at the
door of the Senate, dissatisfaction with the measure
found vent in renewed demands for the curbing of the
Speaker's authority.

   The storm broke during the regular session of 1909–
1910.   Several insurgent members showed irritation
under the rulings and other acts of the Speaker; till
finally a leader of the group, George W. Norris of
Nebraska, introduced, March 19, 1910, a resolution

[1] *House Jour.*, 61 Cong., 1 Sess., 9–10.

to increase the number of members of the Committee on Rules from five to ten, to provide for the election of all members by the House, and to exclude the Speaker from membership.[1] Objection was made that the resolution was out of order, and after a dramatic parliamentary battle lasting throughout almost an entire night, the contention was sustained by the chair. On appeal from the decision, the Democrats and insurgent Republicans adroitly joined forces and accomplished the Speaker's defeat; whereupon they carried a rule closely following the lines of Norris's motion. The next step was a resolution to declare the speakership vacant and to proceed to the election of a new incumbent. This was a tactical mistake, for it shifted the attack from a system to a personality. Cannon met the issue squarely and defied his enemies to depose him. It became clear that further action would break the Republican power in the House. Hence only eight of the insurgents supported the motion, which was lost by a vote of 155 to 192.

The outcome of this dramatic episode was the transfer of most control over legislative procedure from the Speaker, or at all events from an oligarchy composed of the Speaker and his friends, to a committee chosen and controlled by the membership of the House. When, in 1911, the Democrats signalized their return to mastery in the House by stripping from the presiding officer the appointment of all remaining standing committees and vesting this function in the Ways and Means Committee, subject to ratification by the

[1] *House Jour.*, 61 Cong., 2 Sess., 457–458.

House, the chamber took fuller control over its affairs than it had exercised at any time since the Civil War.[1]

Of itself, the contest over "Cannonism" need not have affected greatly the position of the Republican party. But it was symptomatic of a state of public feeling which, as the congressional and state elections of 1910 drew near, caused Republican leaders grave anxiety. Throughout large portions of the Middle West and in several of the far western states insurgency was rampant. The new tariff law was roundly disliked. The Administration's efforts to curb the trusts and to promote conservation were considered feeble. The Ballinger-Pinchot controversy roused suspicion of administrative inefficiency. Many people felt that the President spent too much time in travel. Others criticised him for not sweeping away small matters with despatch, in order that larger affairs might have proper attention.

More serious was the feeling that the influences about the President were reactionary, and that he had chosen to ally himself with the protected interests, the capitalists, the East. His sincerity and good intentions were never doubted, but the interests seemed to get the better of him, and men wondered whether he had in him the steel which the battle demanded. No other president had laid out at the beginning of his term a program so extensive and orderly. But he seemed to rely too much on party regularity as a means of carrying this program into effect; he was willing

[1] *Cong. Record*, 62 Cong., 1 Sess., pt. i., pp. 9–57; see p. 179.

to waive "revision downward" for the sake of other legislation, whereas the West put such revision ahead of everything else.

The fault was not wholly the President's. People expected too much of him, and expected the most contrary things. Low-tariff men wanted him to be one of them; stand-patters called on him to uphold high protection. Conservationists looked to him for drastic measures in support of their cause; water-power and other exploiting interests breathed easier when he entered office. Furthermore, he suffered by contrast with his more daring and brilliant predecessor. The glamour of the Roosevelt régime was sorely missed; the people could not make up their minds to like a rubber-tired administration.

As the congressional and state elections of 1910 approached, the Republican Congressional Campaign Committee and other managers brought to bear both persuasion and threat in an effort to rebuild the party fences.[1] Success was slight. The country was not in a partisan mood, and people refused to be driven by the party lash. The bulk of the party members in Ohio, Indiana, Illinois, Iowa, Wisconsin, Minnesota, Kansas, and the Dakotas, though coming of a stock that had voted the Republican ticket for three generations, were ready to put up independent candidates if they could not control the nominations; and wise candidates chose to make their campaigns on platforms which were in accord with the prevailing senti-

[1] Foraker, *Notes of a Busy Life*, II., chap. xlvii; Hansbrough, *The Wreck*, 115–134.

ment of their own communities. From the time when, at special elections in March and April, two strongly Republican districts in Massachusetts and New York were carried decisively by the Democrats, the drift of the country toward the opposition party grew steadily plainer.

At the November elections the Democrats fulfilled predictions by winning decisive victories in all sections and obtaining full control of the national House of Representatives. In Massachusetts, Connecticut, New York, New Jersey, Ohio, and a number of other normally Republican states, Democratic governors were elected; the victor in New Jersey was the ex-president of Princeton University, Woodrow Wilson. To the Sixty-second Congress were elected 227 Democrats, 173 Republicans, and one Socialist. Several prominent Republican "regulars," including Cannon, were returned; but the party quota contained many insurgents. In the Senate, the nominal Republican majority was cut from twenty-eight to ten. This was decidedly more than the usual loss of ground in an "off-year" election. It was a sweeping reversal of party fortunes, fully confirming surface indications that the country was dissatisfied with the Taft Administration and in revolt against the elements controlling the Republican party.

The Democratic victory was won mainly on the tariff, which meant that this issue would continue in the forefront. The short session of 1910–1911 gave all elements a chance to define afresh their position on the subject. It developed that the plan of the

Administration Republicans was to maintain a permanent tariff board, charged with the task of studying scientifically the problems involved in tariff legislation, and eventually to use this information in a cautious revision of the Payne-Aldrich law, schedule by schedule. The Democratic purpose was to proceed without delay to a general revision, with a view to establishing a totally different standard of rates on which subsequent investigations and rate changes should be based.

The question was kept to the fore during the session by the efforts of Taft to secure legislation for commercial reciprocity with Canada. President Roosevelt and Secretary Root had sought to bring about closer relations between the United States and her northern neighbo.; and under President Taft's direction Secretary Knox negotiated, in January, 1911, an agreement providing for reduction or abolition of duties on many Canadian food products and on wood-pulp, paper, rough lumber, and other manufactures; this to be compensated by lower Canadian duties on agricultural implements and some other commodities. Arrangement of reciprocity by treaty would raise troublesome questions as to the power of the Senate over commerce; hence the agreement was to be carried into effect in both countries by ordinary legislation.

On the whole, the plan was favorably regarded by American manufacturers. But the farming and lumbering interests of the West, Northwest, and parts of rural New England warmly opposed it, on the ground that it set up new competition in their products without giving them any compensating advantage.[1] Accordingly, a Canadian reciprocity bill, drawn to give the scheme effect, was resisted at every stage by the western insurgents. February 14, the Administration forces, supported by the Democrats, and acting under a special rule practically preventing debate, carried the measure in the House by a vote of 221 to 92.[2] But the session closed, March 4, without action in the Senate. Contrary to the plain desire of almost all members of the two houses, and of the people at large, the President carried out a threat which he had repeatedly made by calling the new Congress into session April 4 to enact the desired legislation.

When Congress assembled, the Democratic House promptly elected Champ Clark of Missouri Speaker, and Oscar W. Underwood of Alabama, John J. Fitzgerald of New York, and Robert L. Henry of Texas, chairmen, respectively, of the Ways and Means, Appropriations, and Rules Committees; and these four men became the recognized majority leaders of the chamber. The opportunity of the Democrats was alluring. For the first time in sixteen years they were in control of the popular branch of Congress. Their opponents were hopelessly divided. The country had pronounced unmistakably in their favor on the issue of the hour, the tariff. The Administration was play-

[1] Hibbard, "Reciprocity and the Farmer," *Am. Econ. Rev.*, 4th series, No. 3, pp. 221–233.
[2] *House Jour.*, 61 Cong., 3 Sess., 303.

ing squarely into their hands by persisting in the reciprocity program after it had become fairly certain that the tariff arrangements on which that program was based would soon be superseded.

With a view to safeguarding the advantages that had been gained and building upon them in preparation for the campaign of 1912, the House majority, under the astute leadership of Underwood, mapped out a policy with two main features: (1) to support the reciprocity agreement, inasmuch as it involved tariff reductions, and because it could reasonably be expected to bring the Payne-Aldrich law into further disrepute; (2) to pass tariff bills which would win the support of the Republican insurgents and in other ways embarrass the Administration.   Both parts of the plan were carried out successfully. The Reciprocity bill was passed in the House, April 21, by a vote of 268 to 89,[1] and in the Senate, July 22, by a vote of 53 to 27;[2] the Senate minority consisting of twelve insurgent Republicans, twelve regular Republicans, and three Democrats.   Reciprocity unexpectedly broke down at the Canadian end; for it was made the issue in a general election of September 21, and the Liberal government which had negotiated the agreement was decisively beaten.[3]   But in the United States the Democrats got whatever advantage there was in supporting it, while the Taft Administration was made to suffer the fresh

---

[1] *House Jour.*, 62 Cong., 1 Sess., 140–141.

[2] *Senate Jour.*, 62 Cong., 1 Sess., 133.

[3] Skelton, "Canadian Attitude toward Reciprocity," *Jour. Polit. Econ.*, XIX., 77–97, and "Canada's Rejection of Reciprocity," *ibid.*, 726-731.

discomfiture of defeat in a cause for which it had
sacrificed much.[1]

In pursuance of the second portion of its program,
the Democratic majority brought forward three important tariff measures.   The first, known as the
Farmer's Free List bill, placed on the free list agricultural implements, lumber, flour, meat, boots and shoes,
and many other commodities used extensively by farmers.   It was passed, May 8, by a vote of 236 to 109.[2]
The second, a Woolens bill, revised the notorious
"Schedule K" by reducing the average duty on wool
and woolen manufactures from ninety to forty-eight
per cent., and was passed June 20 by a vote of 221 to
100.[3]   The third, a Cotton Schedule bill reducing the
duties on cotton manufactures, chemicals, metals,
paints, and other articles, was passed August 3 by a
vote of 202 to 90.[4]   In the Senate, combined Democratic and insurgent votes carried all of these measures
with less difficulty and delay than had been expected.
All, however, were killed by vetoes of the President,
on the ground that they were improperly drawn and
were based on no exact information on the industries
and interests affected, such as the Tariff Board might
eventually supply.   The country regarded the bills as
very satisfactory, and the President's position was
further weakened by his vetoes.   He seemed to care
more for the form of revision than for revision itself.
In their handling of the subject the Democrats showed

---

[1] Hansbrough, *The Wreck*, 130–160.
[2] *House Jour.*, 62 Cong., 1 Sess., 193–194.
[3] *Ibid.*, 279.   [4] *Ibid.*, 339.

unanimity, self-restraint, and sincerity; from it they gained a highly advantageous tactical position.

Meanwhile the radical Republicans matured plans to capture control of their party and prevent the renomination of Taft in 1912. On January 21, 1911, a group of insurgent senators and representatives met at the home of Senator La Follette in Washington and established a National Progressive Republican League, whose object was announced to be "the promotion of popular government and progressive legislation."[1] Ex-President Roosevelt declined membership, although in a notable speech at Ossawattomie, Kansas, five months earlier he had sounded the call for a "new nationalism," and had put himself in line with the latest phases of the progressive movement by advocating a graduated income tax, conservation, labor legislation, the direct primary, and the recall of elective officers. The league grew rapidly in numbers and influence, and was soon described as "the culmination of the progressive movement in the Republican party and the beginning of the new Progressive party."[2]

The question of national leadership remained to be settled. At a conference held April 30, 1911, in Senator Bourne's committee-room at the Capitol, it was agreed that Senator La Follette, on the whole the ablest and most outspoken member of the group, should be put forward as a candidate against Taft for the Republican nomination in the following year.[3] Sup-

---

[1] La Follette, *Autobiography*, 495.
[2] De Witt, *Progressive Movement*, 70.
[3] La Follette, *Autobiography*, 516–521.

port was liberally promised, and during the ensuing summer the La Follette campaign was definitely launched. Headquarters were opened in Washington; progressive clubs were organized in a number of states; and in the Middle West, where during the autumn and winter the candidates spoke extensively, the cause gained ground rapidly. A national conference of two hundred Progressive Republicans, held at Chicago October 16 on call of the La Follette campaign manager, declared the senator to be "the logical Republican candidate for president of the United States," called for the formation of La Follette organizations in all states, and advocated a direct primary for the nomination of presidential candidates.[1]

Everything looked favorable for the La Follette candidacy except the preference of the eastern Progressives for ex-President Roosevelt, whose less radical views were more acceptable to them, and whose abilities they regarded as superior to those of La Follette.[2] At the launching of his campaign La Follette was given to understand by persons who were presumed to speak authoritatively that under no circumstances would Roosevelt enter the field. But he could not be oblivious to the fact that during the ex-President's prolonged absence in Africa and Europe (March, 1909, to June, 1910) the press abounded in half-humorous, half-serious allusions to "back-from-Elba," and he could not ignore the manner in which the ex-President,

[1] La Follette, *Autobiography*, 532.
[2] *Am. Year Book*, 1911, pp. 68–71.

after his return, threw himself into political affairs, notably in the New York gubernatorial election of 1910. Positive suspicion was aroused by Roosevelt's refusal to identify himself with the Progressive Republican League and by his half-heartedness, in general, in coming to the support of the organized progressive cause.

For a time, none the less, La Follette's star kept rising. On January 1, 1912, a Progressive Republican League was established in Ohio; and within a few days a similar organization appeared in Illinois. In a rambling and acrimonious speech delivered at the annual dinner of the Periodical Publishers' Association in Philadelphia, February 2, 1912, the senator, however, weakened his candidacy irreparably. His friends said that the strain of the campaign had broken him down physically, and strove to induce the country to forget the incident. But the elements that had been desirous of pushing him aside now found their opportunity. They spread the impression that he was not able to run, and even that he had withdrawn from the contest; and denials proved of no avail.

The truth is that the bulk of progressive sentiment had been shifting rapidly to Roosevelt; quite apart from the Philadelphia speech, La Follette's candidacy was doomed. The Wisconsin senator was a man of courage and ability, and he had achieved much during his three terms in the governorship of his state. His ambition was boundless, and he knew well how to keep in the spot-light's narrow circle. He was an indomitable fighter. But the country knew him as an ultra-radical and either feared him or doubted his presidential capacity. The trend from him toward Roosevelt was for months perceptible; yet even the shrewdest political observers were surprised by the extent, as well as the apparent suddenness, of the defection.

To La Follette himself the turn of affairs brought much bitterness. He felt that his supporters had trifled with him; and he was firmly of the opinion that Roosevelt had been using him all the while as a stalking-horse to test the situation, with the intention of entering the race himself at the opportune time. Pointing scornfully to the trust record of the Roosevelt Administration and to his rival's cordial indorsement of the Payne-Aldrich tariff, he denied to the ex-President the right to bear the name "Progressive," and contended that by transfer of allegiance to such a leader true progressivism was being betrayed in the house of its friends.

Fulmination and sober argument alike failed to stay the Roosevelt tide. February 10, seven Republican governors—Bass of New Hampshire, Glasscock of West Virginia, Osborn of Michigan, Hadley of Missouri, Stubbs of Kansas, Aldrich of Nebraska, and Carey of Wyoming—together with seventy other Republican leaders representing twenty-four states, met in conference at Chicago to forward Roosevelt's nomination. As an outcome, the seven governors issued a statement urging all persons who desired "prosperity and progress" to join in demanding that the ex-President be nominated, while to Roosevelt himself they communicated their conviction that a large majority of the people favored his election, and urged him to say whether, should the nomination come to him unsought, he would accept it.[1]

For days the ex-President hesitated, while golden opportunities to secure delegates slipped by. At last, February 24, he announced that he would accept the nomination if it were offered him by the Republican convention, and that he would adhere to this decision until the convention should have expressed a preference. Under the conditions, this meant that he was a candidate, and that he was ready to enter a contest for Republican leadership against his intimate friend and co-laborer of other years, Mr. Taft.[2]

[1] *Review of Reviews*, XLV., 391; *Outlook*, Vol. 100, p. 475.
[2] *Am. Year Book*, 1912, p. 4.

CHAPTER XI

THE ELECTION OF 1912

(1911–1912)

EVERYTHING pointed to a new party, whether to spring from a mere secession of Republican progressives or to take the form of a union of progressives drawn from all parties. And not only did some observers expect such a party to arise and sweep the country in the autumn elections; enthusiasts said that the new party already existed, having both the principles and the men, and lacking only name, machinery, and corporate consciousness. Yet even in the early months of 1912 the Republican progressives had no intention of withdrawing from, or otherwise disrupting, the old party. They were bent on securing the nomination of some leader, preferably Roosevelt, known to be in sympathy with their views; and they intended to keep up the effort to carry their principles into nation-wide legislation. But they proposed to regenerate their party and then work through it, not to abandon it.

The Republican pre-convention campaign resolved itself at the outset into a contest between Taft and Roosevelt. Senator La Follette remained a candidate,

187

but with only a meagre following outside his own state.
Other persons mentioned included ex-Governor Charles
E. Hughes (who in 1910 had been appointed a justice
of the federal Supreme Court), Senator Cummins of
Iowa, and former Vice-President Fairbanks; but no
one of them was seriously considered.

The two principal contestants promptly fell into
acrimonious debate, Roosevelt charging Taft with reaction and subservience to bosses, Taft denouncing
Roosevelt's plan for the recall of judges and judicial
decisions and warning the country against political
emotionalists who "would hurry us into a condition
which would find no parallel except in the French
Revolution." It was a sorry controversy, and the
public freely criticized both participants.

Meanwhile, preparations were under way for the
Republican national convention, which was to meet
at Chicago on June 18. The managers of the Taft
campaign gave their first attention to the capture of
the delegations of the southern states. The task offered little real difficulty, because in most of those
states the party was notoriously weak and its activities
were dominated by the federal office-holders, who in
turn were under control of the Administration. Yet
the number of delegates was large; for, according to
long-established practice, it was based on total population, and not on the Republican strength of the
state. Under inspiration from Washington, the southern conventions were held during the first three months
of the year; and in almost all cases they elected delegations pledged to Taft. Realizing that the old-

fashioned convention system would clinch nation-wide
control of the party organization in the hands of the
President, Roosevelt and his adherents urged the election of delegates by direct vote of the party members; and the campaign became the first in which the
presidential preference primary was brought into
actual-service. It was used in twelve states.[1]

The results of the primaries were overwhelmingly
favorable to Roosevelt. March 19, he carried Illinois
by a majority of 138,410 over President Taft. The
next day he obtained 67 of the 76 delegates of Pennsylvania. Decisive victories followed, April 19, in
Nebraska and Oregon. In Maryland, on May 6, and
in California, on May 14, he won by a substantial
plurality. On May 21 came the climax in the crush-
ing defeat of the President in his own state, Ohio.
Other triumphs were achieved in New Jersey on May
28 and South Dakota on June 4. In Massachusetts
the preferential vote of April 30 was favorable to Taft
by a small majority; and Taft delegates were chosen
in eighteen districts, although Roosevelt obtained the
eight delegates-at-large and ten of the district delegates. In Indiana, Michigan, Texas, Washington, and
some other states in which the progressives considered
themselves wronged, contesting delegations were
named; while, on one pretext or another, such delegations were made up in most of the states of the
South. At the opening of the convention the progressive forces were in a position to argue with much
plausibility that the primaries had shown the rank and

[1] See p. 159.

file of the party to be opposed to the Taft Administration and its political alliances, and to be in favor of the nomination of Roosevelt.

When, on June 6, the National Committee assembled at Chicago to take the customary steps preparatory to the convention's work, it found, in a total of 1,078 delegates' seats, 210 nominally contested. Many of these contests, however, were groundless, and somewhat less than half of the number were actually brought before the committee. Whether or not because the committee favored the nomination of Taft, the outcome of a week's deliberations was that enough seats were assigned to that candidate to insure him a majority in the convention. It was easy to show that the Taft delegations from the South had been chosen by dubious methods. The Republican regulars retorted, however, that these methods were brought to bear under President Roosevelt's direction in behalf of the candidacy of Taft in 1908; and that the contesting Roosevelt delegations stood upon foundations even less secure. Whatever the merits of the controversy, a system which gave the southern states and territories more delegates in a Republican convention than were allotted to New York, Pennsylvania, Illinois, Ohio, Massachusetts, Indiana, and Iowa combined was indefensible.

June 15, Roosevelt went to Chicago to watch proceedings; and three days later the convention began its work. The first clashes resulted in victories for the regulars. On the opening day the convention refused to give seats temporarily to certain Roosevelt contestants;[1] it also elected as temporary chairman Senator Root, charged by the progressives with being put forward as the representative of privilege, over the progressive candidate, Governor McGovern of Wisconsin.[2] In his "keynote" speech Root reviewed at length the achievements of the Taft administration, declared that the best traditions of the McKinley and Roosevelt administrations had been maintained, and called for a restoration of party harmony and loyalty;[3] but the progressives were not visibly affected.

On the question of the temporary chairmanship the roll was called as made up by the National Committee, and all Roosevelt contestants were ignored. It was clear that nothing short of a complete reorganization of the convention could prevent the nomination of Taft. But such reorganization was impossible; for although hours running into days were spent in dumb-show pretense of dealing with contested seats, the Taft delegates whose seats were in dispute enjoyed the right to vote equally with delegates whose seats were not questioned, and all the contests but one were settled in Taft's favor. It was not the first time that a National Committee had organized a convention and used it for its own purposes. But it was the first time that the calcium light was thrown on the whole proceeding, so that the public could get an intimate view behind the scenes. The cry of "steam roller," repeatedly raised in the Coliseum, was echoed from one end

[1] Fifteenth Republican National Convention, *Official Report of Proceedings*, 32–42.
[2] *Ibid.*, 42–88.   [3] *Ibid.*, 88–100.

of the country to the other, and millions of voters drew the conclusion that the convention's proceedings were outrageously unfair.

When, finally, it became apparent that no more Roosevelt delegates would be seated, the ex-President issued a statement (June 20) declaring that the bosses were thwarting the will of the people, and advising his followers not to act with the fraudulent majority. Thereafter most of the Roosevelt delegates were present in the convention only as spectators. After four days of rigmarole over contested seats, the convention formally adopted the report of the Committee on Credentials, sustaining at every point the action of the National Committee. Henry J. Allen of Kansas thereupon announced that the Roosevelt supporters would no longer share responsibility for the convention's acts, and read a statement from his chief declaring that in view of the refusal of the convention to purge its roll of eighty or ninety "stolen" delegates, the body as composed had "no claim to represent the voters of the Republican party."[1]

These tumultuous preliminaries were the important part of the convention's work; the rest was performed quickly and according to program. Root was chosen to remain in the chair as permanent presiding officer. A progressive platform offered by the Wisconsin delegation was tabled after brief debate, and the platform reported by Charles W. Fairbanks of Indiana for the Committee on Resolutions was adopted by a vote of 666 to 53, with 343 delegates not voting. Two

[1] *Review of Reviews*, XLVI., 141.

candidates, Taft and La Follette, were placed in nomination, and a vote was taken, resulting as follows:
Taft, 561, Roosevelt 107, La Follette 41, Cummins 17,
and Hughes 2, with 344 delegates not voting.[1] The
nomination of Taft was announced; Vice-President
Sherman was renominated, virtually without contest;
and the convention adjourned.

The vote as stated does not reveal on its face the
closeness of the struggle. Competent observers were
of the opinion that the seating of as few as twenty
Roosevelt contestants would have brought the ex-
President near enough to the Taft vote to carry him
over the line by a stampede. A break in the Taft ranks
might easily have come. There was no real enthusiasm
for the President, whereas the candidate against whom
the convention was organized was constantly cheered
with a fervor which refused to be bottled up. The
southern delegations would have been quick to turn
their support to a more promising candidate.

The platform bore little evidence of the conflict
amidst which it was drawn up[2]. It declared the "un-
changing faith of the party in government of the
people, by the people, and for the people"; and it
promised social and economic legislation for which the
progressives in many states had been contending. It
was silent, however, on the presidential primary; and
while advocating better means of removing unworthy
judges, it pronounced the judicial recall "unnecessary

[1] Fifteenth Republican National Convention, *Official Report of Proceedings*, 402.
[2] *Ibid.*, 342–351; *Republican Campaign Text-Book*, 1912, pp. 271–277.

and unwise." The position taken on the tariff was identical with that of the Taft Administration; the tariff bills passed by the Democratic House in 1911 were denounced "as sectional, injurious to the public credit, and destructive of business enterprise." The trust plank carried only the impression that the party favored strengthening the Sherman law. Other recommendations were: currency reform; a federal trade commission; extension of the merit system; more stringent regulation of immigration; a parcels post; and more effective restraint of corporations from contributing funds to be used in national elections.

On the evening of June 22, immediately after the adjournment of the Republican convention, the Roosevelt delegates and alternates, with some thousands of followers and spectators, came together in Orchestra Hall. The delegates adopted resolutions declaring that the nomination of Taft had been accomplished by fraud, and Roosevelt made an impassioned speech in which he said that the time had come when "not only all men who believe in progressive principles, but all men who believe in those elementary maxims of public and private morality which must underlie every form of successful free government, should join in one movement." The next day the delegates, before dispersing to their homes, set up a committee to lead in determining the future course of action; in effect they then and there launched the Progressive party. July 8, this committee issued a call, signed by men of prominence representing forty states, and addressed

to the progressively-inclined people of the United
States without regard to past political differences,
fixing August 5 as the time, and Chicago as the place,
of the first Progressive national convention. Before
the date arrived the cleavage between the Republicans
and Progressives spread rapidly through the country,
and in Illinois, Michigan, Iowa, Indiana, New Jersey,
and elsewhere, full Progressive state tickets were placed
in the field.

Chicago had been the scene of many political gath-
erings, but never of one like that of August 5 to 7,
1912. Some two thousand men and women, duly
elected as delegates, came together in the Coliseum to
set a new party on its feet, to map out its program, and
to name its candidates. For the first time on such an
occasion professional politicians were in the minority;
the bulk of the delegates had never before taken part
in politics; more than a score of them were women.
"A family reunion," some sentimentally called the
assemblage; "a prayer-meeting," said others. It indeed was much like a gigantic revival meeting, with its
old-fashioned enthusiasm, its prayers, hymn-singing,
patriotic songs, and all the inspiration and fervor of a
great body of earnest people moved by a common
cause.[1] The convention hall was a blaze of color;
the oratory was spontaneous and at times thrilling;
no dramatic possibilities were overlooked.

August 6, Roosevelt was introduced as the convention's "guest," and for an hour there was a riot of
enthusiasm, punctuated by the booming, rhythmic cry,

[1] *Review of Reviews*, XLVI., 310.

"We—want—Teddy." The candidate delivered a powerful address, termed by him a "confession of faith," in which he reiterated the charge that both the Republican and Democratic parties were boss-ridden and privilege-controlled, and set forth at length the view that the country was facing "a great economic evolution" and that, to the end that it might go forward on the path of social and economic justice, the people must be allowed to rule. On the following day the convention officially selected for the party the name "Progressive," adopted a platform, nominated candidates, and adjourned. By acclamation, Roosevelt was named for president, and Governor Hiram Johnson of California for vice-president.

The Progressive platform represented the result of prolonged labor, participated in by many men and women of ability and conviction, and was both comprehensive and definite.[1] It advocated the direct primary; a nation-wide presidential-preference primary; popular election of United States senators; the short ballot; the initiative; the referendum; the recall, including the recall of judicial decisions; woman's suffrage; registration of lobbyists; greater publicity of campaign funds, both before and after elections; and "a more easy and expeditious method of amending the federal Constitution." It urged legislation on minimum wage standards; child labor; industrial health and accidents; industrial education; social insurance; agricultural credit and co-operation; and the organization of a national department of labor. It favored

[1] Stanwood, *History of the Presidency*, II., 288–298.

strengthening the Sherman law; denounced the Payne-Aldrich tariff; and demanded protective duties no higher than necessary to equalize conditions of competition between the United States and foreign countries and to maintain for labor an adequate standard of living.

The whole course of affairs leading up to the several conventions indicated that 1912 was to be a Democratic year. Nevertheless, from the moment when, at the Washington meeting of the National Committee, January 8–10, Bryan sought fruitlessly to exclude from membership a Pennsylvania reactionary, it was evident that the Democrats would have to face the same issue of progressivism that had disrupted their opponents. One of the first Democratic candidates in the field was Governor Judson Harmon of Ohio, a conservative. Missouri had two candidates, ex-Governor Joseph W. Folk and Speaker Champ Clark, both regarded as progressives; but at an early date Folk withdrew. A candidate of whose progressiveness there could be no doubt was Governor Woodrow Wilson of New Jersey. Other persons mentioned were Governor Marshall of Indiana, Governor Burke of North Dakota, Governor Foss of Massachusetts, Governor Baldwin of Connecticut, Congressman Underwood of Alabama, and Mayor Gaynor of New York City. Bryan was not a candidate, but his power in the party promised to be a leading factor in the contest.

In the pre-convention campaign the advantage lay distinctly with Clark. His victories in the primaries of Illinois, Nebraska, Iowa, and California were matched by Wilson triumphs in Pennsylvania, Wisconsin, Oregon, and New Jersey. But when all primaries and conventions had been held the Speaker was found to have the pledges of more delegates than any other candidate, although far from the two-thirds required by Democratic rules for nomination.

The Democratic convention, which assembled at Baltimore June 25, proved not only the longest, but also, like the Republican gathering of the preceding week, one of the most dramatic, since the Civil War. Violent controversy arose at the outset over the temporary chairmanship. The National Committee put forward Alton B. Parker, Democratic candidate for president in 1904. Bryan opposed him as a reactionary, and after a hard fight barely failed to prevent his election.[1] To ease the situation the Nebraskan was offered the permanent chairmanship. This, however, he refused, contenting himself with a fresh demand that the convention purge itself of reactionary influences. Eventually the position went to an ardent Bryan follower, Senator Ollie James of Kentucky.

On the second day the progressive element scored an important victory by securing the adoption of instructions to the chairman to make exceptions, in the enforcement of the unit rule, in favor of states which had provided by statute for "the nomination and election of delegates and alternates to national political conventions in congressional districts."[2] The tensest

[1] Democratic National Convention of 1912, *Official Report of Proceedings*, 3-19.
[2] *Ibid.*, 76.

moments of the session came on the evening of the
27th, when Bryan strove to carry a resolution which
(1) reaffirmed the party's position as "the champion of
popular government and equality before the law";
(2) declared against the nomination of any candidate
representing, or under obligation to, any member of
the "privilege-hunting and favor-seeking class"; (3)
demanded the withdrawal from the convention of certain capitalists alleged to belong to this class.[1]   After
angry debate, the third section of the resolution was
given up; the other two were adopted.

In these proceedings Bryan rose to greater heights
of leadership than he had attained in any of his own
three candidacies for the presidency. At his further
suggestion the usual convention procedure was reversed,
and the nominations were made before the platform
was adopted. The convention contained 1,092 delegates, and 728 votes were necessary to nominate. The
balloting continued from June 28 to July 2. On the
first ballot Clark received 440½ votes, Wilson 324,
Harmon 148, Underwood 117½, with 56 scattering.
On the tenth, New York transferred its vote from Harmon to Clark. After the fourteenth, Bryan, who as
a member of the Nebraska delegation had been voting
for Clark, created a fresh sensation by announcing in
an impassioned speech that he would thereafter withhold his vote from the Missouri candidate as long as
New York's vote, alleged to be contaminated by pluto-
cratic influences, should be cast for him. Despite the

[1] Democratic National Convention of 1912, *Official Report of Pro-*
ceedings, 129–138; Stanwood, *History of the Presidency*, II., 260–271.

best efforts of the Speaker and his friends to overcome
the effect of this move, the balance began to turn;
and on the twenty-eighth ballot Wilson's vote for the
first time pushed ahead of Clark's.   The end came with
the forty-sixth ballot, on which Wilson received 990
votes, Clark 84, and Harmon 12.[1]   After two ballots
on the vice-presidential candidates failed to yield a
choice, Governor Thomas R. Marshall of Indiana was
nominated by acclamation.

The figures recording the results of the balloting
are dry enough; the ballots themselves were taken
amidst convention pandemonium perhaps unequalled
in American political history.   "It was halloing," says
a journalist describing the scene, "yelling, screaming,
roaring, raised to the nth power; they 'hollered,'
simply hollered, for an hour at a time.   When a telling
speech was successfully shouted or a significant vote
was cast, they carried banners up and down and
around the aisles; they reared mammoth pictures of
candidates against the galleries; they sent up toy
balloons, and tossed pigeons into the air; they carried
a girl about the hall; men and women shied hats
through the air; horns, whistles, and infernal con-
trivances without name contributed to the diabolical
din. . . . 'Demonstration' followed 'demonstration' and
passed into 'counter-demonstration' without altering a
vote.   Uproar that shattered the voice of a new chairman every five minutes, and wore out fresh platoons
of police every hour; the efforts of bands drowned under

[1] Democratic National Convention of 1912, *Official Report of Proceedings*, 353.

the vocal din, and the chromatic clamor of banners assailed the delegates and left them stubborn at their posts. At Chicago they stood pat to the end. At Baltimore they changed, but they refused to stampede. They changed slowly, and only under the slowly increasing realization that Woodrow Wilson was the right man."[1] It was never charged that the Baltimore convention was a cut-and-dried affair, or that it was boss-ruled.

Once more the platform was mainly the work of Bryan. It stressed the tariff, and promised "immediate downward revision"; it demanded new trust legislation which would make private monopoly impossible; it urged banking and currency reform and physical valuation of railways; it indorsed pre-election publicity for campaign contributions, called for a constitutional amendment making the President ineligible for re-election, and pledged Wilson to this principle; it approved the exemption from tolls of American ships engaged in coastwise traffic passing through the Panama Canal, and favored "an immediate declaration of the nation's purpose to recognize the independence of the Philippine Islands as soon as a stable government can be established."[2]

Aside from the Progressives, no new party appeared in the campaign of 1912; and the existing minor parties played unimportant rôles. The Socialists held

---

[1] *World's Work*, XXIV., 366.

[2] Democratic National Convention of 1912, *Official Report of Proceedings*, 365–376; *Democratic Campaign Text-Book*, 1912, pp. 2–42; Stanwood, *History of the Presidency*, II., 260–271.

their convention at Indianapolis May 12–18, and adopted a platform which was the product of ingenious compromise between the moderate and revolutionary wings of the party. Their nominees were Eugene V. Debs of Indiana and Emil Seidel of Wisconsin. The Socialist Labor party held a convention in New York City in early April and nominated Arthur E. Reimer of Massachusetts and August Gillhaus of New York. The Prohibitionists assembled at Atlantic City and renominated their candidates of 1904 and 1908, Eugene W. Chafin, now of Arizona, and Aaron S. Watkins of Ohio.[1]

It was not to be expected that the intense public interest aroused by the spectacular Republican and Democratic conventions would be sustained throughout the campaign. Considering the novelty of the situation, however, the post-convention contest was extraordinarily tame. The defeat of Taft and the triumph of the Democrats over a divided opposition seemed inevitable, and the tenseness which accompanies a contest felt to be really close did not develop. The chief element of uncertainty was the showing of the new Progressive party, and especially of its presidential candidate. Probably at no other national election in the country's history have so many people voted for a cause felt to be already lost, or in a spirit of revenge, or for a candidate supported under protest.

Cherishing a forlorn hope, the Republicans carried through their campaign to the bitter end. While federal office-holders were resigning on all hands to aid in

[1] Stanwood, *History of the Presidency*, II., 272–285.

organizing the Progressive party, and while necessary
reconstructions of the old party organization were being
undertaken, Charles D. Hilles, the President's private
secretary, was made chairman, and George R. Sheldon,
a New York banker, was again made treasurer, of the
campaign committee.   General advisers were found in
Senator Penrose of Pennsylvania, Senator Crane of
Massachusetts, Senator Smoot of Utah, and other members of the "Old Guard."   In notifying the President
of his renomination (August 1), Senator Root affirmed
that the action of the Chicago convention had been
entirely in accord "with the rules of law governing
the party, and founded upon justice and common
sense."

Neither the President nor the members of his cabinet
took an active part in the campaign. In his acceptance
speech, however, the candidate defended the record
of his Administration, denounced the "new and dangerous" tenets espoused by Roosevelt, and expressed
gratitude that, despite the assaults made upon it at the
Chicago convention, the Republican party had been
"saved for future usefulness."   In later addresses and
interviews he defended his tariff vetoes, charged that
the Progressive party was a product of personal ambition and vengeance, characterized its platform as a
"crazy quilt," and predicted that the fear of "hard
times" under a Democratic Administration would be
sufficient to prevent the election of Wilson.

The Progressives perfected a national organization
on lines made familiar by the usage of the older parties,
with Senator Joseph M. Dixon of Montana, who had

14

managed Roosevelt's pre-convention campaign, as
chairman of the National Committee. In New York,
Ohio, and some other states a separate ticket was put
in the field. In Wisconsin and elsewhere the Republican nominees declared for Roosevelt and received the
Progressive support. After the middle of August
Roosevelt was almost continuously on the stump,
visiting every section of the country, expounding the
Progressive program, and attacking the platforms and
leaders of the old parties, although his speaking tour
was abruptly terminated, October 14, by a wound
received at the hand of a maniac at Milwaukee.

The Democratic campaign was interesting because
likely to be successful, and because of the personality
of the chief candidate. After holding a professorship
of jurisprudence and politics in Princeton University,
Wilson was promoted, in 1902, to the presidency of his
institution; and in 1910 he was elected governor of
his state. His vigorous conduct of that office attracted nation-wide attention. His first act was to
break with and defy the machine of his own party;
and notwithstanding the control of the upper house
of the legislature by the Republicans, he secured a
public utilities law, a corrupt practices act, an employers' liability and workmen's compensation act,
and much other progressive legislation. His political
opponents dubbed him a mere academician, a "peda-
gogue," and a theorizer. But he revealed himself to
be no less a man of affairs than a scholar. He had a
vast fund of political information and exceptional
powers of speech; and he became one of the best cam-

paigners in the history of American politics. In his acceptance speech, delivered at Sea Girt, New Jersey, August 7, he brushed aside the Baltimore platform with the observation that "a platform is not a program," and spoke broadly in commendation of the rule of the people and the reasonable regulation of business enterprise. It was sufficiently clear that, although a progressive, he was an exponent of neither radical principles nor extremist measures.

The management of the Democratic campaign was placed in the hands of a committee under the chairmanship of William F. McCombs, who had looked after the candidate's pre-convention interests. During September and October Wilson made extensive speaking tours through the West, emphasizing the changed economic condition of the country; declaring himself to be favorable to "big business" which should not seek to stifle competition nor to control the government, but opposed to trusts; advocating tariff revision which should eliminate "cunningly devised and carefully concealed special favors"; and proclaiming the gospel of a "new freedom," by which was meant the liberation of private enterprise from domination by trusts and other corporate powers. On more specific lines, he advocated popular election of senators; the initiative and referendum, where likely to be found useful as "a gun behind the door"; and the recall of administrative officers. To the recall of judges he, like Taft, was strongly opposed.

The closing incidents of the campaign foreshadowed Democratic victory; and in the election, November 5,

Taft carried but two states (Vermont and Utah),
yielding eight electoral votes. Roosevelt carried five
states—Pennsylvania, Michigan, Minnesota, South
Dakota, and Washington—and received 11 of the 13
electoral votes of California, giving him 88 electoral
votes in all. Wilson carried all of the remaining 40
states, with a total of 435 votes, which represented the
largest vote, and also the largest majority, in the
electoral college ever obtained by a party candidate.

The popular vote presented, however, a different
aspect. The figures were: Wilson, 6,286,214; Roosevelt, 4,126,020; Taft, 3,483,922; Debs, 897,011;
Chafin, 208,923; and Reimer, 29,079.[1] The outstanding fact is that in a large proportion of the states in
which the Democrats were victorious—in all, indeed,
except those in the South—they won by pluralities,
not by majorities; and that while Wilson had a plurality of 2,160,194 votes over his closest competitor, his
total fell short of the combined votes for all other
candidates by 2,458,741, and of the combined votes
for Roosevelt and Taft by 1,323,728. It is further to
be observed that the Wilson vote was 181,732 smaller
than the Bryan vote of 1896, and 122,892 smaller than
the Bryan vote of 1908. The stay-at-home vote was
large; and the Socialists drew from the major parties
to such an extent that their vote was more than doubled
over that of 1908.

From the presidential returns it might have been
argued that the nation showed no overmastering desire

[1] McLaughlin and Hart, *Cyclopædia of American Government*, III.,
45–46.

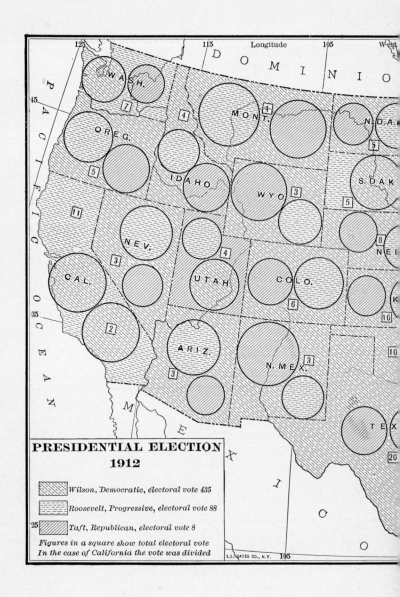

125   115   Longitude   105   West

D O M I N I O

45

P A C I F I C

O C E A N

35

WASH.

7

OREG.

5

11

CAL.

2

IDAHO

4

NEV.

3

UTAH

4

ARIZ.

3

MONT.

4

WYO.

3

COLO.

6

N. MEX.

3

N. DA.

5

S. DAK.

5

NEB.

8

K

10

10

TEX

20

M

E

X

I

C

O

25

PRESIDENTIAL ELECTION
1912

Wilson, Democratic, electoral vote 435

Roosevelt, Progressive, electoral vote 88

Taft, Republican, electoral vote 8

Figures in a square show total electoral vote
In the case of California the vote was divided

L.L. POATES CO., N.Y.   105

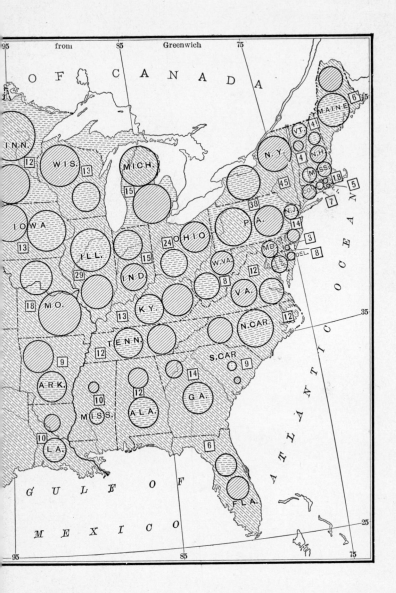

OF CANADA

from · 85 · Greenwich · 75

MAINE · 6

VT. · 4

N.Y. · N.H. · 4

MINN. · 12 · WIS. · 13 · MICH. · 15 · 45 · MASS. · 18 · 5 · CONN. · 7

IOWA · 13 · ILL. · 29 · IND. · 15 · OHIO · 24 · PA. · 38 · N.J. · 14 · 3 · MD. · DEL. · 8

MO. · 18 · KY. · 13 · W.VA. · 8 · VA. · 12 · N.CAR. · 12 · 35

ARK. · 9 · TENN. · 12 · S.CAR. · 9 · GA. · 14

MISS. · 10 · ALA. · 12

LA. · 10

GULF OF · 6

FLA.

MEXICO · 25

95 · 85 · 75

ATLANTIC OCEAN

for Democratic rule. The real character of the Democratic victory appeared only in the congressional and state results. Control of the national House of Representatives was kept, with 291 seats in a total of 435; and such Republican wheel-horses as Speaker Cannon and William B. McKinley, the manager of Taft's pre-convention campaign, were defeated. Control of the Senate was at last secured, the quotas being fifty Democrats, forty-four Republicans, and one Progressive, with an Alabama seat vacant. In twenty-one of the thirty-five states which elected governors Democratic chief executives were chosen; and these included New York, Massachusetts, Connecticut, Ohio, Indiana, Illinois, Michigan, and Nebraska.

The victory lay with progressivism; yet not with the Progressives. The Republican leaders had strong intimations of the new drift of public sentiment before Roosevelt's retirement from the White House. In the elections of 1910 they were given solemn warning. The movement to prevent Taft's renomination was understood by everybody else. But they were constitutionally unable to see, or refused to see; and the party was run on the rocks. Rooseveltian progressivism made a powerful appeal; yet there was something incongruous about it. While in the presidency Roosevelt had never shown much interest in the vicious tariff situation. His concern for direct government had developed tardily. In his manner and method and temperament there was a strong suggestion of the boss; and people with a sense of humor were amused at his ferocious attack on his own error of 1908. His attempted leadership of progressivism came a few years too late. Even at that, it would probably have been successful had not the Democrats, through much travail, found in Governor Wilson a progressive leader in whom a deciding proportion of the people placed full confidence.

CHAPTER XII

THE DEMOCRATS IN POWER

(1913-1914)

MARCH 4, 1913, the Democrats found themselves in control of the presidency and both houses of Congress for the first time since the middle of Cleveland's second administration. On this earlier occasion business was depressed, the majority party was divided on the repeal of the Sherman silver-purchase law, and constructive legislation was difficult. But the Wilson Administration had a clear field. The Republican party, which as late as 1908 appeared invincible, was disrupted and in danger of extinction; Democratic majorities in both houses were ample for every need; the incoming President commanded the full confidence of his party and the respect of all men; the country was prosperous; the Administration was heir to legislative projects relating to banking reform, child labor, and rural credit, which could be depended on to win public favor; on the supreme issue of the tariff it was in a position to meet squarely the country's unmistakable demand.

In short, the Democrats, although brought into control through the division of their opponents and buttressed in office by pluralities rather than majorities, had a splendid opportunity so to commend themselves as to become a majority party and to stay in power for many years. Such dangers as beset their path arose principally from two sources—their inexperience in the management of national affairs, and cleavage between their radical and conservative elements. A difficulty of another kind was the sheer size of their House majority; unnecessary numbers were likely to increase the task of leadership and discipline.

As President-elect, Wilson continued to show strong progressive inclinations. He took counsel with only fellow-partisans of a progressive turn of mind; and shortly before his inauguration he published a collection of revised campaign speeches, under the title of *The New Freedom*, in which he sketched out a broad program of reform with a view to "fitting a new social organization to the happiness and prosperity of the great body of citizens." He retained the governor's office in New Jersey until March 1, and made the closing weeks of his stay at Trenton notable by carrying through the legislature a group of bills—popularly termed "the Seven Sisters"—aimed at the better regulation of trusts and holding companies.[1]

The inauguration, March 4, was auspicious. The weather was agreeable; the spectators were more than usually numerous; the spirit of the occasion was irreproachable. The inaugural address was brief, eloquent, and lofty in sentiment. The establishment of Democratic control was interpreted to mean "much

[1] *Statutes of New Jersey*, 1913, chaps. xiii.-xix.; *Am. Year Book*, 1913, p. 344.

more than the mere success of a party." The nation, the new President asserted, had come to a realization of the great social and economic evils which the phenomenal expansion of its wealth and power involved, and was proposing to use at this juncture the Democratic party "to interpret a change in its own plans and point of view." "Our duty," he urged, "is to cleanse, to reconsider, to restore, to correct the evil without impairing the good, to purify and humanize every process of our common life without weakening or sentimentalizing it. . . . We have made up our minds to square every process of our national life again with the standards we so proudly set up at the beginning and have always carried at our hearts. Our work is a work of restoration."

Protest was specially lodged against a tariff which "cuts us off from our proper part in the commerce of the world, violates the first principles of taxation, and makes the government a facile instrument in the hands of private interests; a banking and currency system based upon the necessity of the government to sell its bonds fifty years ago and perfectly adapted to concentrating cash and restricting credits; an industrial system which . . . holds capital in leading strings, restricts the liberties and limits the opportunities of labor, and exploits without renewing or conserving the natural resources of the country; a body of agricultural activities never yet given the efficiency of great business undertakings or served as it should be through the instrumentality of science taken directly to the farm, or afforded the facilities of credit best suited to its practical needs; watercourses undeveloped; waste places unreclaimed, forests untended, fast disappearing without plan or prospect of renewal, unregarded waste heaps at every mine."[1] Stress was laid, too, on the need of "conservation of human health and human rights" in the struggle for existence, as a matter, not of pity, but of simple justice. The address was full of feeling, yet strong and sensible. It included most of the tenets of the progressive movement.[2]

Interest in the new cabinet centered in William J. Bryan as Secretary of State. This appointment was inevitable; for it was mainly to Bryan that Wilson owed his nomination at Baltimore, and the Administration's program of legislation was certain to need the support of the Nebraskan and his friends. But there was no pretense that by training, experience, or temperament the appointee was specially fitted for the position; and to most persons it seemed doubtful whether he would be content for any length of time to play the rôle of an administrative subordinate.

The cabinet group included three business men: William G. McAdoo of New York was made Secretary of the Treasury; William C. Redfield of New York, Secretary of Commerce; and Josephus Daniels of North Carolina, Secretary of the Navy. There were two lawyers: Lindley M. Garrison of New Jersey, Secretary of War, and Albert S. Burleson of Texas, Postmaster-General. David F. Houston of Missouri, an economist and university president, was made Sec-

[1] *Am. Year Book*, 1913, p. 14.   [2] *Nation*, XCVI., 222.

retary of Agriculture; and William B. Wilson of Pennsylvania, a representative of organized labor, became
Secretary of Labor. Only two of the new department
heads were men of experience in federal administration. Franklin K. Lane of California, a conservation-
ist, a progressive Democrat, and a former member of
the Interstate Commerce Commission, was made Secretary of the Interior. James C. McReynolds of
Tennessee, who as Assistant Attorney-General prose-
cuted the American Tobacco Company, became Attorney-General. The group was a good working body of
men, but without claim to distinction. One-third of
its members (Bryan, Burleson, and Daniels) owed their
appointment solely to political considerations.

Shortly after his election Wilson announced that
he would convoke the Sixty-third Congress in special
session to undertake a revision of the tariff on the lines
laid down in the Democratic platform. This special
session began April 7, and lasted until the opening of
the next regular session, December 1. For both length
and achievement it became one of the most notable
in the history of the country. Already, in a special
session of the Senate, called March 4 to confirm appointments, the leadership of the upper chamber had
passed definitely from the ultra-conservatives of the
two parties to the progressive or radical elements. A
new "steering committee" of seven progressive and two
conservative Democratic members was set up; assign-
ments to the regular committees were to be made by
this committee, subject to final action by the caucus;
and every committee was henceforth to choose not

only its chairman, but its conferees and its sub-committees.

The new House was organized on similar lines. At a Democratic caucus, March 5, A. Mitchell Palmer of Pennsylvania was named for chairman of the majority caucus; Oscar W. Underwood of Alabama was again assigned to the post of chairman of the Ways and Means Committee and floor leader; and Champ Clark was renominated for the speakership. At the opening of the session, April 7, Clark was duly elected speaker over the Republican candidate, James R. Mann of Illinois, by a vote of 272 to 111. As in the preceding Congress, committee chairmanships went almost wholly to the South, not for sectional reasons, but because southern Democrats, as a rule, had been longest in service, and in Republican Congresses had held ranking places as minority members.

Life-long study of political science, and extended observation of the workings of the American system of government, had convinced Wilson of the need of closer relations between the President and Congress. Accordingly, he broke with the precedent which called for the sending in of written messages, and revived the usage of Washington and the elder Adams by appearing before the legislative branch and addressing it orally. Under this practice communications from the White House became brief, direct, and fundamental, contrasting agreeably with the diffuse, and sometimes wearisome, essays transmitted by Presidents Roosevelt and Taft. The first address after the new manner was delivered April 8, and was a crisp statement of the

principles which ought to be observed in the forthcoming tariff legislation, together with a forceful appeal for vigorous and prompt fulfillment of the party's
promises to the country.

The special session of 1913 made its chief task the
revision of the tariff. It, however, yielded some important miscellaneous legislation, notably the "Newlands Act" relating to the arbitration of labor disputes;[1]
and a measure for the reform of the currency and banking system was carried to a point where enactment became easy in the next regular session.[2]

In handling the tariff question the new Administration, like its predecessor, received its baptism of fire.
The opportunity was alluring; the obligation was clear;
but the task was hazardous. The situation was more
favorable than in 1909, in that the will of the nation
had been more decisively expressed. The business
world, too, showed less apprehension; indeed, its feeling that it could get along, no matter what was done,
was the best evidence that something ought to be done.
There were still, however, no means of making a tariff
that would be really scientific; and practical interests,
as usual, lined up for a tug of war.

The new bill was introduced by Chairman Underwood in the House of Representatives on the opening
day of the session. In a sense, it had been in preparation more than two years; for most of its schedules
followed closely the bills put forward by the Democrats
in 1911 and vetoed by President Taft. The drafting
of the actual bill was begun by the Democratic mem-

[1] See p. 87.   [2] See p. 229.

bers of the Ways and Means Committee early in the closing session of the Sixty-second Congress, which opened December 2, 1912; and with the aid, in the later stages, of President Wilson and of the Democratic members of the Senate Committee on Finance, the work was pushed to completion in early April.

The bill was drawn with more regard for public interests, and less consideration of private advantage, than any in a generation. The tariff of 1897 betrayed the fact that its chief author, Dingley, was a woolen manufacturer. The act of 1909 showed that Aldrich allowed his cotton and woolen manufacturing constituents to write the schedules in which they were interested. Underwood represented an iron and steel district; yet his bill courageously provided for heavy reductions in the metals schedule. "Jokers" were few; the measure was made with all the cards on the table.

The goal aimed at was defined in the President's message of April 8. "We must abolish everything that bears even the semblance of privilege or of any kind of artificial advantage and put our business men and producers under the stimulation of a constant necessity to be efficient, economical, and enterprising, masters of competitive supremacy, better workers and merchants than any in the world. Aside from the duties laid upon articles which we do not, and probably cannot, produce, therefore, and the duties laid upon luxuries and merely for the sake of the revenues they yield, the object of the tariff duties henceforth laid must be effective competition, the whetting of American arts by contest with the arts of the rest of the world."[1]   In a statement which accompanied the bill, Underwood said that the framers had acted, not on the doctrine of Taft and his Tariff Board, that tariff rates should be fixed to cover the differences in cost between foreign and domestic production plus a reasonable margin of profit, but on the view of the Democratic platform of 1912, that tariff duties should be designed primarily to produce revenue, yet without injury to legitimate industry.[2]

In short, the tariff was a question of morals as well as of expediency; protection, being a form of privilege, was in principle wrong; business and trade should be allowed to be controlled by natural, rather than by artificial, forces; and the revenue basis must be arrived at by such stages as would permit business to readjust itself in all proper ways.

The Underwood bill was well received by an interested public.   In the House, where debate was opened on April 22, the Democrats gave it unstinted support.   The Republican and Progressive opposition was swamped, and on May 8 the measure, slightly amended, was passed by a vote of 281 to 139.[3]   The vote followed party lines closely, although two Wisconsin Republicans and four Progressives were recorded for the bill, and five Democrats (four representing the sugar interests of Louisiana) voted with the opposition.

As in 1909, the brief and uneventful debates in the House were followed by a long and exciting contest in

---

[1] *Senate Jour.*, 63 Cong., 1 Sess., 15.
[2] *Cong. Record*, 63 Cong., 1 Sess., pt. i., pp 328–332.
[3] *House Jour.*, 63 Cong., 1 Sess., 139.

the Senate. The Democratic majority in the upper chamber numbered only six, and the party forces represented all shades of tariff opinion. The Louisiana members objected to free sugar, and the interests which they represented promised votes for a high duty on citrus fruits if producers of those fruits would reciprocate on sugar; members from wool-growing states opposed free wool; New Englanders thought the reductions on cottons excessive. Encouraged by the division of their opponents, the Republicans brought all their artillery into action against the bill. Cummins subjected it to a drastic analytical criticism; Burton, Smoot, and others assailed it, from the standpoint of particular schedules, or upon the lines of broad policy. Lobbyists were insidiously active. Nothing but the astute leadership of the President and the inability of the "stand-pat" and progressive elements of the opposition to act together kept the revisionist program alive.

In amended form, the bill passed the Senate September 9, by a vote of 44 to 37.[1] La Follette and Poindexter voted for it, and Ransdell and Thornton of Louisiana against it; otherwise party lines were unbroken. In conference committee the Senate's changes, including a new income tax schedule, were mainly sustained. The bill was finally passed in the House, September 30, by a vote of 255 to 104,[2] and in the Senate, three days later, by a vote of 36 to 17.[3] On

[1] *Senate Jour.*, 63 Cong., 1 Sess., 186.
[2] *House Jour.*, 63 Cong., 1 Sess., 305.
[3] *Senate Jour.*, 63 Cong., 1 Sess., 203.

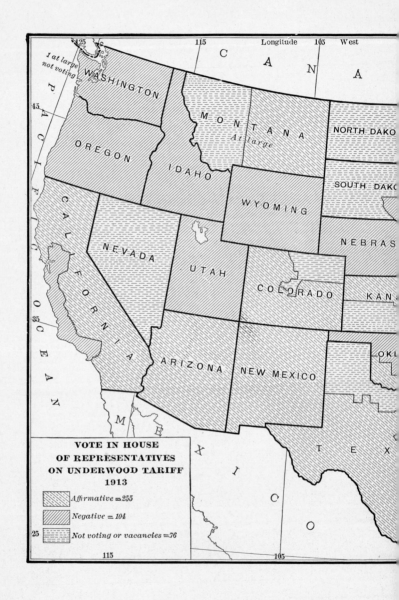

VOTE IN HOUSE
OF REPRESENTATIVES
ON UNDERWOOD TARIFF
1913

Affirmative = 255

Negative = 104

Not voting or vacancies = 76

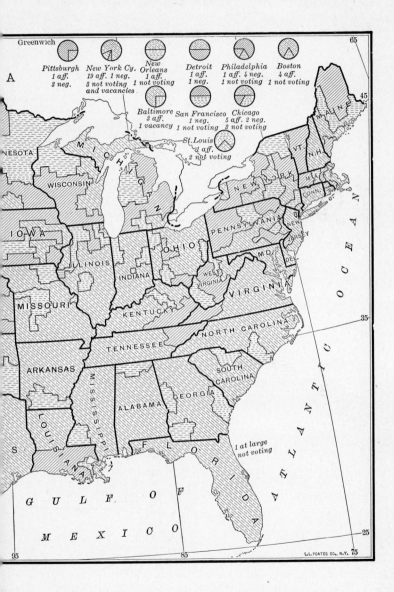

Greenwich

Pittsburgh
1 aff.
3 neg.

New York Cy.
19 aff. 1 neg.
3 not voting
and vacancies

New
Orleans
1 aff.
1 not voting

Detroit
1 aff.
1 neg.

Philadelphia
1 aff. 4 neg.
1 not voting

Boston
4 aff.
1 not voting

Baltimore
3 aff.
1 vacancy

San Francisco
1 neg.
1 not voting

Chicago
5 aff. 2 neg.
3 not voting

St. Louis
1 aff.
2 not voting

A

MINNESOTA

WISCONSIN

MICHIGAN

IOWA

ILLINOIS

INDIANA

OHIO

MISSOURI

KENTUCKY

ARKANSAS

TENNESSEE

MISSISSIPPI

ALABAMA

LOUISIANA

GEORGIA

FLORIDA

1 at large
not voting

NORTH CAROLINA

SOUTH
CAROLINA

VIRGINIA

WEST
VIRGINIA

PENNSYLVANIA

NEW YORK

MD.

DEL.

NEW
JERSEY

VT.

N.H.

MAINE

MASS.

CONN.

R.I.

ATLANTIC OCEAN

GULF OF MEXICO

65

45

35

25

95

85

75

L.L. POATES CO., N.Y.

the evening of October 5 the act was signed by the President, in the presence of the cabinet and the Democratic leaders of the two houses, and with words of hearty commendation. Aside from the coal and sugar schedules, which took effect January 1 and March 1, 1914, respectively, the measure went into operation at once.

The new tariff was not based throughout on scientifically ascertained data, nor were its fourteen schedules framed on principles which were wholly consistent.[1] But its authors argued plausibly that its faults were much less serious than those of the Payne-Aldrich Act, and that it brought the scale of rates down to a level where alone it was worth while to spend time in working out nice adjustments. It was a protective measure; but the schedules were really revised downward. The new rates showed 958 reductions, 86 increases (mainly in the chemical schedule), and 307 items unchanged. The free list was enlarged by more than a hundred items.[2]

For years the increased cost of living had been a nation-wide problem, and the Democrats contended that a prime cause of soaring prices was the protective tariff. Accordingly, the Underwood Act was framed not merely on the conventional principle of taxing luxuries heavily and necessities lightly, but expressly with a view to making it easier for the common man

---

[1] *U. S. Statutes at Large*, XXXVIII., pt. i., p. 114.
[2] Taussig, "The Tariff Act of 1913," *Quart. Jour. Econ.*, XXVIII., 1–30; Mussey, "The New Freedom in Commerce," *Polit. Sci. Quart.*, XXIX., 600–625; Willis, "The Tariff of 1913," *Jour. Polit. Econ.*, XXII., 1–42, 105–131, 218–238.

15

to maintain his family in comfort. To this end, the rates were notably reduced on food, clothing, and raw materials. Thus the rates on many agricultural products—wheat, butter, cheese, vegetables, and fruits—were lowered sharply; while corn, wheat, potatoes, flour, meats, and other important foodstuffs were relieved altogether. In the sugar schedule, an effort was made to conciliate the cane-growers of Louisiana and the beet-sugar producers of the Middle West, and at the same time to meet the demand of the country for free sugar, by immediately reducing the sugar rates by a fourth and placing the commodity on the free list from May 1, 1916.

The rates on cotton manufactures were reduced by about one-half; and the much-discussed Schedule K was revised so as to lower the duties on woolens by more than half and to place raw wool, in accordance with time-honored Democratic maxim, on the free list.[1] In the metal schedule, iron ore and steel rails were put on the free list, and the rates on pig-iron were reduced by half. In the wood schedule, unmanufactured products, including lumber, were made free; and rates on manufactures were lowered—on household furniture, from thirty-five to fifteen per cent.

The act made some important administrative changes. It abolished the maximum and minimum provisions of the Payne-Aldrich law, and empowered the President to negotiate (subject to ratification by a majority vote in each house of Congress) trade agree-

[1] Taussig, "Report of the Tariff Board on Wool and Woolens," *Am. Econ. Rev.*, II., 257–268.

ments with foreign nations, making mutual concessions "looking toward freer trade relations and further reciprocal expansion of trade and commerce." It made provision for a special additional duty not to exceed fifteen per cent. *ad valorem* to prevent "dumping"; and in cases where articles of foreign production were aided by bounties, the advantage was to be off-set, on importation of the articles into the United States, by additional duties. American ship-building was encouraged by the removal of duties on foreign ship-building materials; and American shipping was favored by the remission of five per cent. of the duties on goods imported in vessels of American registry. The existing reciprocity agreement with Cuba was left intact, and absolute free trade with the Philippines was established by the removal of the restrictions imposed in the Payne-Aldrich law upon the amounts of insular sugar, tobacco, and rice entitled to free entry into the United States.

When the bill was introduced, Treasury officials estimated that in the first year of its operation customs receipts would fall off by $38,000,000 (approximately one-eighth), leaving a deficit of $68,790,000; and the reductions of duties could not have been so sweeping but for the timely opportunity to balance the budget, and by the same stroke to fulfill a long-standing party pledge, by levying a tax on incomes. Since the Supreme Court, in 1895, pronounced the income-tax law of 1894 unconstitutional, the Democrats had never ceased to advocate the placing of a larger share of the burden of taxation on wealth. The most obvious means of doing this was an income tax. Many influential Republicans, including President Roosevelt, favored such a tax; and in 1909 the Senate insurgents urged it with such vigor that they and the Democrats brought Congress to vote for and submit to the states a constitutional amendment empowering Congress to "lay and collect taxes on incomes, from whatever source derived, without apportionment among the several states, and without regard to any census or enumeration." After almost four years of discussion in the state legislatures, this Sixteenth Amendment was proclaimed in effect by Secretary Knox, February 25, 1913 [1]—just in time to enable the new Democratic Administration to lay an income tax as such, rather than an income tax disguised as an excise tax (on the analogy of the corporations tax of 1909), such as the leaders planned to impose if the amendment failed, or if its final adoption remained much longer in doubt.

The Underwood Act accordingly laid a tax on the unexempted net incomes of all persons residing in the United States and of citizens of the United States residing abroad, and on the incomes of corporations, joint stock companies, and associations, without exemption. Radicals of all parties demanded larger use of this form of tax than was at first proposed, and the Senate discussion resulted in heavier rates. The amount of exempted individual income was reduced from $4,000 to $3,000, save in the case of husband and wife living together. The normal rate was fixed at one per cent.; but incomes exceeding $20,000 were

[1] *U. S. Statutes at Large*, XXXVII., pt. ii., p. 1785.

made subject to a progressive surtax, on the following scale: one per cent. on incomes between $20,000 and $50,000; two per cent. between $50,000 and $75,000; three per cent. between $75,000 and $100,000; four per cent. between $100,000 and $250,000; five per cent. between $250,000 and $500,000; and six per cent. above $500,000. The objection that the taxation of both individual and corporation on the same income is double taxation was met by permitting individuals to deduct from their taxable income corporate dividends, or other income on which the tax was paid by the corporation.[1]

It is too much to ask of a tariff law that it be universally popular; and the act of 1913 was strongly disliked by the sugar, wool, and other interests which considered themselves injured by it. But, on the whole, it met the popular demand, and its adoption was a striking evidence of the power of an aroused public sentiment. It seemed likely to mark a new epoch in the history of the country—an epoch in which American industry was to convince itself, no less than the world at large, that it could stand on its own feet.

In operation, the Underwood law showed many defects.[2] Unscientific classifications and loose phraseology caused confusion. The clause discriminating in

[1] Hill, "The Income Tax of 1913," *Quart. Jour. Econ.*, XXVIII., 46–68; Seligman, "The Federal Income Tax," *Polit. Sci. Quart.*, XXIX., 1–27.

[2] Curtis, "The Administrative Provisions of the Revenue Act of 1913," *Quart. Jour. Econ.*, XXVIII., 21–45; Hoffman, "Customs Administration under the 1913 Tariff Act," *Jour. Polit. Econ.*, XXII., 845–871.

favor of American shipping proved unworkable. The
income-tax sections were found to be little more than
a framework of general principles, and had to be construed and carried out by the Commissioner of Internal
Revenue, often with controversy and inconvenience;
besides, they were not water-tight against evasion.
Finally, before the law had been in operation a year
the European war disrupted trade and cut off all opportunity to judge the normal results of the new rates.

An interesting by-product of the debates on the act
was an extensive, though not very fruitful, inquiry
into the activities of lobbyists at the national capital.
On May 26 President Wilson issued a statement denouncing the "extraordinary exertions" of an "in-
sidious and numerous lobby" to procure changes of the
Underwood bill in the interest of manufacturers and
other producers.[1]   May 29, on motion of Cummins,
the Senate authorized an inquiry; and on July 9 the
House was led, chiefly by stories of influence brought
to bear on its members by agents of the National
Association of Manufacturers, to take similar action.
The inquiries covered a period of thirty years, and
startling facts were laid bare: powerful aggregations
of capital scheming for the protection of privilege, and
stooping to the corruption of boy pages of the House
and humble doorkeepers of committee-rooms; lavish
outlays of money for secret, unfair, and sometimes
criminal purposes; elections tampered with; legislation throttled; books and correspondence burned to
avert detection; ambitions soaring to the dictation of

[1] *Review of Reviews*, XLVIII., 7.

cabinet appointments. The House committee submitted a report, December 9, which exonerated all persons then members save one, and he soon resigned.[1]
The Senate investigation yielded no tangible results.
But the discussion made for a higher conception of
political ethics in Congress and throughout the country.[2]

The Republican plan for a permanent tariff commission found no place in the Underwood law.   Taft's
Tariff Board had been brought to an end by Democratic failure to provide funds, and as late as 1915
President Wilson declared that the nation had all the
machinery that was needed for the investigation of
tariff problems.   Gradually the leaders of the party,
including the President, changed their minds on the
subject, and a general revenue act of September 7,
1916, created a bi-partisan Tariff Commission of six
members, appointed by the President for terms of
twelve years.[3]   The duties of the board are purely
investigative, and include study of the fiscal, administrative, and industrial effects of the tariff laws; the
relations between the rates of duty on raw materials
and finished or partly finished products; the comparative advantages of specific and *ad valorem* duties; and
other matters submitted by the President, by the Ways
and Means Committee of the House, or by the Finance
Committee of the Senate.   The Commission was organized early in 1917 under the chairmanship of F. W.
Taussig, of Harvard University, a leading authority on

[1] *House Reports*, 63 Cong., 2 Sess., No. 113.
[2] O'Laughlin, "'The Invisible Government' under Searchlight,"
Review of Reviews, XLVIII., 334–338.
[3] *U. S. Statutes at Large*, XXXIX., pt. i., p. 795.

tariff history and administration. The strong bias
of parties on the tariff question made its position somewhat precarious; but it was gratifying that the major
parties had at last come into agreement that expert
and continuous investigation is essential to sound
tariff-making.

CHAPTER XIII

FINANCIAL, INDUSTRIAL, AND COLONIAL POLICY
(1913–1917)

POLITICAL scientists and practical statesmen alike recognize that the American system of government cannot be operated in strict conformity with the principle of separation of powers upon which it is ostensibly based. Experience shows that Congress, when left to its own devices, tends to disintegrate into its sectional elements and to flounder in a bog of contrary purposes. Powerful leadership, on national lines, is indispensable. Under normal circumstances, this leadership can be supplied only by the President; which means that the President must be not only the head of the administrative system and the leader of his party, but the directing force in legislation. If the government over which he presides is to work smoothly and effectively, he must write the great measures and must see that they are converted into law. In their practical way of looking at things, the people nowadays expect the President to manage Congress, and if he does not do so they pronounce him a failure.

President Roosevelt recognized and acted upon these facts more fully than had any occupant of the White House since Lincoln; and largely on that account his presidency became a notable epoch of constructive legislation and national revival. President Taft inclined to a legalistic view of the chief executive's functions, and hesitated to assert legislative leadership. He failed to get the legislation which the nation demanded; accordingly, the record of his Administration was dimmed, and his own political fortunes were blasted.

President Wilson promptly assumed a leadership such as not even Roosevelt had conceived. His reasons were twofold: first, he believed that such leadership would yield unity, responsibility, and dispatch similar to that of the English cabinet system; and second, he thought leadership an especial need when his party was new to power and bent on gaining the esteem of the country by a careful legislative policy. Many times his intervention in the work of lawmaking was denounced as dictatorial by his political opponents, and it was disliked by some members of his own party. But his personal activity became a principal factor in his administration's imposing record of constructive and remedial legislation; and his conception and example of presidential leadership in legislation became his chief contribution to American political methods.

Next after the Underwood tariff came banking and currency reform. This was something that the country had long needed. The Taft administration failed to bring it about, and after the election of 1912 the Democrats advanced it to a prominent place in their plans. During the final session of the Sixty-second Congress (December 2, 1912 to March 4, 1913) a Demo-

cratic sub-committee of the House Committee on Banking and Currency, under the chairmanship of Carter
Glass of Virginia, held hearings and in other ways
brought together information and opinions as a basis
for action.

Early in the special session convened April 7, 1913,
President Wilson urged Congress to give the business
interests of the country a banking and currency system
"by means of which they can make use of the freedom
of enterprise and of individual initiative" about to be
bestowed on them by the pending tariff measure.[1]
Three days later the Owen-Glass federal reserve bill,
drafted on lines approved by the President and Secretary McAdoo, was introduced.[2] Sharp differences
of opinion developed among the House Democrats,
but an amended measure won the votes (September 18)
of 248 of them, besides 24 Republicans and 14 Progressives.[3] The Senate acted slowly; but the bill was
passed in definitive form by the House, December 22,
by a vote of 298 to 60;[4] and by the Senate, on the following day, by a vote of 43 to 25.[5] It received the
President's signature December 23, and was hailed
as the Administration's second great legislative
triumph.[6]

[1] *Senate Jour.*, 63 Cong., 1 Sess., 100.
[2] For an important group of papers dealing with the history and bearings of the bill see Acad. Polit. Sci., *Proceedings*, IV., No. 1 (1913).
[3] *House Jour.*, 63 Cong., 1 Sess., 285.
[4] *Ibid.*, 63 Cong., 2 Sess., 87.
[5] *Senate Jour.*, 63 Cong., 2 Sess., 62.
[6] *U. S. Statutes at Large*, XXXVIII., pt. i., pp. 251–275; Sprague,
"The Federal Reserve Act of 1913," *Quart. Jour. Econ.*, XXVIII.,
213–254.

The main objects of the new law were: (1) to reorganize banking power in such a way that funds would be available to meet extraordinary demands; (2) to provide a currency which would expand and contract automatically as needed. To meet the first of these ends, it was necessary to concentrate bank reserves and place them under such control that, as occasion required, they could be brought to bear in aid of local banks. The Aldrich plan of a central reserve bank with branches was popularly regarded as an invention of the "money trust," and the act of 1913 provided rather for the centralization of reserves in regional banks, specially created for the purpose, and known as federal reserve banks. The number of districts, each containing a reserve bank, was eventually fixed at twelve.

The reserve banks were really banks of bankers; their capital (a minimum of $4,000,000) was subscribed by such banks as joined the system, not by individuals. All national banks were required to join, and state banks and trust companies might join if they desired. Mobilization of reserves was secured by authorizing the reserve banks to receive deposits from member-banks and from the United States government, though not from individuals; and member-banks were required to keep on deposit in the reserve banks funds intended ultimately to amount to from one-half to two-thirds of their total legal reserves. The reserve banks became thus great regional reservoirs from which a large part of the banking strength of the district could be directed at any time to the places where it was most needed; and under the central control of a Federal Reserve Board the banking strength of one district could be made available in other districts.

When the act was passed, the country's currency consisted of: (1) coin, United States notes, and Treasury notes, issued by the federal government; (2) notes issued by the national banks and secured by deposits of United States bonds in the Treasury at Washington. Whatever the condition or needs of business, the volume of currency remained about the same. To secure greater elasticity, provision was now made for gradually substituting for the national bank notes "federal reserve notes," issued to the regional banks by the Federal Reserve Board on the security of commercial paper deposited with the regional banks by the local banks. When business was flush and such paper plentiful, the currency expanded; when business fell off and paper became scarce, the currency contracted; for when the paper was taken up, the currency secured by it was withdrawn from circulation by the reserve bank. Elasticity was thus combined with precautions against inflation. [1]

The new system was duly installed November 16, 1914. No one doubted the soundness of its purpose; the only question was as to the adaptation of the machinery to the desired ends. Some experts would have preferred a central reserve bank. On the other hand, there was some public apprehension lest the Federal Reserve Board should use its great powers arbitrarily.

[1] Kemmerer, "The Bank-Note Issue of the Proposed Federal Reserve Banks," Acad. Polit. Sci., *Proceedings*, IV., 160-168.

So far as judgment could be based on two years of operation under abnormal circumstances, the system was highly successful. Changes in financial and commercial relationships flowing from the European war altered the underlying conditions and, coupled with the unusual and extreme expedients adopted by foreign governments, subjected the American money market to varying pressures which could not have been foreseen. None the less, the reserve system proved a "going concern." The regional banks were operated substantially as a unit, at little expense to the country; and as a result interest rates were harmonized, currency demands were promptly met, crop-moving difficulties were overcome (especially in the South), standardization of commercial paper was begun, and progress was made toward the unification of the underlying banking resources of the country, and the accumulation of gold reserves under uniform control.[1]

The next task was trust regulation; and in an optimistic message of January 20, 1914, the President called on Congress to approach it with the feeling that the antagonism between the government and business was ended, and that each was ready to meet the other half-way "in a common effort to square business

[1] Willis, "The New Banking System," *Polit. Sci. Quart.*, XXX., 591–617; "The Federal Reserve Act," *Am. Econ. Rev.*, IV., 1–24; "What the Federal Reserve System Has Done," *ibid.*, VII., 269–288; Hamlin, "The Federal Reserve Act," First Pan-American Financial Conference, *Proceedings*, 152–164; Laughlin, "The Banking and Currency Act of 1913," *Jour. Polit. Econ.*, XXII., 293–318, 405–435; Sprague, "The Federal Reserve Banking System in Operation," *Quart. Jour. Econ.*, XXX., 627–644; "Location of Federal Reserve Districts," *Senate Docs.*, 63 Cong., 2 Sess., No. 485.

methods with both public opinion and the law." Five
tentative bills—popularly known as the "Five Brothers"—were put forward: (1) creating an Interstate
Trade Commission, with powers to investigate the organization and operation of corporations engaged in
interstate commerce, except carriers; (2) forbidding interlocking directorates in interstate corporations and railroads, and in banks and trust companies which were members of a reserve bank; (3) more accurately defining
various terms used in the Sherman Anti-Trust Act; (4)
adding to the Sherman Act sections against unfair competition by means of local price-cutting, discounts, and exclusive agreements; (5) authorizing the Interstate Commerce Commission to regulate issues of railway securities.

Legislation on these lines proved less easy than had
been expected, and only by a fresh display of leadership
did the President keep his measures steadily before
Congress and the country. The House passed the
Trade Commission bill in one form; the Senate, in
another. But the measure finally signed by the President, September 26, substantially represented the
Administration's views.[1] April 14, 1914, Clayton of Alabama, chairman of the House Committee on the Judi-
ciary, introduced a general anti-trust bill, which, after
much seesawing, was carried in the Senate, September
28, by a vote of 35 to 24,[2] and in the House, some days
later, by 245 to 52.[3] It was signed by the President
October 15.[4]

[1] U. S. Statutes at Large, XXXVIII., pt. i., pp.717–724.
[2] Senate Jour., 63 Cong., 2 Sess., 537.
[3] House Jour., 63 Cong., 2 Sess., 975.
[4] U. S. Statutes at Large, XXXVIII., pt. i., pp. 730–740.

The Federal Trade Commission Act provided new machinery for the investigation and regulation of all corporations engaged in interstate and foreign commerce, except banks and common carriers, which were already subject to strict federal control. The Bureau of Corporations, created in 1903, was abolished, and in its stead was set up a Federal Trade Commission of five members, with power (1) to investigate the organization and management of the corporations coming within the scope of the law; (2) to readjust the business of any corporation alleged to be violating the anti-trust laws, and to issue decrees in equity suits brought under the direction of the Attorney-General; (3) to require annual or special reports; (4) to prevent persons, partnerships, or corporations from using unfair methods of competition in commerce, and to secure aid in the enforcement of its orders by resort to the circuit court of appeals of the circuit in which the offense was alleged to have been committed.[1] Like the Interstate Commerce Commission and the Federal Reserve Board, the Trade Commission was not placed in any one of the ten executive departments.

The Clayton Anti-Trust Act perfected existing anti-trust legislation in several ways. It prohibited every sort of discrimination in prices where the effect would be to lessen competition or to tend to create a monopoly; it forbade any corporation to acquire the whole, or any portion, of the stock of another corporation in restraint

---

[1] Stevens, "The Trade Commission Act," *Am. Econ. Rev.*, **IV.**, 840-856; Fayne, "The Federal Trade Commission," *Am. Polit. Sci. Rev.*, **IX.**, 57-67.

of competition; it prohibited (save under certain conditions) interlocking directorates of banks, common
carriers, and other corporations. Speaking broadly, in
the first two of these matters it laid down restrictions
which were already recognized by the courts. But in
the third it went beyond all previous legislation and
decisions. Authority to enforce the law was given
to the Interstate Commerce Commission, in relation
to common carriers; to the Federal Reserve Board, in
relation to banks, banking associations, and trust companies; and to the Federal Trade Commission, in relation to corporations of other kinds.

The act derived further importance from its provisions touching the status of organized labor; indeed,
no measure of Congress ever met the demands of
labor more completely. It sustained a time-honored
contention of the labor leaders by declaring that the
labor of a human being is not a commodity or article
of commerce; it prohibited injunctions in labor disputes growing out of the terms and conditions of employment, unless necessary to prevent irreparable injury to property rights for which there was no remedy
at law; it proclaimed that strikes, picketing, and boy-
cotting were not violations of any federal law; it exempted from the operation of the anti-trust laws all
labor, agricultural, and other associations not conducted for profit.[1]

[1] Stevens, "The Clayton Act," *Am. Econ. Rev.*, V., 38–54; Durand,
"The Trust Legislation of 1914," *Quart. Jour. Econ.*, XXIX., 72–97;
Young, "The Sherman Act and the New Anti-Trust Legislation," *Jour.
Polit. Econ.*, XXIII., 201–220, 305–326, 417–436.
16

Of these two great measures, the first embodied the views of the more conservative Democrats, the second the views of the radicals. One put emphasis on prevention, the other on punishment. Both were favorably received by the country. All important parties had declared for a trade commission, and there was general confidence that the new agency would aid greatly in settling the trust problem. The only important feature of the Administration's program of corporation control which was not adopted was the regulation of issues of railroad securities.

While the Federal Trade and Anti-Trust bills were pending, the outbreak of war in Europe brought upon the country unexpected problems. Extensive legislation became necessary on army reorganization, naval expansion, merchant marine, and revenue. None the less, Congress kept its earlier program steadily in hand. Statutes on public lands, conservation, and reclamation were revised; new acts were passed on child labor, seaman's protection, agricultural education, highway improvement, rural credit, and many other matters.

Constant attention was claimed by the dependencies, especially the Philippines, Porto Rico, and Alaska. The questions touching the Philippines were two: Should the islands be given independence? How should they be governed while remaining in American hands? The Democrats were on record as favoring an early declaration of intention to set the islands free, and the election of Wilson in 1912 aroused much enthusiasm among the natives. But most people in the United States expected the victorious party to prove, on this issue, less radical in deed than in word.

In 1913 Cameron Forbes was succeeded as governor-general by Francis Burton Harrison. In his inaugural address at Manila, October 6, Harrison explained that the United States regarded itself simply as a trustee in the Philippines, and promised that no step would be taken save with a view to the islands' welfare and their ultimate independence. These ideas were enlarged upon by the President in his message of December 2. He declared that the country must move toward a grant of independence "as steadily as the way can be cleared and the foundation thoughtfully and permanently laid."[1] Ex-President Taft, ex-Governor Forbes, and other Republicans sharply criticized the Administration's policy, on the grounds (1) that the Filipinos could not be made ready for independence for at least a generation; (2) that it was dangerous to raise false hopes; (3) that the substitution of natives for experienced American officials would endanger the foundations of good government that had been laid.

From 1908 the government of the islands consisted of a Commission appointed by the President, and serving as both an executive body and the upper house of the legislature, and an elected assembly, established in 1908 in pursuance of the Philippine Civil Government Act of 1902. In 1913 President Wilson gave the Filipinos for the first time a majority of the nine seats in

[1] *House Jour.*, 63 Cong., 2 Sess., 10.

the Commission; and October 14, 1914, the House of
Representatives passed, by a vote of 212 to 60, a
somewhat startling Philippine bill, reported by Jones
of Virginia for the Committee on Insular Affairs.
This bill declared in its preamble the purpose of the
United States to recognize the independence of the
islands as soon as stable government should have been
established. Meanwhile, the Commission was to be
abolished and a bicameral, elective legislature was to
be set up on the model of the legislature of an organized
territory.[1]

The Sixty-third Congress expired March 4, 1915,
before the Jones bill reached a vote in the Senate; but
on February 3, 1916, a new measure of similar purport
was passed, by a vote of 52 to 24.[2] The Senate bill
contained a striking provision, introduced as an amendment by Senator Clarke of Arkansas, and adopted with
the aid of the casting vote of Vice-President Marshall,
to the effect that complete independence should be
granted the Philippines within two or, at the discretion
of the President, four years. But the House rejected
the Clarke amendment and revived the original Jones
bill, which, following conference, was passed by the
Senate, August 16, by a vote of 37 to 22, and approved
August 29.[3]

This measure became, in effect, a new charter of
government for the islands. Chief executive functions
remained in the governor-general, who was named

[1] *House Jour.*, 63 Cong., 2 Sess., 986.
[2] *Senate Jour.*, 64 Cong., 1 Sess., 196.
[3] *U. S. Statutes at Large*, XXXIX., pt. i., pp. 545-556.

(as were the justices of the Supreme Court and a few other officials) by the President; but the appointing powers of that officer were much increased, and the power of veto was for the first time lodged in him independently. For the Commission was substituted a Senate of twenty-four members, of whom twenty-two were to be elected by popular vote for terms of six years. Formerly, the franchise was restricted by educational and property qualifications to approximately 225,000 inhabitants. It was now extended to all male residents who spoke and wrote a native dialect—a total of more than 800,000. The formal declaration of the intent of the United States to withdraw from the islands when they should have attained stable government stood; and the implication was that the withdrawal would take place at a reasonably early date. Nevertheless, the failure of the Clarke amendment indicated that the country, in 1916, had by no means made up its mind to set the Philippines adrift.

American policy in the Philippines ran directly counter to the practice of older colonizing powers in the control of tropical dependencies. The islands were governed with a view, mainly, to their own welfare. Their people were admitted to an early and large share in the control of their own affairs. Every effort was made to develop in the mixed populations a capacity to govern themselves; repression and exploitation gave place to disinterested, constructive tutelage. The plan was abundantly justified by the results. The islands became orderly and prosperous; education advanced with rapid strides; the people were generally contented.

The reconstruction of the government and the suffrage in 1916 was hailed as the dawn of a new era.[1]

Porto Rico affords further illustration of the success of American colonial administration. Conditions there, it must be admitted, were exceptionally favorable. The island was better off under the Spanish régime than either the Philippines or Cuba, and less reconstruction was required. The population was largely white (in 1899, 589,426 white; 304,352 mestizo; and 59,390 negro), and hence differed sharply from the populations of most Caribbean countries, notably Jamaica, where but one person in fifty was white. There was a substantial middle class; and the resources of the island enabled a dense population to maintain a standard of living much above the average in Caribbean lands. None the less, American rule brought vast improvements in government, in taxation, in education, and in economic conditions.[2]

Civil government in Porto Rico was organized under the Foraker Act of April 12, 1900. Residents of the island were given the status of "citizens of Porto Rico," and government was vested in: (1) a governor appointed by the President; (2) an executive council of eleven members appointed by the President and Senate (at least five to be Porto Ricans), and serving as the upper house of the insular legislature; (3) a House of Delegates of thirty-five members elected

---

[1] Worcester, *The Philippines Past and Present*, II., chap. xxxv.; Le Roy, *The Americans in the Philippines*, II., chap. xxvi.
[2] Lloyd Jones, *Caribbean Interests of the United States*, chap. vii.

biennially.[1] The people accepted American sovereignty gladly, expecting greater freedom under the benign rule of a republic. Serious difficulty arose at only two points: the preponderance of Americans in the executive council was galling to local pride; and the denial of full rights of American citizenship caused confusion. The Porto Rican was not an alien and he was not a citizen; having no allegiance to forswear, he could not, under existing law, become a citizen. He was left, like Mohammed's coffin, dangling between earth and heaven.

Hence there was discontent; and as years passed without relief the islanders became restless. Bad feeling found expression in obstructionist tactics in the House of Delegates; and when that body fell to holding up appropriations it became necessary for Congress to pass a measure (approved July 15, 1909) providing that in case the insular House failed to vote the supplies of any year, a sum equal to the appropriations of the preceding year should none the less be available. President Taft several times urged a grant of citizenship; and in his first annual message President Wilson gave the subject a place in his legislative program. A presidential order of 1914 met one cause of complaint by reconstructing the executive council so as to give the Porto Ricans a majority. But the question of citizenship called for legislation; and Congress was slow to act.

[1] Latané, *America as a World Power* (*Am. Nation*, XXV.), 140–144; Willoughby, *Territories and Dependencies of the U. S*, chap. iv.; Rowe, *The U. S. and Porto Rico*, chaps. vii.–viii.; Allen, "How Civil Government was Established in Porto Rico," *No. Am. Rev.*, Vol. 174, pp. 159–174.

The desired end was attained March 2, 1917, when President Wilson signed a Porto Rican civil government bill. The measure gave the island a bill of rights, altered the structure of the government, met in full the demand for citizenship, and broadened the suffrage. The principal change in the structure of government was the replacing of the executive council as the upper legislative chamber by a Senate of nineteen members elected by the people. This was in line with the policy already adopted in the Philippines. Full American citizenship was conferred on all inhabitants, with provision for exemption of persons who within one year should indicate their desire not to avail themselves of the new right. And it was felt to be safe to extend the suffrage to all males of twenty-one years or over "who have heretofore been known as the people of Porto Rico"; rich Castilian and mountain peon were alike included. No other nation ever set up in a tropical colony an electoral system of such liberality.[1]

At the opening of the twentieth century the sole unorganized continental territory of the United States was Alaska; and during the ensuing decade and a half several important questions centered about the development of this valuable but largely unknown possession. In 1903 a long-standing dispute between the United States and Canada over a portion of the Alaskan boundary was adjusted by decision of an Alaskan Boundary Tribunal, on terms which gave about two-thirds of the contested area to the United

[1] Capo-Rodriguez, "Relations between the United States and Porto Rico," *Am. Jour. Internat. Law*, IX., 883–912; X., 65–76, 312–327.

States.[1] By this time the riches of the dependency began to be known, and it became necessary to enact
much legislation for their protection; for a decade
Alaskan resources loomed large in the conservation
program. In 1903 the Homestead law was extended
to the territory, although for a good while the demand
for land by settlers was very small. The best timber
lands were set off as national reserves, and efforts were
made to protect coal and other mineral lands from
unlawful seizure. For the development of the territory on a scale commensurate with the extent and
variety of its natural resources the thing chiefly needed
was a permanent population; and this was supplied
very slowly. The total population in 1910 was 64,356,
including 25,331 Indians. The estimated white population in 1915 was 44,000.[2] Mining, fishing, and railway
construction continued to be the principal occupations;
agriculture made little headway.

As population took on a more settled character
demand arose for some measure of self-government.
As a first concession, the territory was authorized, in
1906, to send an elected delegate to Congress;[3] and in
1907 President Roosevelt advised the establishment of
a local legislature. It was President Taft's opinion
that the territory was not ready for an elective legislature; consequently he advocated a commission type of
government like that which existed until 1908 in the
Philippines. Other counsels prevailed, and on August

[1] Latané, *America as a World Power* (*Am. Nation*, XXV.), chap. xi.
[2] Secretary of the Interior, *Annual Report*, 1916, p. 60.
[3] *U. S. Statutes at Large*, XXXIV., pt. i., pp. 169–170.

24, 1912, he signed a measure creating a territorial legislature of two houses: a Senate, composed of two members elected from each of the four judicial districts for a term of four years; and a House of Representatives, composed of four members from each of the judicial districts, elected for two years.[1] The powers of this body were very limited, and its acts were subject to veto by the governor and to annulment by Congress. Nevertheless, it satisfied the local demand for a legislative agency better informed upon Alaskan affairs than was Congress. The first session of the new legislature was opened March 3, 1913, at Juneau; and the first measure passed extended the elective franchise to women.

Alaska has been serviceable in furnishing opportunity for an interesting experiment in government ownership of railroads. The territory's progress was held back by inadequate transportation, and the organic act of 1912 provided for the appointment of an Alaskan Railways Commission to make a thorough investigation of the transportation problem, with special reference to routes from the seaboard to the coal fields and to the interior.[2] The commission's report was transmitted to Congress February 6, 1913, and was accompanied by a recommendation by President Taft that railroads to a total length of 733 miles, to connect the interior with tide-water, be constructed by the United States government at an estimated cost of $35,000,000, and afterwards be leased to private operators.

[1] *U. S. Statutes at Large*, XXXVII., pt. i., pp. 512–518.
[2] *Ibid.*, 517.

March 2, 1914, an act was approved authorizing the President to construct, maintain, and operate, railroads in the territory, not to exceed one thousand miles in length, and at an expense not to exceed $35,000,000.[1] Full power was conferred to select routes, to acquire necessary land and other property, to maintain subsidiary telegraph lines and terminal facilities, to fix rates, and to lease any part of the proposed system for a period not to exceed twenty years for operation under the existing interstate commerce laws. An Alaskan Engineering Commission reported in February, 1915, upon possible routes; and in April President Wilson selected the Susitna route, extending from Seward to Fairbanks, with a branch line into the Matanuska coal fields. Under the direction of the Commission, construction was at once begun, and before the close of the year a line forty-five miles in length was completed. A short line operating out of Seward was also purchased. For the first time the United States became, in days of peace, a railway owner and operator.[2]

[1] *U. S. Statutes at Large*, XXXVI., pt. i., pp. 305–307; Brooks, "The Development of Alaska by Government Railroads," *Quart. Jour. Econ.*, XXVIII., 586–596.

[2] Secretary of the Interior, *Annual Report*, 1916, p. 67.

CHAPTER XIV

THE GUARDIANSHIP OF THE CARIBBEAN

(1907-1917)

FOUR fundamental facts underlie the relations of
the United States with the governments and peoples of Latin America. The first is the geographical
and political separateness of the Americas from Europe
and from Asia. Political isolation is not quite complete; for three European nations—Great Britain,
France, and the Netherlands—hold American territory. Furthermore, the effect of physical detachment
has been greatly reduced by improvements in communication and transportation. None the less, America is still a world within a world. A second fact is the
difference of race and inheritance between the peoples
of north and south. There is no inherent or necessary
antagonism between the populations that speak English and those that speak Spanish, and they may be
brought to common action in many matters; yet differences of mental and moral traits, as of institutional
equipment, mark them off sharply one from another.

A third condition is the preponderance of the United States in population, in industry, in wealth, and
in material strength. This preponderance affects all
inter-American relations; yet it must not be exag-

gerated. The area of the United States is but one-third that of Latin America. Of 175,000,000 people living in the twenty-one republics, 75,000,000, or almost forty-three per cent., are inhabitants of Latin American countries. In 1914, when the in-and-out foreign commerce of the United States was valued at four and a quarter billion dollars, that of Latin America was valued at almost three billions.[1]

A fourth condition is the growing control of the United States over Latin American territories and peoples. Porto Rico was taken from Spain in 1898. The Virgin Islands were purchased from Denmark in 1916 and occupied in the following year. Cuba and Panama, although nominally independent, are subject to supervision which makes them virtual protectorates. Haiti is a full-fledged protectorate. Santo Domingo and Nicaragua are under fiscal control. Construction of the Panama Canal has added the Isthmus to the country's coast-line; while acquisition of naval bases has resulted in planting the stars and stripes at Guantanamo in eastern Cuba, on the Corn Islands off the east coast of Nicaragua, and in the Gulf of Fonseca within striking distance of the Canal's western terminus. In short, quite apart from the possession of the Philippines, the United States is, in a very real sense, a "Spanish power."

Liberated with the aid of American arms, the people of Cuba entered upon their career as an independent republic May 20, 1902.[2] The first President, Thomas

[1] *Statistical Abstract of the U. S.*, 1914, p. 688.
[2] Latané, *America as a World Power* (*Am. Nation*, **XXV.**), **175–181.**

Estrada Palma (inaugurated May 20, 1902) distributed patronage equitably among the three rival parties
and managed to preserve public order. His re-election
in 1905 became the signal, however, for a factional
uprising; and in the following year he found it necessary
to appeal to the United States for assistance. In
August, 1906, President Roosevelt sent Secretary Taft
and Robert Bacon, then Assistant Secretary of State,
to the island to reconcile the contending elements.
The mission failed; for while Palma resigned, the insular Congress adjourned without filling the office, and
the government was left in chaos.

In this situation the only course for the United
States was to act under that clause of the Platt Amendment which conferred "the right to intervene for the
maintenance of a government adequate for the protection of life, property, and individual liberty. . . ."[1]
On September 29 Secretary Taft proclaimed a provisional government; and two weeks later the duties
of provisional governor were assumed by Charles E.
Magoon, former governor of the Panama Canal Zone.
To maintain order and to assist in the work of reconstruction, a body of United States troops was stationed
in the island.

The occupation lasted somewhat more than two
years, and cost the United States six million dollars.
During this interval peace was re-established; progress
was made in the study of problems of drainage and

[1] *U. S. Statutes at Large*, XXXI., pt. i., pp. 897–898; Wood, "The
Purpose of the Platt Amendment," *Am. Jour. Internat. Law*, VIII.,
585–591.

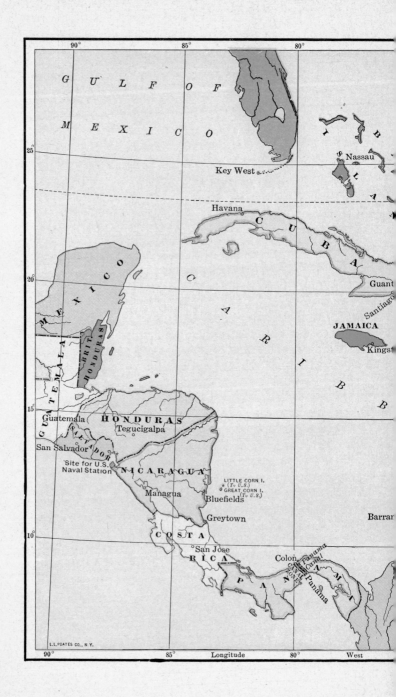

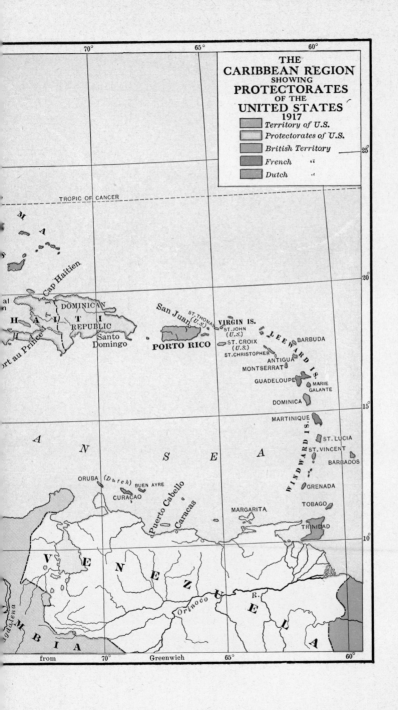

THE
CARIBBEAN REGION
SHOWING
PROTECTORATES
OF THE
UNITED STATES
1917

Territory of U.S.
Protectorates of U.S.
British Territory
French "
Dutch "

70°   65°   60°

25°

TROPIC OF CANCER

20°

Cap Haitien

DOMINICAN
REPUBLIC

HAITI

San Juan   ST.THOMAS
(U.S.)   VIRGIN IS.
PORTO RICO   ST.JOHN
            (U.S.)
            ST.CROIX
            (U.S.)
            ST.CHRISTOPHER

BARBUDA

LEEWARD IS.

ANTIGUA
MONTSERRAT

Santo
Domingo

Port au Prince

GUADELOUPE   MARIE
              GALANTE

DOMINICA

15°

MARTINIQUE

A   N   S   E   A

WINDWARD IS.

ST.LUCIA
ST.VINCENT
BARBADOS

ORUBA (Dutch) BUEN AYRE
      CURAÇAO

Puerto Cabello
      Caracas

GRENADA

TOBAGO

MARGARITA

TRINIDAD

10°

V   E   N   E   Z   U   E   L   A

Magdalena

Orinoco   R.

MBIA

from   70°   Greenwich   65°   60°

reclamation; new sanitary measures were introduced; public improvements were put under way in many cities and towns; the harsh criminal law was revised; and a careful study of the vexed question of the franchise by a commission of Cubans and Americans was made the basis of a new electoral law. At the outset it was proclaimed that the provisional government would be maintained "only long enough to restore order, peace, and public confidence."[1] Nevertheless, President Roosevelt asserted in his annual message to Congress, December 3, 1906, that while the United States had no desire to annex Cuba, it was "absolutely out of the question that the island should continue independent" if the "insurrectionary habit should become confirmed."[2] Both in the United States and in the island, it was widely supposed that the occupation would be of long duration; many expected it to end in annexation.

In his message of December 3, 1907, however, the President reported that "peace and prosperity" already prevailed in the country;[3] and a few weeks later he announced that the occupation would be ended on or before February 1, 1909. As a preliminary, a general election—the third in the republic's history—was held November 14, 1908. A new Congress was chosen; and the Liberal candidate, Gen. José Miguel Gomez, whose defeat by President Palma in 1905 had led to the revolution of 1906, was elected president by a

[1] *Outlook*, LXXXIV., 293.
[2] *Foreign Relations*, 1906, pt. i., p. xlv.
[3] *Ibid.*, 1907, pt. i., p. lxiv.

large majority. On January 13, 1909, the Congress was assembled; and two weeks later the administration of affairs was turned over to the Cuban authorities and the embarkation of the American soldiery was begun.

In succeeding years the political inexperience of the Cuban people bore much evil fruit. Politics absorbed an excess of energy; passion controlled in public affairs; extravagance and mismanagement flourished; brigandage and insurrection required constant watchfulness. The restoration of cock-fighting as a national sport, and of lotteries as a means of "improving the condition of the common people," were widely demanded as a natural and proper use of the regained powers of independent legislation. Thrice in 1911 and 1912 American intervention was imminent.

When, in 1913, the Democrats assumed control at Washington, some people supposed that the United States would cease to watch so closely over Cuban affairs. The Wilson Administration shortly proved the notion groundless. On the very day, indeed, on which Bryan took oath as Secretary of State, he despatched to President Gomez a strong note urging him to veto a pending amnesty bill which would have allowed him to pardon without trial certain persons accused of looting the Treasury; and at the last moment the measure was killed. In point of fact, so long as the Platt Amendment should stand, the United States could not evade the obligation to preserve Cuban independence and to see that a government adequate for the protection of life, property, and liberty was maintained in the island.

President Menocal's term (1912–1916) was a period of progress, and only the ceaseless bickerings of factions and the steady rise of the public debt gave ground for apprehension. The American people were therefore disappointed when, at the close of the Menocal administration, the Cubans again proved unable to handle a national election without serious disorder. The election fell on November 1, 1916, and was preceded by a spirited campaign. The Conservatives supported President Menocal for a second term; the Liberals pinned their hopes to Dr. Alfredo Zayas, a pliant follower of ex-President Palma. The Liberals put forward an attractive program of progressive legislation, and charged their opponents with seeking to establish themselves permanently in power. Nevertheless, the Conservatives won an apparent victory, and Menocal entered upon his second term. Gomez refused to accept the result and started an insurrection which soon became so serious that the United States felt it necessary to land marines at Santiago and other ports for the protection of life and property. The force of the rebellion, however, was finally broken without the direct aid of American arms, and Gomez and other insurrectos were imprisoned. In a published statement President Menocal declared that the United States acted toward Cuba in the crisis "with the utmost delicacy and firmness," and that "a very long step has been taken toward overcoming the old-time prejudice that certain portions of the Cuban people

17

have entertained toward Americans since the intervention of 1906."[1]

Cuba is only a part of the far-flung circle of tropical islands and mainland in which the United States has a lively interest. The decision in 1903 to construct an interoceanic canal gave new value to orderliness and security in all countries adjacent to the Isthmus or commanding its approaches; and in the next decade and a half the United States asserted itself in this portion of the Latin-American world with steadily increasing vigor. Two features of the situation called specially for vigilance. One was the fondness of the Caribbean peoples for revolution and lawlessness, which often touched the lives and property of foreigners. The second was the weak financial position of most of the Caribbean states, and their inability to meet the claims of their creditors. Both of these conditions had for some time led to protests, threats, naval demonstrations, and even intervention, by European powers; barring special precautions, they were likely to continue to do so. But the United States must prevent other nations from attacking or endangering her new interest, the Canal. This meant that she must avert foreign interference in the western hemisphere which might lead to such attack; and this, in turn, meant that she must preserve in the neighborhood of the Canal such political stability, financial integrity, and prosperity as would leave to foreign states no reason or pretext for hostile action. Such, in brief, were the considerations which led

[1] *Outlook*, Vol. 115, p. 502.

Roosevelt and Taft to assume a degree of responsibility for Central American and West Indian affairs never before known; and the argument had no less weight with the Democratic Administration of Wilson.

As the new Caribbean program gradually took form, several elements in it came to view. The first was tactful but firm insistence that the rights of the United States be fully observed. The principal opportunity for emphasis at this point presented itself in Venezuela, where the collection of American claims was obstructed by arbitrary acts of the government of President Castro. Diplomatic relations of the two countries were interrupted; and only after Castro was driven out by a *coup d'état* (in which the United States had no part) was a protocol signed, February 15, 1909, making a favorable settlement.[1]

A second policy was the encouragement of efforts by the Central American states to establish and maintain peaceful relations among themselves. In August, 1907, at the close of a dreary war between Honduras and Nicaragua, President Roosevelt and President Diaz of Mexico urged the chief executives of the five Central American republics to hold a Central American conference to formulate a general treaty of arbitration and friendship.[2] The proposal was received with favor, and on November 14 the Conference—attended by delegates from Honduras, Nicaragua, Guatemala, Salvador, and Costa Rica—convened in Washington.

[1] *Foreign Relations*, 1909, pp. 609–630; Scott, "The Venezuelan Situation," *Am. Jour. Internat. Law*, III., 436–446.
[2] *Foreign Relations*, 1907, pt. ii., pp. 638–639.

The result was two treaties and six conventions, signed December 20; and all were promptly ratified by every one of the five states.[1] The treaties provided for general peace and amity for a period of ten years; and the most important of the conventions undertook to create a Central American Court of Justice, to be composed of five judges appointed (one from each state) for five years, and to have its seat at Cartago, in Costa Rica. In the presence of high commissioners of the United States and Mexico, this tribunal, to which the several states were pledged to refer their disputes, was inaugurated May 25, 1908. A "temple of peace," designed for its use, was erected at Cartago with funds supplied by Andrew Carnegie.[2]

A third phase of the newer policy was financial assistance or supervision for weaker and imperilled nations. Aside from Cuba, the earliest action of this kind was in the negro republic of Santo Domingo. Throughout the nineteenth century the history of this little state was most unhappy. Revolutions alternated with dictatorships; anarchy was chronic; life and property were continually menaced; economic degeneracy went hand in hand with political failure and social demoralization. In 1905 the national debt was $32,000,000, and not even the interest charges could be met. Furthermore, European nations—chiefly France,

---

[1] Internat. Bureau of Am. Repubs., *Monthly Bulletin*, XXV., No. 6, pp. 1345–1368; *Am. Jour. Internat. Law*, II., Supplement, 219–265; Scott, "The Central American Peace Conference of 1907," *ibid.*, II., 121–144.

[2] "Central American League of Nations," World Peace Foundation, *Pamphlet Series*, VII., No. 1.

Italy, and Belgium—were threatening to intervene in defense of their claims; and it was reported that one or more of them would soon seize the customs-houses. At this juncture President Morales called upon the United States to shield his country against the disaster of foreign occupation.

Some people urged that the Dominicans had brought their troubles upon themselves; that if European governments desired to take steps to enforce payment of their claims they had full right to do so; and that, therefore, the United States should adhere to its habitual policy of non-interference. President Roosevelt, however, took a different view. He recognized that the Dominicans were weak and in need of tutelage, and he believed it to be the moral duty of the United States to respond to their appeal. He considered also that the practical interests of the United States were deeply involved. This country, too, had Dominican claims; the harassed republic was adjacent to Porto Rico, and European lodgment in its ports might have serious consequences.

Accordingly, in February, 1905, a protocol was drawn up, under which the United States was to adjust all claims of foreign creditors and to assume control of the customs-houses, turning over forty-five per cent. of the receipts to the Dominican government for running expenses and applying the remainder (after covering the costs of administration) to liquidation of the national debt.[1] When the Senate refused to ratify this treaty, the arrangement was put into effect as a

[1] *Foreign Relations*, 1905, pp. 334–343.

modus vivendi by executive agreement. The results
were excellent, and public opinion in the United
States was won over to such an extent that a new treaty
drawn up in February, 1907, was promptly ratified and
put in operation.[1]

Already the weeding out of fraudulent claims had
reduced the Dominican foreign obligations to $17,000,-
000, including principal and interest. The whole was
refunded into a loan of $20,000,000, arranged by
Kuhn, Loeb & Company of New York, and five per
cent. bonds were issued for the amount, payable in
fifty years. The treaty stipulated: (1) that so long
as any of these bonds should be outstanding, all customs duties should be collected by a "general receiver"
and assistants appointed by the President of the
United States; (2) that only such portions of the proceeds should be turned over to the Dominican government as should not be needed in paying interest on the
bonds, in purchase or retirement of bonds, and in
meeting the costs of the receivership; and (3) that
until the bonded debt should be paid in full, the republic should not increase its debt or alter its customs
laws without the consent of the United States.[2]

From 1905, therefore, the Dominican customs-
houses remained in charge of American officials. One

[1] *U. S. Statutes at Large*, XXXV., pt. ii., pp. 1880–1885; *Foreign Relations*, 1907, pt. 1, pp. 307–322.

[2] *Am. Jour. Internat. Law*, 231; Internat. Bureau of Am. Repubs.,
Monthly Bulletin, XXV., No. 1, pp. 130–132; Hollander, "Convention
of 1907 between the U. S. and the Dominican Republic," *Am. Jour.
Internat. Law*, I., 287–296, and "The Readjustment of San Domingo's
Finances," *Quart. Jour. Econ.*, XXI., 405–426.

of the main incentives of revolution was the hope of seizing the revenues of the government; that was now partly cut off, and the country entered upon a period of reasonable prosperity. Notwithstanding reductions of tariff rates in 1910, annual collections rose from $2,502,000 in 1906 to $4,109,000 in 1913.[1]

In December, 1909, José Santos Zelaya of Nicaragua, whose presidency had been for seventeen years a curse to native and foreigner alike, was swept from power by revolution.[2] The government which succeeded found the public finances hopelessly disordered; and when, in 1910, it won recognition by the United States, it turned to that country for assistance. The result was a convention (May 6, 1911) providing that loans by American bankers should be made more secure by placing American officials in charge of the Nicaraguan customs-houses.[3] The Senate refused to ratify the convention. But under an executive agreement, similar to that of 1905 with Santo Domingo, President Taft despatched to Nicaragua a representative to take charge of the customs; and it was arranged that the proceeds should be employed in the common interest of the government of Nicaragua, the British creditors, and a group of American bankers who were to aid in financing the conversion of the country's currency system from a paper to a gold basis. A convention of the same type with Honduras was also rejected by

[1] "Development of the Dominican Republic," *Special Consular Reports*, No. 65 (1914); Lloyd Jones, *Caribbean Interests of the United States*, chap. viii.

[2] *Foreign Relations*, 1910, pp. 738–767.

[3] *Am. Jour. Internat. Law*, V., Supplement, 291–293.

the Senate, and in this case no further action was taken.

During the closing days of the Taft administration a new treaty with Nicaragua was signed. In consideration of a payment of three million dollars, to be expended on public works and education, the southern republic agreed to give the United States: (1) an exclusive and perpetual right to construct an interoceanic canal across its territory; (2) the right to use the Gulf of Fonseca on the Pacific as a naval base; and (3) substantial control of finances and foreign relations. In short, Nicaragua was to become essentially a protectorate of the United States.

The Senate failed to act, and the task of establishing more regular relations between the two countries was inherited by President Wilson. Change of administration brought no change of policy, and on July 20, 1913, the treaty, slightly modified, was resubmitted for ratification. Action failing, the instrument was redrafted and again submitted in 1914. Finally, on February 18, 1916, it was ratified by the Senate, and on April 11 by the Nicaraguan Congress.[1] The United States obtained—in addition to the exclusive canal right, a naval base in Fonseca Bay, and the control of fiscal administration—a ninety-nine-year lease of the Corn Islands, adjacent to the eastern terminus of the Panama waterway, and admirably adapted for a naval base. The new political relations between the two countries were described in terms closely resembling

[1] *U. S. Statutes at Large*, XXXIX., pt. ii., pp. 51–55; *Am. Jour. Internat. Law*, X., Supplement, 258–260.

those of the Platt Amendment applying to Cuba; and the right of intervention for the preservation of Nicaraguan independence was clearly asserted.

Meanwhile, similar problems presented themselves in Haiti, where political and economic conditions had long been even worse than in Santo Domingo. By 1914 the republic's finances were in utter collapse; and in the early summer of that year both Germany and France demanded that they be allowed to take control of the customs. The early outbreak of war in Europe caused this purpose to be abandoned. But disorders in the republic increased, and in the summer of 1915 the administration of the customs was taken over by the United States. On September 16, a treaty was signed at Port-au-Prince frankly converting Haiti into a protectorate of the United States. The chief provisions were: (1) a Haitian receivership of customs under American control; (2) appointment of an American financial adviser, and American supervision of all expenditure of public moneys; (3) a native constabulary commanded by American officers; (4) a pledge on the part of the Haitian government to cede or lease no territory to a foreign power; and (5) a promise by the United States to "lend an efficient aid for the preservation of Haitian independence and the maintenance of a government adequate for the protection of life, property, and individual liberty."[1] The treaty was to last ten years, and an equal additional period if its objects were not accomplished within that time. Pending ratification, its terms were put in operation

---

[1] *U. S. Statutes at Large*, XXXIX., pt. ii., pp. 44–51.

under a *modus vivendi*. The Haitian Congress ratified it in November, 1915, and the American Senate February 28, 1916.

The arrangement marked a distinct expansion of the policy of Caribbean control; for responsibility was assumed not only for honest customs administration and prompt meeting of obligations abroad, but for wise management of the country's internal finances and for the maintenance of an adequate police. Haiti had been a pariah among nations. The population was almost wholly black, and twice as great as that of Santo Domingo. The burden assumed by the United States was therefore more weighty than most people understood.[1]

From the measures that have been described it was but a step to a general police·supervision in the Caribbean countries. In a message to Congress in 1904 President Roosevelt emphasized the possibility that "chronic wrongdoing" or impotence resulting in "a general lessening of the ties of civilized society" might force the United States to the exercise of an international police power in the western hemisphere;[2] and within a decade many steps were taken in that direction which were unlikely to be retraced. The methods employed were diverse. One was the supervision of elections. In Panama the national elections were supervised by American officials in 1908, and again in 1912; and, contrary to the wishes of the native government, the elections of Santo Domingo in 1913 were watched

[1] Lloyd Jones, *Caribbean Interests of the United States*, chap. ix.
[2] *Foreign Relations*, 1904, p. xli.

by an American commission of "friendly observers."
A second method was non-recognition, used to weaken
the position of dictators and provisional governments
and discourage the violence to which they commonly
owed their power. A third was the sending of regular
and special agents of the State Department to investigate disorders and to mediate between contending
factions. A fourth was the stationing of warships on
the coasts of offending countries, and the landing of
troops.

Most of these armed demonstrations took place in
Santo Domingo, Nicaragua, and Haiti. In Santo
Domingo a battalion of American marines was despatched to the Haitian border in the spring of 1912
to restore the disordered customs service. Thereafter
not a year passed without at least one precautionary
visit from American cruisers. In the summer of 1916
marines were landed, and for months they were used
to protect lives and property endangered by factional
strife; until finally, in November, their commander
proclaimed a military government under American
auspices, to be maintained until after the elections of
January, 1917.[1]

During the successive stages of the contest in Nicaragua which culminated, in 1909–1910, in the overthrow of Zelaya, the United States kept war-ships near
the coasts to protect life and property of Americans
and other foreigners; and upon one occasion marines
were landed to prevent the rival armies from fighting

[1] Stoddard, "Santo Domingo: Our Unruly Ward," *Review of Reviews*,
XLIX., 726–731.

a battle in Bluefields, a principal seat of American business interests.[1] In the summer of 1912, when the work of reconstruction was interrupted by revolutionists and the republic was again plunged in civil war, 2,500 American marines and bluejackets were despatched to the country; and they were employed, not only to guard the legations and patrol the American-owned railway and steamboat lines, but to wage war upon the rebel forces. The revolution was suppressed, and after two months the American troops were withdrawn. A permanent legation guard of one hundred marines, however, was left at Managua.[2]

Steadily, quietly, almost unconsciously, the United States was drawn by dealings with the Caribbean nations far out of the traditional course of isolation and non-interference. Republican and Democratic statesmanship alike yielded to the logic of circumstances. Opinion on the new policy was divided, and confusion arose from failure to distinguish two underlying purposes. One was to safeguard not only the Monroe Doctrine, but practical rights in Porto Rico, the Panama Canal, and Cuba, by maintaining political and economic stability in and around the Caribbean. The other was to give special protection to American capital invested in the Caribbean lands.

Upon the first of these objects there was substan-

[1] *Foreign Relations*, 1910, p. 752.
[2] Ham, "Americanizing Nicaragua," *Review of Reviews*, LIII., 185–191; Thompson, "Renovating Nicaragua," *World's Work*, XXXI., 490–504; Brown, "American Diplomacy in Central America," Am. Polit. Sci. Assoc., *Proceedings*, VIII., 152–163, and "American Intervention in Central America," *Jour. of Race Development*, IV., 409–427.

tially only one view. The argument was that the task assumed was imposed by the conditions and the times; that so long as the United States would not allow other powers a free hand in the western hemisphere, we were in honor bound to maintain order and security in the American states; that not territory and power, but the political stability and financial security of these states was sought, in the interest of both natives and foreigners; and that the proprietorship of the Canal laid upon the nation a special obligation to shield the waterway from extra-American attack and competition.

Upon the use of the power of the government to protect the interests of private investors in backward countries, judgment was less favorable. "While our foreign policy," asserted President Taft, "should not be turned a hair's-breadth from the straight path of justice, it may be well made to include active intervention to secure for our merchandise and our capitalists opportunity for profitable investment which shall inure to the benefit of both countries concerned." Taft followed out this view systematically, but under a rapid fire of criticism. He was charged with fostering "dollar diplomacy," with permitting the government to be made the cat's-paw of adventurous business interests, and with sacrificing the national dignity and security. Government encouragement and guarantee of loans and other investments in Latin America meant to put the army and navy at the service of private interests. It raised the question, too, whether the United States would be willing to allow other nations to back up private enterprise in the Latin American states in the same manner. If the debts of American citizens were to be collected by force, either European powers must be permitted to collect debts of their nationals in the same manner, or the United States must make such collections for them. Either alternative offered difficulties. Hence opponents of the Taft policy urged that the United States, once committed to the active support and defense of money-lenders, mine operators, plantation owners, and other concession-holders and exploiters in the Caribbean lands, would be found to have entered upon a perilous path, from which withdrawal would be difficult or impossible; while the actions that such a policy would force upon her would rouse the suspicions of Latin American peoples and ruin the chances of building up a genuine Pan-American spirit.

These considerations carried much weight with the Wilson Administration. For a time it drew back from the course marked out by its predecessor, and at no stage did it base its acts in behalf of American influence in the Caribbean on the desire to propagate American business and financial power in that quarter. It recognized that the advantage of the private investor might be promoted by measures which also served the larger interest of the country, but it felt that such assistance should be subsidiary, or even incidental. After 1913 our Caribbean policy was, therefore, less frankly shaped to back up the enterprises of "big business." Such actual changes as took place, however, were in motive rather than method; for the broader demands of the national interest still irresistibly impelled the government to spread the ægis of its authority over the whole of the Caribbean region.[1]

[1] On the relation of Caribbean policy to the Monroe Doctrine, see pp. 279–283 cf.; Hart, *Monroe Doctrine*, chap. xx.

CHAPTER XV

LATIN AMERICAN ISSUES AND POLICIES

(1907–1917)

THE opening of the Panama Canal, August 15,
1914, marked the completion of one of the most
stupendous engineering projects ever undertaken, and
realized a dream centuries old. It brought into action
a weighty factor in the relations of the United States
with the great maritime and commercial nations of
Europe and Asia, and it put a new face on the country's
dealings with Latin America.

The diplomacy and legislation leading up to the
beginning of work on the waterway in 1906 have been
described in an earlier volume of this series,[1] and may
be summarized as follows: (1) creation of the Isthmian
Canal Commission of 1899, to investigate afresh the
several proposed routes; (2) ratification, December 16,
1901, of the second Hay-Pauncefote treaty, abrogating
the Clayton-Bulwer treaty and recognizing the right
of the United States to construct a canal and exercise
exclusive control over it;[2] (3) agreement of the French
Canal Company, in 1902, to sell its property and

[1] Latané, *America as a World Power* (*Am. Nation*, XXV.), 204–223.
[2] *U. S. Statutes at Large*, XXXII., pt. ii., pp. 1903–1905.

franchises to the United States for $40,000,000; (4)
report of the Canal Commission, in 1902, virtually
in favor of the Panama route; (5) enactment, June 28,
1902, of the Spooner bill, authorizing the President
to purchase the property and rights of the French
Canal Company, to secure by treaty with Colombia
perpetual control of a strip of land across Panama not
less than six miles wide, and to proceed with the construction of the canal; (6) negotiation of the Hay-
Herran convention ceding for ninety-nine years the
use of the desired strip,[1] and the refusal of the Colombian Congress to ratify it, in 1903; (7) prompt revolt
of Panama, and the recognition of the republic's independence by the United States, November 13, 1903;
(8) signing of a treaty with Panama (ratified February
23, 1904) granting to the United States in perpetuity
a ten-mile strip;[2] (9) appointment of an Isthmian Canal
Commission, in 1904, to undertake the work of construction; (10) decision, in 1906, in favor of a lock, rather
than a sea-level, canal; (11) introduction of measures of
sanitation in 1904–1907, under the direction of Dr. W.
C. Gorgas; (12) reorganization of the Canal Commission in 1907, with army engineers predominating, and
with Col. George W. Goethals as chairman.

By 1908 the details of policy and administration
were settled, and thereafter work progressed rapidly.
An Atlantic Division carried forward construction between the Caribbean Sea and the Gatun locks and

[1] *Senate Docs.*, 63 Cong., 2 Sess., No. 474, p. 277.
[2] *U. S. Statutes at Large*, XXXIII., pt. ii., pp. 2234–2241; *Foreign Relations*, 1904, pp. 543–551; Thayer, *John Hay*, II., chaps. xxv., xxix.
18

dam; a Central Division operated between Gatun and the Pedro Miguel locks, and excavated the Culebra Cut; and a Pacific Division worked between the Pedro Miguel locks and the western ocean. By the opening of 1912 construction was so far advanced that it was necessary to take up several questions concerning the waterway's maintenance and operation. Chief among these were: (1) How should the Canal Zone be governed? (2) Should the Canal be fortified? (3) Under what arrangements of tolls, or other charges, should the Canal be operated?

These matters were gathered into a comprehensive act of Congress (August 24, 1912) for "the opening, maintenance, protection, and operation of the Panama Canal, and for the sanitation and government of the Canal Zone."[1] The question of government was disposed of easily. On the completion of construction, the Canal Commission was to be dissolved; and the President was authorized to appoint a governor of the Canal Zone, to serve four years, and to have power to select subordinates needed for the enforcement of law and the protection and operation of the waterway. The Zone became thus an American "crown colony," without a suggestion of self-government. To prevent the Canal traffic from falling under undue control of the railroads, the Interstate Commerce Commission was given increased authority over the relations of rail and water carriers, even to the extent of denying the use of the Canal to steamship lines which should take

[1] *U. S. Statutes at Large*, XXXII., pt. i., pp. 560–569; *Am. Jour. Internat. Law, VI.*, Supplement, 277–290.

advantage of railroad affiliations to restrict competition. American building and ownership of shipping were encouraged by a "rider" providing for free registry of foreign-built ships not over five years old at the time of application, if owned wholly by American citizens or American corporations, and employed exclusively in the foreign trade. Ship-building materials were to enter the country free of duty.

One of the reasons for building the Canal was the military advantage to be derived from easy water communication between the Atlantic and the Pacific. Could this advantage be gained unless the waterway was fortified against capture or destruction? Had the United States the right to undertake such fortification? The question of right was long and hotly discussed.[1] The unratified Hay-Pauncefote treaty of February 5, 1900, expressly forbade fortification. But the revised treaty, ratified December 16, 1901, made no mention of the subject; and the conclusion finally reached was that fortification would violate neither letter nor spirit of the country's engagement with any foreign power. Fortification was urged by the War Department, by President Taft, by ex-President Roosevelt, and by many other influential persons. Unless fortified, it was urged, the waterway might be seized in time of war and used against its builders. Furthermore, fortification would release the guard-ships for other ser-

[1] Hart, "Have We the Right to Fortify the Panama Canal?" *World Today*, XX., 287–292; Davis, "Fortification of Panama," *Am. Jour. Internat. Law*, III., 885–908; Kennedy, "The Canal Fortifications and the Treaty," *ibid.*, V., 620–638; Olney, "Fortification of the Panama Canal," *ibid.*, V., 298–302.

vice.[1] On the other hand, fortification was opposed on the ground of expense; and it was argued that in time of peace forts were not needed and in time of war they would prove inadequate; also that fortification would be a concession to the spirit of militarism.[2] The decision was to fortify, and a beginning was made with a three-million-dollar appropriation in 1911. By 1914 the work was substantially complete.[3] Great Britain cordially acquiesced.

The most difficult questions dealt with in the Canal Act of 1912 was tolls. It was understood from the beginning that the Canal was not to be so managed as to yield the United States a large net revenue. But it was always expected that commercial shipping would pay enough for the use of the waterway to cover up-keep, and perhaps interest charges. In two reports submitted to President Taft, August 7, 1912, Emory R. Johnson, an expert on transportation, recommended a charge of $1.20 per net ton for loaded merchant vessels (with a reduction of forty per cent. in the case of vessels in ballast), and that the same rate be imposed on American and foreign vessels.[4] The Canal Act practically carried out this suggestion, and the President was given power to fix a rate not to exceed $1.25 per ton; but free use of the Canal was granted

[1] Secretary of War, *Annual Report*, 1911, p. 15.

[2] *Independent*, LXXI., 125–128; Olney, "Fortification of the Panama Canal," *Am. Jour. Internat. Law*, V., 298–301.

[3] Secretary of War, *Annual Report*, 1913, p. 479.

[4] *Panama Canal Traffic and Tolls* (*Senate Docs.*, 62 Cong., 2 Sess., No. 575); *Relation of the Panama Canal to the Traffic and Rates of American Railroads* (*Senate Docs.*, 62 Cong., 2 Sess., No. 875).

to vessels engaged in the coastwise trade of the United States. November 13, 1912, President Taft issued a schedule of rates on the lines proposed by Johnson.

While the bill was pending, Great Britain lodged informal protest against preference to American shipping, and requested that action be delayed until a detailed statement upon the subject could be submitted. The basis of the protest was the third article of the Hay-Pauncefote treaty of 1901, which stipulated that "the Canal shall be free and open to the vessels of commerce and of war of all nations observing these Rules [*i. e.*, the regulations embodied in the Convention of Constantinople, October 28, 1888, on the free navigation of the Suez Canal], on terms of entire equality, so that there shall be no discrimination against any such nation, or its citizens or subjects, in respect of the conditions or charges of traffic or otherwise."[1] The contention of the British government was that exemption of American vessels, even though only in the coastwise trade, would be a discrimination against British and other foreign vessels contrary to this guarantee.

In a memorandum issued when the Canal Act was signed, President Taft defended the exemption clause. The Canal, he pointed out, was built entirely by the United States, on territory specially acquired for the purpose. The "rules" referred to in the Hay-Pauncefote treaty had been adopted by the United States solely as the basis of the Canal's neutralization. The United States had engaged not to discriminate in any

[1] *Am. Jour. Internat. Law*, VI., 976.

way, with respect to the Canal's use, against foreign
nations. The coastwise trade of the country, however, was a purely domestic activity, from which foreign shipping had long been excluded by law. Its
exemption from tolls involved nothing more than the
regulation by the United States of its own commerce
"in its own way and by its own methods"—an incident of domestic policy, comparable to the subsidizing
of the merchant marine in Great Britain, Germany,
and other European states.[1]

Great Britain's formal protest, presented by Ambassador Bryce, December 9, 1912, urged: (1) that
while the Hay-Pauncefote treaty left the United States
free to build and protect the Canal, it expressly maintained the principle of Article VIII of the Clayton-
Bulwer treaty, guaranteeing to Great Britain the use
of the waterway on terms of complete equality with
the United States; (2) that exemption of American
coastwise shipping would throw upon British and other
foreign shipping an undue share of the burden of the
Canal's upkeep, involving violation of the treaty provision that the conditions and charges of traffic "shall
be just and equitable."[2] Secretary Knox's rejoinder
(January 17, 1913) sought to narrow the controversy
to a consideration of the actual, provable injury done
to British and other shipping, and contended that only
after it should have been shown by experience that
the discrimination was more than theoretical would
Great Britain have a grievance worthy of diplomatic

[1] *U. S. Statutes at Large*, XXXII., pt. ii., p. 1904.
[2] *Senate Docs.*, 63 Cong., 1 Sess., No. 11, pp. 11–19.

consideration, and perhaps of submission to an **arbi**-tration tribunal.[1] In a series of "observations," **under** date of February 27, Ambassador Bryce insisted that the grievance of the British government was already of such proportions as to call for settlement, and pressed for a reference of the issue to the Hague Tribunal.

At this stage the British government rested its case. In the United States, however, numerous jurists and public men, including members of both houses of Congress, thought the exemption clause of doubtful propriety, if not actually a violation of treaty obligations.[2] When the Wilson Administration came in, the voice of dissent was freshly raised; and despite the fact that the Democratic platform of 1912 indorsed the exemption,[3] the President appeared before Congress, March 5, 1914, and urged the repeal of the controverted clause, as not only a violation of treaty obligations, but a product of mistaken economic policy.[4] After a contest which thoroughly tested the President's power over his party, a repealing bill became law, June 15, 1914.[5] The surrender, however, was not complete; for the measure affirmed the full right of the United States "to discriminate in favor of its vessels by exempting the vessels of the United States or its citizens from the pay-

[1] *Senate Docs.*, 63 Cong., 1 Sess., No. 11, pp. 3–10; *Am. Jour. Internat. Law*, VII., Supplement, 100–102; *Senate Docs.*, 63 Cong., 2 Sess., No. 474.
[2] Root, "Panama Canal Tolls," World Peace Foundation, *Pamphlet Series*, III., No. 3; *Nation*, XCVI., 26.
[3] *Democratic Campaign Text-Book*, 1912, p. 36.
[4] *Senate Jour.*, 63 Cong., 2 Sess., 136; *House Docs.*, 63 Cong., 2 Sess., No. 813.
[5] *U. S. Statutes at Large*, XXXVIII., pt. i., pp. 385–386; *Am. Jour. Internat. Law*, VIII., 249–250.

ment of tolls for passage through said canal." The repeal was based on expediency, or perhaps courtesy, rather than legal obligation, and the gratification felt by foreign peoples was tempered by the realization that the issue was rather postponed than closed.[1]

Under the terms of the Canal Act of 1912, the Canal Commission passed out of existence April 1, 1914; whereupon the first governor of the Canal Zone, Col. Goethals, since 1907 chairman of the Commission, assumed office. On the succeeding August 15, the waterway was thrown open to the commerce of the world. The total cost of construction, estimated (including sanitation and police) at $144,233,458 by the Commission of 1899–1901, was (including appropriations for the fiscal year 1915) $361,874,861.

The opening of the Canal for purposes of commerce antedated by less than two weeks the outbreak of the European war. Traffic conditions were, therefore, from the beginning abnormal. In particular, there was a sharp decline of commercial intercourse between western Europe and the Pacific countries. It had been estimated that under normal conditions the tonnage passing through in a year would be about 10,500,000. Actually, 1,258 vessels (of which 540 were British and 526 American), of 4,390,405 net tons, and carrying

[1] Brief discussions of the subject include: Baty, "The Panama Tolls Question," *Yale Law Jour.*, XXIII., 389–396; Hains, "Neutralization of the Panama Canal," *Am. Jour. Internat. Law*, III., 354–394; Latané, "Neutralization Features of the Hay-Pauncefote Treaty," *Am. Hist. Assoc. Reports*, 1902, I., 291–303, and "The Panama Canal Act and the British Protest," *Am. Jour. Internat. Law*, VII., 17–26; Kennedy, "Neutralization and Equal Terms," *ibid.*, 27–50; Wambaugh, "Exemption from Panama Tolls," *ibid.*, 233–244.

5,675,261 tons of cargo, passed through during the first eleven and one-half months. The net tolls collected during this period amounted, none the less, to $4,909,150.96, which almost sufficed to cover the costs of operation and maintenance.

The construction of the Canal brought the United States into another controversy which yielded less readily to negotiation than that with Great Britain. Throughout the second Roosevelt and Taft administrations the government of Colombia clung resolutely to its charge that the revolt of Panama in 1903 was fomented from Washington, and not only refused to recognize the independence of the new state, but demanded that the United States apologize and make reparation.[1]   Several attempts to smooth over the difficulty failed.   In 1909 a treaty was signed which fell short of ratification, and in 1913 overtures by the United States for a tripartite convention among the nations concerned met with no response.   Colombia held out for reference of the entire dispute to the International Tribunal at The Hague.

Hope of a settlement was aroused in both countries by the coming in of President Wilson; and on April 7, 1914, the American minister signed a treaty at Bogota in which the United States expressed "sincere regret that anything should have occurred to interrupt or to mar the relations of cordial friendship that had so long subsisted between the two nations." The United States agreed to pay the southern republic $25,000,000, and conceded the right in perpetuity to

[1] Latané, *America as a World Power* (*Am. Nation*, XXV.), 215-217.

use the Canal freely for military transportation, and to use it for commercial purposes on the same terms as the United States herself. Colombia was to recognize the independence of Panama and accept a boundary line defined in the treaty.[1]

At Bogota this agreement was promptly ratified. At Washington President Wilson applied strong pressure in the Senate, but without avail; and in the summer of 1917 the treaty was still pending. Public opinion was divided. Some people held that the United States was responsible for the revolt of the Panamanians in 1903, and that the Colombian grievance was well founded.[2] Others considered that the conduct of the United States had been technically correct, but that to conciliate Latin American opinion we could afford to be generous.

Most persons, however, refused to concede that the United States owed Colombia either an apology or money, and felt that it was the part of weakness, from which no desirable result could come, to yield to a demand that was unjust merely because the nation making it was small, and one whose friendship was specially desired. The phrase "sincere regret" seemed a censure of Roosevelt; although, strictly, the treaty "regretted," not any action of the United States, but simply the interruption of the friendly relations of the two countries. It was objected that the United States

---

[1] *Diario Oficial*, Apr. 14, 1914, pp. 793–799; *Am. Year Book*, 1914, pp. 76–78; *Review of Reviews*, XLIX., 683–686.

[2] Taylor, *Why the Pending Treaty with Colombia should be Ratified* (1914); Chamberlain, "A Chapter of National Dishonor," *No. Am. Rev.*, Vol. 195, pp. 145–174.

should grant to no foreign state such exceptional privileges in the use of the Canal as were proposed for Colombia. The promise to pay $25,000,000 carried no explanation of why that particular sum—or, indeed, any sum—should be paid. It was pointed out, too, that Colombia conceded nothing save acceptance of Panaman independence, which had already been for more than a decade a *fait accompli;* and that even the long-discussed right to a canal route by way of the Atrato River (valueless except as a safeguard against future international complications) was not conferred. The desire of the Administration to heal the Colombian rupture and to promote Latin American confidence in the justice and good-will of the United States met sympathy. But there was strong doubt whether such a settlement would lead to that desirable result.[1]

In the decade 1906–1916 relations between the United States and Latin America as a whole grew closer, and reciprocal attempts to strengthen them went on steadily. Trade, international banking, and other forms of business dealings were developed on new and promising lines.[2] Intellectual intercourse was promoted by visits of university professors and other scholars, by increased attendance of students from southern lands at colleges and universities in the United

[1] Roosevelt, "The Panama Blackmail Treaty," *Metropolitan Magazine*, Vol. XLI., pp. 8, 69. In view of its authorship, this argument against the ratification of the treaty of 1914 has exceptional interest. Cf. Thayer, "John Hay and the Panama Republic," *Harper's Magazine*, Vol. 131, pp. 167–175.

[2] Kinley, "The Promotion of Trade with South America," *Am. Econ. Rev.*, I., 50–71; Shepherd, "Our South American Trade," *Polit. Sci. Quart.*, XXIV., 667–693.

States, and by Pan-American scientific congresses, such
as were held at Santiago in 1908 and at Washington
in 1915. Opportunity for official or semi-official expressions of good-will was afforded by trips of statesmen, notably of Secretary Root to South America in
1906 and to Mexico in 1907, of Secretary Knox to the
Central American capitals in 1912, of ex-Ambassador
Bacon to South America in 1913, and of ex-President
Roosevelt to South America in 1913–1914.

International friendship was stimulated also by general Pan-American congresses. In 1906 the Third International Conference of American States met at Rio
Janeiro; a Fourth Conference, held at Buenos Aires in
1910, was timed to coincide with a celebration of the
one-hundredth anniversary of Argentine independence.
At Buenos Aires all of the twenty-one American republics were represented except Bolivia. In both gather-
ings the United States was ably represented; the delegation of 1906 was led by Secretary Root.

Other meetings were held specially to promote closer
economic relations; and a Pan-American Financial
Conference at Washington, in 1915, set up as an agency
for the carrying out of its purposes an International
High Commission, organized in twenty national sections, each consisting of nine jurists and financiers
under the chairmanship of the minister of finance.[1]

An International Bureau of the American Republics,
established at Washington in 1890, proved useful, and
at the Rio Janeiro conference of 1906 its work was
enlarged to include compiling and distributing com-

[1] First Pan-American Financial Conference, *Proceedings*, 1915, p. 301.

mercial and legal information, preparing reports, performing tasks specially entrusted to it by the successive conferences, and acting as a permanent committee of the conferences to fix the time and place of meetings and to make up the lists of subjects to be discussed. In 1907 John Barrett succeeded William C. Fox as director, and three years later the Bureau (renamed in 1910 "Bureau of the Pan-American Union") moved into a splendid building erected, on a site furnished by the United States, with funds supplied chiefly by Andrew Carnegie. The institution is supported by proportional grants from all the independent states in the western hemisphere, and is managed by a governing board composed of the diplomatic representatives of these states in Washington, with the Secretary of State of the United States as *ex-officio* chairman. In each American capital is an official Pan-American Committee, which promotes ratification of the acts of the conferences, supplies information for the use of the Bureau, and submits projects for the consideration of the Bureau and of the conferences.[1]

The Monroe Doctrine continued in the twentieth century to be, speaking broadly, the cornerstone of American international policy. None the less, uncertainty concerning the Doctrine's meaning and scope steadily grew. Some writers and publicists urged that the Doctrine no longer squared with the facts of the international situation—that it was obsolete and should be deliberately abandoned.[2] Some who took this view

---

[1] Pan-American Union, *Bulletin*, XXXI., 798–801.
[2] Bingham, *Monroe Doctrine*, 55–72.

thought that prevention of European and Asiatic encroachment in the western hemisphere should be undertaken by the United States only in conjunction with
three of the southern nations which had become strongest and most progressive, the "A B C powers,"
Argentina, Brazil, and Chile. But most people were
unwilling to admit that the Doctrine was outgrown.
The most common notion was rather that, while the
pronouncement of President Monroe in 1823 had no
bearing in the twentieth century, there was none the
less a Doctrine of Permanent Interest which underlay
American foreign policy from Washington to Wilson;[1]
that from this Doctrine the United States derived the
self-imposed task of preventing foreign aggression in
the western hemisphere; that the exact content and
significance of the Doctrine were variable, taking color
from new situations as they arose; and that the Doctrine might as well be labelled with the name of Monroe
as any other.

That the Doctrine was still alive was proved not
alone by frequent allusions in speeches and state
papers, but by forceful reassertions and by definite acts.
In 1911 the creditors of an American company holding
a tract of land on the Mexican coast, in the vicinity
of Magdalena Bay, sought from the Taft Administration permission to sell their rights to a Japanese fishing
company. There was no evidence that the Tokio
government was in any way concerned; but assent
was withheld, and on August 2, 1912, the Senate passed,
by a vote of 51 to 4, a resolution introduced by Senator

[1] Hart, *Monroe Doctrine*, 349-370.

Lodge, as follows: "That when any harbor or other place in the American continents is so situated that the occupation thereof for naval or military purposes might threaten the communication or the safety of the United States, the government of the United States could not see, without grave concern, the possession of such harbor or other place by any corporation or association which has such a relation to another government, not American, as to give that government practical power of control for naval or military purposes."[1] There could be no doubt that one branch of Congress, at all events, believed in the Doctrine of Permanent Interest. Furthermore, when in 1913 an English house, S. Pearson and Son, Ltd., which had vast holdings of oil-producing lands in Mexico, sought an exten‧ sive oil concession in Colombia, it was turned from its purpose chiefly by adverse opinion in the United States. In both cases the fear was that alien business interests might prove an entering wedge for political interference or domination.

These two episodes very well illustrate the principal change which the so-called Monroe Doctrine underwent in the first decade and a half of the century. Previously, the Doctrine was wholly political. It aimed to prevent foreign interference with the American governmental systems and the extension of foreign sovereignty to American soil. Purely economic engagements and operations were unknown to it. But the United States was gradually forced to recognize

[1] *Senate Jour.*, 62 Cong., 2 Sess., 511; Hart, *Monroe Doctrine*, 349–370.

that the investment of foreign capital in a backward country may easily lead to economic absorption, and that economic absorption is likely to result in open or disguised political control. Latin America bristles with opportunities for such manipulation.

Hence the new Doctrine is economic as well as political. Concretely applied, it means two things: (1) European and Asiatic peoples are to be discouraged from acquiring lands and other vested interests in America on such a scale as to suggest political control; (2) weaker states whose financial looseness might tempt creditor nations to intervene in their affairs are to be brought under American protection and put in a position to meet their obligations fully and promptly. How far, up to 1917, the second of these ideas was carried has appeared in the preceding chapter.

These deliberate extensions of the Doctrine aroused apprehension in Latin America, and official statements sought to disclaim aggression. "My government," declared Secretary Knox to the Nicaraguan Congress in 1912, "does not covet an inch of territory south of the Rio Grande." "The United States," said President Wilson at Mobile, October 27, 1913, "will never again seek one additional foot of territory by conquest."[1] In an address to the Second Pan-American Scientific Congress at Washington, January 6, 1916, the President spoke of the "fears and suspicions" that had been aroused in Latin America because the Monroe Doctrine contained "no promise . . . of what America was going to do with the implied and partial pro-

[1] World Peace Foundation, *Pamphlet Series*, VI., No. 1, p. 12.

tectorate which she apparently was trying to set up
on this side of the water"; and he asserted emphati-
cally that part of the plan of the United States was
that all the states of the western hemisphere should
unite in "guaranteeing to each other absolute political
independence and territorial integrity."[1]

These declarations were balanced by others intended
to convince the world that the United States would not
permit the Doctrine to be used by any nation as a
shield against the consequences of its misdeeds. President Roosevelt declared that the Doctrine did not
compel the United States to intervene to prevent
punishment of a tort committed against a foreign
nation, "save to see that the punishment does not
assume the form of territorial occupation in any
shape"; and President Taft said that the Doctrine
must never be made to serve the ends of irresponsible
or dishonest American governments.[2]

But after all explanations were made and reassurances offered, the fact remained that with every new
turn that the Doctrine took, the pre-eminence of the
United States in American affairs was further exalted.
The task of reconciling this tendency with the growing
power, stability, and pride of the greater nations south
of Panama seemed likely to give the guides of American foreign policy many anxious hours.

[1] *Am. Year Book*, 1916, p. 88.
[2] Taft, *The United States and Peace*, 11–13; Merriman, "The Monroe
Doctrine—Its Past and Present Status," *Polit. Quart.*, No. 7, pp. 17–40;
Robertson, "South America and the Monroe Doctrine," *Polit. Sci.
Quart.*, XXX., 82–105; Shepherd, "New Light on the Monroe Doc-
trine," *ibid.*, XXXI., 578–589.
    19

CHAPTER XVI

THE MEXICAN IMBROGLIO
(1910–1917)

FOR forty years after the collapse of Napoleon III.'s proposed Latin American empire in 1867, the relations of the United States and Mexico were close and, in the main, friendly. More than two score agreements, conventions, and treaties were concluded, and in 1908 the series was capped by a general treaty of arbitration.[1] A visit of Secretary Root to Mexico in 1907, and a meeting of Presidents Taft and Diaz on the Rio Grande border in 1910, brought out strong expressions of good-will on both sides. None the less, controversy arose between the two nations in 1911, and the "Mexican problem" became the most burdensome inheritance of the Wilson Administration. The issues of foreign policy centering about the border republic were forced into the background only by the staggering demands of the war in Europe.

From the winning of independence in 1821 to 1876, Mexico had about eighty presidents; revolutions tripped on one another's heels. But under the firm rule of Porfirio Diaz (1877–1880, 1884–1911) the country found comparative quiet; and while no one sup-

[1] *U. S. Statutes at Large*, XXXV., pt. ii., pp. 1997–1999.

posed that it was advancing, like Argentina or Brazil
or Chile, out of chaos into the status of a strong and
progressive nation, the world was not prepared to
witness its relapse into anarchy.

Mexico is a land of great natural wealth; Humboldt
rightly called it "the storehouse of the world." Four
hundred years of intermittent working have only
scratched the surface of the mineral resources; millions of acres are unsurpassed for rubber production,
fruit-growing, and diversified agriculture; vast districts are adapted to cattle and sheep grazing. Native
capital and enterprise were lacking for the development of these resources. Hence the country early became one of the world's great fields of international
business enterprise. The Diaz government held out
every inducement in the form of concessions; it was
strong enough to guarantee the safety of investments;
and the opportunity to make large profits drew in
enormous amounts of American, British, German, and
French capital. Most of this money was employed in
silver, gold, and copper mining, oil and rubber production, stock-raising, fruit-growing, cotton-mills, and
railroads and other public utilities; and to carry
on these enterprises thousands of people of foreign
nationality—chiefly Americans, but many English-
men, Frenchmen, Germans, and Spaniards—became
residents of the country.[1]

Viewed from a distance, the land appeared orderly
and prosperous; actually, its condition was thoroughly

[1] Middleton, "Mexico, the Land of Concessions," *World's Work*,
XXVII., 289–298.

bad. In the first place, government was autocratic
and corrupt. Diaz was a hard-working, abstemious,
iron-willed man who had risen to power from the
modest estate of a farmer. He differed from a score
of other dictators only in being astute enough to play
off contending forces one against another, and thus
to hold his advantage for a good part of a lifetime.
He dealt liberally with the foreign investing interests,
and in turn was backed up by them; he curried favor
with the few Mexicans of wealth by appointments and
honors; he kept the bandit elements in his pay, not
hesitating to make notorious leaders of robber bands
governors of states. Popular government was only a
matter of form: the constitution was disregarded
when found inconvenient; elections were farces; proposals to overhaul the political machinery were frowned
down; public opinion found no opportunity for expression; power rested with the dictator-president and
a clique of corrupt politicians, the "scientificos," buttressed by the vested interests, native and foreign.
Diaz freely admitted that the country did not have
representative government, but he said that his people
were not ready for it.[1]

Economic conditions were unfortunate. Mexico
was rich, but the Mexicans were poor; the land and
its resources belonged chiefly to outsiders, who used
it for their own advantage. A few native magnates
were prosperous, but the masses were wretchedly poor,
densely ignorant, and not even safe in their personal

[1] Murray, "Porfirio Diaz at First Hand," *World's Work*, XXII.,
14571–14591.

rights.   Only a fraction owned land; few had property
of any kind; countless thousands were peons, bound
to labor for persons to whom they had become in-
debted, and with little hope of ever regaining freedom.
In most countries the great majority of citizens have
a direct interest in the keeping of law and order.   But
in Mexico the masses could play at war and revolution
—tear up railroads, demolish plantations, and plunder
towns—without doing harm to anything they owned
themselves.[1]

Thus, Diaz gave his country peace, but not well-
being or hope.   His régime was honeycombed with dissent, and for years the forces bent on its overthrow
lacked only leadership.   In 1910 the republic cele-
brated the centennial of its declaration of independence, and in the same year the venerable President was
re-elected for an eighth term.   Francisco Madero, a
patriot of education and fortune, undertook to stand
as a candidate against him, but was brushed aside.
Madero was not a man to accept such treatment, and
he promptly started a revolt, declaring that he would
never lay down his arms until Diaz should resign or
a free and open presidential election should be held.
He was astute enough to put forward an alluring program of reforms, and rich enough to bring his cause
prominently before the people.   At first, his uprising
was localized in the two northern states of Chihuahua
and Durango, but in 1911 it spread rapidly southward.
Finding that belated concessions were of no avail,

[1] Hart, "Mexico and the Mexicans," *World's Work*, XXVII., 272–
289.

Diaz resigned the presidency (May 11) and sailed for
Europe.[1] In October Madero was duly chosen to the
coveted position, at the first untrammeled election that
the country had known in a generation.

In these events the United States took deep interest.
American lives and property in Mexico called for protection; the neutrality laws had to be enforced and the
frontiers safeguarded. On March 7, 1911, President
Taft ordered the mobilization of twenty thousand
troops on the Rio Grande and stationed war-ships
at Galveston. Despite the killing of American citizens
on American soil by stray bullets fired across the border, he disclaimed any intention to intervene. Following the election of 1911, Madero was recognized as
president; and on March 14, 1912, Taft availed himself of powers conferred by Congress to prohibit purchases of arms and munitions in the United States
by factions which were resisting the new government.[2]

At no time did the Maderist régime command full
support of the Mexican people, and in February, 1913,
it was brought to a close by a revolutionary movement
led by Felix Diaz, nephew of the ex-President, and
General Victoriano Huerta, commander-in-chief of the
federal army. On February 18, Huerta proclaimed
himself provisional president; and five days later
Madero and the deposed vice-president were shot,
while in the custody of officials responsible to Huerta.
From the outset Huerta's ability to establish and main-

[1] *World's Work*, XXII., 14591.
[2] *U. S. Statutes at Large*, XXXVII., pt. ii., p. 1733; *Am. Jour. Internat.
Law*, VI., Supplement, 147–148.

tain order was doubtful. His rule rested on a purely
military basis, and was not of a kind to attract popular
support. Nominally, he was a provisional president;
actually, he was a self-designated dictator, and this fact
was not altered by two so-called elections held during
his ascendancy. Furthermore, the Maderists kept up
opposition, and in the north General Venustiano Carranza, governor of Coahuila, led a party of "Constitutionalists" in denouncing Huerta as a traitor and refusing
to accept his authority. Under altered conditions, civil
war went steadily on, with the principal theatre of hostilities adjacent to the United States border.

Such was the situation when, March 4, 1913, Woodrow Wilson became president; and his first important
foreign problem was the attitude to be taken toward
Huerta. The decision was to refuse recognition, for
three main reasons: the fate of Madero, the failure
to hold a real election, and the dictator's inability to
control all parts of his country. Huerta was believed
to have risen to power by force and murder, and the
redemption of Mexico seemed dependent on his overthrow. "We can have no sympathy," urged Wilson
upon Congress, "with those who seek to seize the power
of government to advance their own personal interests
or ambition. . . . We dare not turn from the principle
that morality and not expediency is the thing that is
to guide us." In its chosen policy the Administration
was not shaken by the fact that within a few months
the United States stood alone among the greater
nations in refusing recognition.

The President's plan of withholding recognition from

rulers who came into power by murdering their predecessors was an innovation in our dealings with Latin-American states. Hitherto the question of recognition was settled on grounds of the new government's strength and probable permanence. The implication of the new principle was that governments should not be recognized if they were based on violence, if they contravened the constitutions or laws of the countries affected, or if they infringed clear principles of morality. Wilson was right in believing that such a policy would embarrass a government like Huerta's, especially by making it difficult to obtain loans. But whether the people of the United States wanted their President to undertake this sort of moral censorship was doubtful.

Within three months after Huerta's accession the northern Mexican states were in general revolt, and by the close of 1913 the Constitutionalist forces, led by Carranza and a former bandit, Francisco Villa, were pressing gradually southward. On the ground that Huerta was the strongest of the rival leaders and the likeliest to re-establish efficient government, the American ambassador, Henry L. Wilson, urged that he be recognized. The Administration was not convinced, and the ambassador resigned. For years thereafter the President sought his information on Mexican affairs, and made his communications to the Mexican factions, through personal representatives without diplomatic rank.[1] In August, 1913, such a representative, John Lind (ex-governor of Minnesota), conveyed to

[1] Wriston, "Presidential Special Agents in Diplomacy," *Am. Polit. Sci. Rev.*, X., 481–499.

Huerta the following terms of a settlement: (1) an immediate cessation of hostilities; (2) a general amnesty; (3) an early and free presidential election; (4) assurance that Huerta would not be a candidate; (5) agreement by all parties to abide faithfully by the results.[1] These proposals were scornfully rejected. August 27, President Wilson read to Congress a full statement of his Mexican policy, explaining that its chief object was to eliminate Huerta.[2] Next day he warned all citizens of the United States to leave Mexican soil. In the annual message of December 2 he foretold the dictator's downfall and expressed confidence that there would be no need to abandon "watchful waiting."[3]

Time passed and the situation did not improve. Was it sufficient to wait for Huerta's power to die a slow death? Was there any guarantee of a better state of affairs afterwards? Should not the United States forcibly intervene to compel a restoration of law and order? For two years the land had been in turmoil; American and foreign lives were imperilled; property was daily confiscated or destroyed; large and lawful interests of many kinds were in jeopardy. Representatives of these interests urged that the United States immediately send troops into Mexico and bring the reign of anarchy to an end, and the passive policy of the President was sharply criticized by the general public. Talk of annexation was revived.

[1] *Am. Jour. Internat. Law*, VII., Supplement, 279-284.
[2] *House Jour.*, 63 Cong., 1 Sess., 256–257.
[3] *Ibid.*, 63 Cong., 2 Sess., 9–10.

On the other hand, supporters of the Administration argued that Huerta's power would speedily collapse; that the expected succession of Carranza would mean orderly government, while intervention would lead to a long, costly, and inglorious war; that strong action would antagonize Latin American sentiment; and that the annexation of Mexican territory was undesirable.

There was the question, also, of the attitude of Europe. Great Britain, France, and Germany were solicitous about the welfare of their nationals in the disordered country; they had war-ships in the Gulf waters, and were prepared to order landings; the Monroe Doctrine was endangered. For three years the American authorities fended off these powers by giving them to understand that the reconstruction of Mexico was an American question; and by common consent the United States was left a free hand. When, in March, 1914, the murder of an English ranchman named Benton by the troops of Villa gave strong excuse for direct action, Great Britain helped avert trouble by accepting the good offices of the United States in fixing responsibility for the crime. Yet it was only after the European powers became involved in war among themselves in 1914 that the danger of their intervention in Mexico was practically removed.

In the early months of 1914 the Constitutionalists gained ground rapidly. In February they secured an outlet to the sea at Mazatlan, and in April they reached the important oil port of Tampico. In recognition of their successes President Wilson, on February 3, revoked in their favor the embargo on arms laid by

President Taft in 1912;[1] and the growing troubles of the Huerta government were heightened.

A trifling incident of the contest for the possession of Tampico served to bring relations between the United States and Huerta to a crisis. On April 10 some American bluejackets landed at the town to purchase gasoline, and were arrested. They were promptly released, and an expression of regret, in which Huerta joined, was tendered. There had been other affronts, however, and Admiral Henry T. Mayo, in command of the American vessels stationed off the port, demanded further apology in the form of a salute to the United States flag. The demand was refused by the local commandant, and subsequently by Huerta. It was reiterated by President Wilson, and after eight days of haggling an ultimatum was presented to Huerta, which failed on a technicality. A breach was not justified by the facts; but, having started on a firm course, the President and his advisers felt obliged to follow it out. The approach of a German steamer to Vera Cruz with a cargo of war material for Huerta's troops supplied the cue for action. On April 21 orders were flashed by wireless to the Gulf fleet, and by sundown the entire city of Vera Cruz was in the possession of American sailors and marines. During the landing and subsequent fighting eighteen Americans were killed. On the following day Congress adopted resolutions declaring justifiable the use of troops to enforce the demand for amends for "affronts and indignities committed against the United

[1] *U. S. Statutes at Large*, XXXVIII., pt. ii., p. 1992.

States," but affirming also that the United States cherished no hostility toward the Mexican people and no purpose to make war upon them.[1]

The capture of Vera Cruz was an act of war. To the peoples of Latin America it looked like the beginning of a war of conquest, and in Mexico it was fiercely resented. Even Carranza protested angrily. Suspicion was not lessened when an army of six thousand men under General Funston was sent to occupy the conquered city; although the Administration avoided further acts which could be construed as belligerent. At this juncture the three "A B C powers," Argentina, Brazil, and Chile, came forward with a proposal to mediate.[2] The offer was promptly accepted by the United States, and Huerta accepted it "in principle."[3]

The outcome was a protocol signed at Niagara Falls, Canada (May 20, 1914), by the mediators and by the representatives of the United States and Huerta, providing for establishment of a provisional government in Mexico by an agreement between Huerta and Carranza, and pledging the United States and the three mediating countries to recognize this government immediately.[4] Carranza, however, stood in the way. His power was daily growing, and he was bent only on the overthrow of Huerta. July 15, the dictator, now hopelessly beaten, resigned and went to Europe; and thereafter the victor had even less reason for accepting a policy involving his own probable retirement.

[1] *U. S. Statutes at Large*, XXXVIII., pt. i., p. 770.
[2] World Peace Foundation, *Pamphlet Series*, VI., No. 1., p. 27.
[3] *Ibid.*, 29.   [4] *Ibid.*, 35–36.

The mediation, none the less, served two useful purposes: it drew the two countries from the brink of war and afforded opportunity for deliberation; and it demonstrated the willingness of the United States to co-operate with its neighbors, and proved to these neighbors that the nation was not bent on conquest.

August 20, 1914, Carranza entered Mexico City in triumph. Then came the turn which people familiar with Latin American revolutionary politics expected. The victors began quarreling among themselves. Within a month Villa was in open revolt, disclaiming presidential ambitions, yet declaring that he would never make peace until Carranza should have been stripped of power; and Villistas fell to fighting Carranzistas all over the northern provinces.

The Administration at Washington was sorely disappointed. It adhered to its purpose to withdraw the troops from Vera Cruz, and the evacuation was carried out November 23. But the forces on the Rio Grande were kept in place, and fresh efforts were put forth to induce the warring factions to come to an understanding. Every suggestion fell upon deaf ears, and affairs went steadily from bad to worse. Carranza abandoned Mexico City for Vera Cruz, and in a single month the capital changed hands three times; titular presidents rose and fell in swift succession. Americans were attacked by lawless bands, not only on Mexican soil, but in Texas, New Mexico, and Arizona.

Finally, in June, 1915, when the entire northern section of Mexico had been made desolate by conflict, and when even in the capital the people were starving because of the stoppage of railway traffic, President Wilson invited the diplomatic representatives of six Central and South American states—the "A B C powers" and Bolivia, Uruguay, and Guatemala—to meet to formulate plans for a provisional Mexican government. By October Carranza was again in possession of Mexico City, with a fair chance of bringing the entire country under control; and the new inter-American conference, sitting at Washington, decided to recommend his recognition. Accordingly, on October 19 the United States and eight of the republics of Central and South America formally recognized "the *de facto* government of Mexico of which General Carranza is head."[1] An American embargo on arms designed for use against the triumphant chieftain was re-imposed,[2] and diplomatic relations, after a break of more than two and a half years, were resumed. Recognition by the principal European nations speedily followed. "Whether we have benefited Mexico by the course we have pursued," said President Wilson in his message of December 7, 1915, "remains to be seen. Her fortunes are in her own hands, but we have at least proved that we will not take advantage of her in her distress and undertake to impose upon her an order and government of our own choosing."[3]

The sense of relief in the United States was short-lived. Carranza professed to have at his command

[1] World Peace Foundation, *Pamphlet Series*, VI., No. 2, p. 88.
[2] *U. S. Statutes at Large*, XXXIX., pt. ii., p. 36.
[3] *Senate Jour.*, 64 Cong., 1 Sess., 6-7.

one hundred thousand men; but he proved wholly
unable to maintain order, and the northern states continued to be overrun by brigands, threatening such
American and other foreign interests as remained.
Villa kept up vigorous opposition; he was furious at
the recognition of Carranza and, with everything to
gain and nothing to lose, was ready to bring on a
general war of his country with the United States.
To this end he swept with a force of several hundred
bandits across the Rio Grande, and on March 9, 1916, fell
on the little town of Columbus, New Mexico, and inflict-
ed considerable losses of both life and property before
retreating into Chihuahua.[1]　This drove the American
government again to positive action.　On March 10
President Wilson announced that, "in aid of the constituted authorities of Mexico," and "with scrupulous
respect for the sovereignty of that republic," an adequate force would at once be sent in pursuit of Villa;
and General Funston, commander of the Southern
Department, was ordered to organize and despatch a
punitive expedition.　Carranza reluctantly gave his
consent.[2]

In army circles the proposed expedition was taken
very seriously.　Experience in the Philippines and elsewhere had shown how difficult a thing it is for American soldiers to operate in barren regions, among populations that take to brigandage.　Villa, although of
diminished prestige, was a military leader of remarkable adroitness.　The Mexican hatred of the "Grin-

[1] *Am. Year Book*, 1916, p. 312.
[2] *Am. Jour. Internat. Law*, X., Supplement, 179–184.

goes" (as Americans are called south of the Rio Grande) could be depended upon to solidify opposition. A general rising such as Villa planned was not inconceivable. Carranza's government, too, might collapse, or be influenced to throw itself into the anti-American cause.

As was predicted, the expedition was inglorious. On March 15 two columns, numbering six thousand men, moved across the New Mexican boundary under command of Brigadier-General Pershing. Other troops were sent in succeeding weeks to hold a line that in a month's time reached Parral, four hundred miles from the point of departure. It was a matter of no difficulty, however, for the bandits to keep out of reach. They knew the country perfectly; they had the sympathy of the inhabitants; and the small, swift-moving bands into which they broke risked only an occasional skirmish.

Meanwhile Carranza objected that neither his *de facto* government nor the local authorities of the invaded territory had been duly notified concerning the intention of the United States;[1] and wearisome negotiations followed in which the First Chief sought to limit the activity of Pershing's forces by agreements as to length of stay, zone of operations, and even the kinds of arms to be used. In driving Villa from the border, he urged, the object of the expedition had been attained; hence the troops should be called home.

Carranza's position was obviously difficult. To ac-

[1] *Am. Jour. Internat. Law*, X., Supplement, 185–186, 197–211.

cept the American expedition meant to link his name
with the detested foreigner and to give his rivals an
opportunity to proclaim themselves the real patriots,
who would resist invaders rather than join with them.
Yet flatly to oppose the American operations meant
to court the fate of Huerta. Months of exchanges of
notes brought no results. Each government held its
ground—Carranza insisting upon the withdrawal of
Pershing's columns, the United States demanding a
guarantee of border security as a condition of withdrawal. Conferences at El Paso, April 29 to May 11,
between Major-Generals Scott and Funston and General Obregon, Carranza's war minister, were of no avail.[1]

The American advance was halted at Parral; and
while the twelve thousand men on Mexican soil were
concentrated in small contingents for defense, fresh
regiments were sent to the border. In early May the
country was startled by a renewal of Villista raids in
Texas. A second punitive expedition penetrated Mexican territory one hundred and sixty-eight miles without encountering a single Mexican soldier.

The long-suffering authorities at Washington resolved upon a fresh step. It was clear that the fifteen-
hundred-mile border could not be protected by the
meager forces of the regular army. Hence on May 9,
1916, the President called into the service of the United
States the organized militia of Texas, New Mexico,
and Arizona; and on June 18 all of the states were requested to mobilize their forces. During the summer

[1] Marvin, "The First Line of Defense in Mexico," *World's Work*,
XXXII., 416–424.

20

about three-fourths of the militia thus called out were sent to the border, where they were assigned by General Funston to patrol duty. The remainder were kept in mobilization camps until October, when they were sent into service and an equivalent number were withdrawn and mustered out. On August 31 there were in the federal service 140,259 National Guardsmen (7,003 officers and 133,256 enlisted men); at the close of the year the forces on the border numbered approximately 110,000.[1]

The mobilization thoroughly tested the country's military system, and the results were far from satisfactory. Large numbers of men of family and business responsibilities were brought into action, while others who had not attained a high economic value were left at home. There was much distress among the families of guardsmen, and relief agencies had to be hurriedly set up. Almost two-thirds of the militiamen were practically without military training. Under a control divided between the nation and the states, the troops could not be properly fitted out and concentrated; three months after the call the units were without the equipment required for action in the field. Shortly before the call, Congress passed a National Defense Act (June 3),[2] inspired by the European war; and the work of mobilization was somewhat impeded by change to a new system. Nevertheless it was clear that the Guard was inherently defective as a line of defense.[3]

---

[1] Secretary of War, *Annual Report*, 1916, p. 11.   [2] See p. 387.

[3] Executive Committee of the Mayor's Committee on National Defense, *The Mobilization of the National Guard, 1916; its Economic and Military Aspects* (New York, 1917).

Hope of a general settlement was revived when, July 12, the Mexican government proposed that a joint commission should draw up a protocol covering the retirement of the American troops and the rights of each nation to send soldiers across the border for the punishment of wrong-doers. The offer was gladly accepted. Three commissioners were appointed on each side, and at meetings held at New London and Atlantic City the difficulties between the two countries were fully discussed. Midway in the course of the parley Carranza ordered his representatives to confine attention to the two subjects of the withdrawal of Pershing's forces and future border patrol. Hence a protocol signed November 24 stipulated only: (1) that Pershing's troops should be withdrawn in forty days from the ratification of the protocol by the two governments, provided American interests in the region of Chihuahua should then be deemed safe; (2) that each nation should provide for the patrol of its side of the boundary by its own armed forces; (3) that the commanders of these forces should be authorized to enter into co-operation against bandits "whenever it is possible."

Carranza hesitated, and finally refused, to approve these terms. He wanted immediate and unconditional withdrawal of the American troops. He wanted also a pledge that the United States would never again send troops into his country. The work of the Joint Commission was, therefore, fruitless. During the winter of 1916–1917, the skies seemed to clear somewhat. On December 2, a Constitutionalist "Congress," com-

posed of delegates elected by the people in every part
of the Mexican republic, convened at Querétaro to re-
vise the constitution of 1857. A wordy instrument was
signed January 31, 1917; it was announced to take
effect May 1; and in March Carranza was elected first
president (with a four-year term) under it.[1] Villa's
activities continued, but they were no longer directed
against the United States. In January the troops under
Pershing's command, after nine months of inactivity,
were brought back upon American soil, while the appearance of normal international relations was fur-
thered by the decision of the new American ambassador, Henry P. Fletcher, to take up his residence in
Mexico City.

The future, none the less, was filled with uncertainty. Villa's power was greater than at any previous
time; fresh attacks on the border were a daily possibility, and there was no prospect of relief from the burden of special patrol; three revolutionary movements,
aside from that led by Villa, were in progress; the new
constitution seemed to many to contain the seeds of
tyranny and fresh rebellion; the country continued
under the rule of a chieftain who had once set aside a
constitution, and who probably would not be averse to
doing so again. The general condition of the land and
people, furthermore, was pitiable. Upward of six years
had passed since the forced retirement of the aged

[1] *Nation*, Vol. 104, p. 571; Gallant, "Mexico's Constituent Congress,"
Review of Reviews, LV., 182–184; Branch, "The Mexican Con-
stitution of 1917 compared with the Constitution of 1857," Am. Acad.
Polit. and Soc. Sci., *Annals*, LXXI., Supplement.

president-dictator Diaz. In that time the country had known not a moment of real peace; large sections had been continuously in the grip of desperate civil war. Vast foreign interests which formerly supplied employment and paid taxes were destroyed. The populace, already poor, was reduced to utter wretchedness. Agriculture was abandoned; trade languished; hundreds of the inhabitants died of sheer starvation.

From its part in the tragic chapter the United States drew small satisfaction and scant credit. It incurred the suspicion or avowed enmity of all the Mexican factions. It shifted policies, and acted upon no apparent policy, to the amazement of Americans and foreigners alike. Twice its troops invaded the revolution-ridden country, only to be drawn back when real war threatened. Thousands of civilians were despatched to the frontier and kept there for months in idleness, to the hardship of themselves and their families. Life and property were but indifferently protected. There was reason for thinking that only the outbreak of the war in Europe in 1914 saved the nation from a position where either it would have been obliged to establish order in Mexico by drastic means or it would have been compelled to permit Great Britain, Germany, and other European powers to intervene for the protection of their nationals.

A redeeming fact was that the nation was able to convince the Central and South American peoples that its purposes were honest; so that the mutual confidence upon which genuine Pan-Americanism must be based, although sorely tested in other parts of the western hemisphere, was not impaired. In addition, the Administration succeeded in preventing a general war between the two countries. Provocation was strong; the investors were insistent; the President felt obliged to keep his mind clear by refusing so much as to talk with men who had personal interests at stake. Such a contest could not have contributed to a stable Mexican government, and it might have made annexation difficult or impossible to prevent. Nevertheless, at the end of five years Mexico was as far as ever from peace, and the United States was still uncertain as to how to deal with a tedious civil war within its nearest neighborhood.[1]

[1] Hart, *Monroe Doctrine*, 335.

CHAPTER XVII

THE PACIFIC AND ASIA

(1907–1917)

TWO sets of circumstances worked together to bring the United States, near the close of the nineteenth century, into the position of a world power. One centered about the Spanish war, and led to the annexation of Porto Rico, Guam, the Philippines, and indirectly Hawaii. The other flowed from an outburst of European aggressiveness in China after the defeat of that nation by Japan, and led to the announcement by Secretary Hay, in 1899, of the principles of the "open door."[1] Both gave fresh importance to our connections with the Orient.

After 1900 the nation energetically followed up its new opportunities and obligations. In that year it co-operated with Great Britain, France, Russia, and Japan in the relief of the Peking legation, besieged by the Boxers, and secured from all of the leading powers a pledge to respect the territorial integrity of the invaded country.[2] The navy was strengthened. The Panama Canal was begun. The Russo-Japanese conflict of 1904–1905 was watched with interest, and

[1] Latané, *America as a World Power* (*Am. Nation*, XXV.), 103; *Foreign Relations*, 1899, p. 142.
[2] Thayer, *Life and Letters of John Hay*, II., chap. ii.

305

the growing importance of the country as a Pacific power was shown by President Roosevelt's success in bringing the belligerents to work out a treaty of peace on American soil. By making a wholesome transformation of social and economic conditions in the Philippines, and by setting up a government there which opened a road for native ability and aspiration, the nation proved that its colonial system, despite charges of "imperialism," was of a different type from that generally prevailing in the dependent territories of the tropical world.

In the Orient there was one strong, progressive, ambitious nation—Japan. As a world power, the United States was obliged to cross the path of this little giant with increasing frequency; and for several years before the European war of 1914 the most disturbing aspects of our foreign relations sprang from our Japanese misunderstandings. The earlier relations of the two countries were very friendly. The service rendered by the United States in bringing the island empire into intercourse with the world was freely acknowledged. Her liberal attitude as to indemnities, tariffs, and extraterritoriality was gratefully remembered. The empire's commercial relations were closer with the United States than with any European country. Between the Chino-Japanese war of 1894–1895 and the Russo-Japanese conflict of 1904–1905—a troubled decade in the Far East—American and Japanese interests were usually in harmony; and in the last-mentioned contest the sympathies of the American people were strongly on the Japanese side.

After the Peace of Portsmouth this tradition of friendliness was put to severe test. The Japanese bearing of self-confidence cooled American enthusiasm. An attitude of aggression toward China engendered suspicion. Rivalry for trade expansion in the Pacific emphasized conflicts of interest. Most serious of all, the rights of Japanese immigrants in the Pacific coast states were brought into heated controversy.

The people of the far West had long believed that their section of the country was in danger of being flooded with Asiatics, and that unless repressive steps were taken they would be saddled with a permanent race problem like the negro question in the South. Exclusion acts wrung from Congress in 1880–1884 were a sufficient safeguard against the Chinese. By 1895, however, high wages began to attract Japanese and Korean laborers, many of whom reached the mainland after a sojourn in Hawaii. In 1900 there were in the coast states only 18,269 Japanese; but after 1903 the influx rose, and native laborers and shopkeepers seemed likely to be displaced on a large scale by orientals. Japanese capitalists, too, were seeking a footing in important industries. In this new form, the "yellow peril" stirred the coast communities profoundly. Organized labor set up a cry for exclusion; and the political leaders, the press, and a large part of the public gave hearty support. Race prejudice played its part, but the mainspring of the protest was the fear of economic competition.[1]

[1] Millis, "Economic Aspects of Japanese Immigration," *Am. Econ. Rev.*, V., 787–804.

On October 11, 1906, the board of education of San Francisco cast a brand into the tinder by passing a resolution that thereafter all Chinese, Japanese, and Korean pupils should be given instruction in an "oriental" school, and not, as previously, in the ordinary schools. Coming at a time when Japanese pride was more than usually exalted, this action was keenly resented. The Tokio authorities made inquiries, and then demanded that Japanese residents in California be protected in the full enjoyment of the rights guaranteed them by the treaty of 1894. In 1907 a tentative settlement was reached in a "gentleman's agreement" to the effect that San Francisco should admit to the ordinary schools oriental children not over sixteen years of age, while the Japanese authorities should withhold passports from laborers bound for the United States, except returning residents and members of their families. An order of President Roosevelt, March 14, 1907, issued under authority of a new immigration act, further restrained the immigration of oriental laborers; and within two years the number of Japanese annually entering the country was reduced to a tenth of its former proportions. February 24, 1911, the United States Senate ratified a new treaty of commerce and navigation with Japan,[1] which was accompanied by a Japanese note to the effect that the Mikado's government was "fully prepared to maintain with equal effectiveness the limitation and control which

[1] *U. S. Statutes at Large*, XXXVI., pt. ii., pp. 1504–1509; *Am. Jour. Internat. Law*, V., Supplement, 100–106; *Japanese Year Book*, 1915, pp. 565–568.

they have for the past three years exercised in regulation of emigration of laborers to the United States."

The real issue in 1906–1907 was not school attendance, but the right of the Japanese to migrate to the Pacific coast states and to enjoy there the same privileges as other aliens. Agitation therefore continued, and in 1913 it bore fruit in a bill introduced in the California legislature prohibiting the holding of land, through either purchase or lease, by aliens ineligible to citizenship under United States law. Several states, including New York and Texas, had laws unconditionally prohibiting ownership of real property by aliens. The Tokio authorities objected to the California proposal, however, on the ground that it was aimed solely at the Japanese (who under the naturalization laws were ineligible to citizenship), and that it was a discrimination in violation of the treaty of 1911. After asking in vain that the measure be modified, President Wilson sent Secretary Bryan to Sacramento to explain to the governor and legislature the views of the officials at Washington. Nevertheless, the legislature passed a substitute measure, known as the Webb alien land-holding bill, which received the governor's signature May 19, 1913.[1]

On its face, the bill passed was less offensive than its original, for it did not contain the phrase "ineligible to citizenship," which had been the basis of the Japanese protest. The real object was attained, however, by the provision that, whereas aliens eligible to citizenship should be allowed to acquire and hold land on

[1] *Statutes of Cal.*, 1913, chap. cxiii., 206–208.

the same terms as citizens, all other aliens should have only such landholding rights as should be guaranteed to them by treaty. No treaty with Japan conferred the right of land ownership; so that Japanese residents of the state, while continuing to be capable of owning real property used for residence or commercial purposes, and while permitted to lease land for a term not exceeding three years, were henceforth disqualified to become land-owners. Existing holdings were not affected.

The law was drawn to minimize legal objections.[1] Its effect, however, was to deny to Japanese residents rights which they, in common with other aliens, had hitherto possessed; and on this ground the Tokio government renewed its protest. The State Department urged that no rights were denied, and that, in any event, the courts were open for the adjudication of the question. But the Japanese authorities preferred to consider the situation on the plane of international and inter-racial honor and fair play; for the real source of their dissatisfaction was the stigma which was felt to have been placed upon the Japanese as a people by the refusal of the United States to admit Japanese settlers to citizenship.

The suggestion of a new treaty was eventually dropped; and after a fruitless exchange of notes, the controversy (overshadowed, from 1914, by the Euro-

---

[1] Collins, "Will the California Alien Land Law Stand the Test of the Fourteenth Amendment?" *Yale Law Jour.*, XXIII., 330–339; Dilla, "Constitutional Background of the Recent Anti-Alien Land Bill Controversy," *Mich. Law Rev.*, XII., 573–584.

pean war) languished. That in the course of time it
would be revived, nobody doubted. Indeed, in the
early months of 1917 the legislatures of Oregon, Idaho,
and one or two other Pacific states debated land-
holding measures resembling that which brought the
difficulty to a head in California.

Certain facts lent the situation an ominous aspect.
Japan and the United States must always confront
each other across the Pacific. Economic competition
between them was certain to increase. An outlet for
surplus population was for Japan a growing necessity.
The Japanese are a proud people, quick to resent any
hint that they are an inferior race. They are extraordinarily polite, and they expect unfailing courtesy
from those who undertake to deal with them as equals.
The events of 1906–1907 and 1913 revealed in both
countries a jingo press, as well as a tendency to indis-
creet and violent acts. Not a few sober-minded Americans were convinced that Japan, having triumphed first
over China, then over Russia, had chosen the United
States as her third great antagonist; and that through
conquests in Latin America, or in some other way, she
would bring on a conflict whenever the time seemed
ripe. Nervous persons recalled that never since the
modernization of her armies had the empire suffered
defeat.

Fortunately, there were offsets to these causes of
alarm. The official attitude of each government toward the other was always correct; diplomatic language
was careful and courteous. For a decade the "gentleman's agreement" was faithfully carried out, and it

yielded every immediate result that could have been attained by statutes or by treaty. The situation was saved by the fact that the Japanese plans for national development admitted of no heavy emigration to the United States; the end in view was rather colonization in Korea and elsewhere, under the Japanese flag. Furthermore, the United States was not alone in seeking to prevent the entrance of orientals; Australia and other British dominions had gone even further. If the country could discover some means of attaining its purpose without branding the Japanese as an inferior people, there was no reason—so far, at all events, as the immigration question was concerned—why earlier friendliness should not be restored. The old relation of mentor and pupil, however, could never be revived; for Japan had outgrown the need of tutelage.[1]

The center of conflicting national interests and policies in the Orient was China. Here the United States found new points of contact with Japan, and was likewise brought into important relations with all of the leading powers of Europe. Chinese affairs in the decade from 1907 group about two principal developments: (1) the revolution which in 1912 overthrew the Manchu dynasty and established a republic; (2) the estrangement from Japan, caused by Japanese aggressions on Chinese rights. In both the United States had deep concern.

The movement for political reform sprang from dissatisfaction aroused by the humiliating defeat of China by Japan in 1894–1895, and by the weakness and in-

[1] Treat, "Japan and America," *Review of Reviews*, LV., 398–401.

competence of the imperial government, especially as brought out by the concessions of territory to Germany, Russia, Great Britain, and France in 1898. The events of the troubled years 1898–1900 showed the need of new machinery of government, but scant headway was made by the reform party until after the Russo-Japanese war of 1904–1905. The cavalier manner in which the belligerents in that contest made Chinese soil the theatre of their hostilities stung the pride of a hitherto languid people, and finally produced a demand for reform as a means of stopping foreign encroachment and preserving national integrity.

In 1905 an imperial commission was appointed to study the governmental systems of Great Britain, Germany, and Japan; and on September 20, 1907, a decree was issued outlining a plan for a national assembly. The imperial court was rent by bitter conflict between the Chinese and Manchu factions. But preparations for the introduction of constitutionalism continued, and on August 27, 1908, it was announced that a parliamentary system would be installed within nine years. The death of the titular emperor, Kwang Hsu, and of the Empress Dowager, Tz'u Hsi (the real ruler) in November, 1908, removed the arch-opponents of the reform program. In 1909 provincial assemblies were held; and in 1910 appeared a provisional national assembly, or senate, which promptly assumed authority to make laws.

The impatience of the reformers hastened events; and in 1911 almost the whole of the empire was plunged in revolution against the ruling Manchu dynasty. At first the imperial party hoped to put off the inevitable by consenting to constitutional government. Before the close of 1911, however, Dr. Sun Yat Sen, a foreign-trained advocate of republicanism, was elected provisional president by a republican convention at Nanking; and early in 1912 the contending factions came to an agreement under which, on February 12, the infant Emperor Hsüan T'ung abdicated and the rule of the Manchus, which had covered a period of two hundred and sixty-eight years, was brought to a close. The nation was proclaimed a republic; Sun Yat Sen was forced to retire and the former minister Yuan Shih Kai was elected provisional president; the seat of the new government was removed from Nanking to Peking, and the historic yellow dragon gave way as a national emblem to a flag of five stripes symbolizing the five races composing the country's population.[1]

To put the new régime upon a secure basis was a very difficult task, and for four years the huge country wavered between republicanism and monarchy, between constitutionalism and reaction. Eventually the republic was saved, although by a hair's-breadth. The struggle was watched with deep interest in the United States. The idea of a great republic in Asia was appealing. Furthermore, the outcome was expected to determine whether China was to become strong enough to take a dignified position among the nations and defend the "open door." The authorities

[1] Text of provisional constitution in *Am. Jour. Internat. Law*, VI., Supplement, 149-154.

at Washington and the American minister in Peking
were active in protecting the interests of foreigners
during the revolution; a congratulatory resolution of
Congress (April 17, 1912) made the United States the
first nation to take official notice of what had occurred; and after 1911 American experts in government—at first, Frank J. Goodnow of Columbia University, and later, W. F. Willoughby of Princeton
University and W. W. Willoughby of Johns Hopkins
University—were present in Peking, by invitation of
the new government, as semi-official advisers on constitutional questions.

One of the republic's chief needs was funds. The
tax system was in chaos; treaties with foreign powers
forbade the customs duties to be placed higher than
five per cent.; the indemnity imposed in punishment
for the Boxer uprising of 1900 was largely unpaid, and
hung like a millstone about the nation's neck. Early
in 1912, therefore, Yuan Shih Kai's government approached the money-lenders of Europe and America
in quest of loans with which to meet operating expenses until an adequate tax system could be installed.
Three years earlier the Taft Administration had successfully backed up a demand of New York bankers
to share in loans which British, French, and German
capitalists were extending to China for railroads and
other enterprises; and it was assumed that American
monied interests would now take a prominent part in
financing the new government.

After extended conferences, bankers of six nations—
Great Britain, Germany, France, Russia, Japan, and

21

the United States—announced the conditions under which they would make a loan of $300,000,000; and participation by the American financiers was at the special request of the Administration. The purposes for which the money was to be used were to be approved by the lenders; the salt taxes were to be set apart for the service of the loan; and to safeguard the interests of investors these taxes were to be administered either by the existing Maritime Customs Service or by a separate service under foreign direction.[1] President Yuan Shih Kai objected to these conditions, on the ground that they infringed the sovereign rights of the republic; and ratification was further obstructed by the radical party in the National Assembly.

Before arrangements could be agreed upon, President Taft was succeeded by President Wilson. The new executive frowned on the American connection with the loan; and in March, 1913, after a conference of Secretary Bryan with leading New York bankers, it was announced from the White House that the United States would not accept any responsibility for the enterprise. The American banks thereupon withdrew from the consortium; so that when, April 25, a loan of $125,000,000 was actually made, representatives of only the five remaining powers shared in it. Thus in the Orient, as in Latin America, Wilson definitely repudiated the "dollar diplomacy" of his predecessor. His fear was that the proposed co-operation between the American and European money-lenders would force the United States into action which would destroy

[1] *Am. Year Book*, 1912, p. 95.

Chinese confidence in her friendship; and he was not moved by the argument that the people that was most liberal in supplying funds for China's development would gain the largest share in shaping the destinies of the new nation. In 1916 the Chinese government, none the less, borrowed in the United States the sum of $5,000,000 as the first instalment of a purely American loan of $30,000,000, to be secured by the wine and tobacco taxes, and to be used in the promotion of industries. The Administration saw no political entanglements in this project and interposed no objections.

There was hope that as a result of her reconstruction China would become more able to defend herself against foreign aggression. The period of transition was, however, one of weakness, and in its dealings abroad the republic was obliged to thread its way through perilous waters. The chief source of difficulty was Japan, and the chief theatre of dispute was Manchuria.

The Japanese looked upon themselves as high-minded liberators who had saved China from servitude to the Europeans, and who, as teachers and guides, were to lead the Chinese people out of their inefficiency and helplessness. The Chinese took a very different view. They knew that the Japanese civilization had been drawn almost entirely from Chinese sources, and they had always regarded the Japanese people as inferior and even tributary. They felt that it was the Japanese who, in the war of 1894, first exposed their weakness to the world. They recalled that it was Japan that deprived them of Formosa and their ancient suzerainty over Korea. They regarded the Japanese rôle in the war of 1904–1905 as entirely selfish. They accused the Japanese (as well as the Russians) of violating the treaty of Portsmouth by using their Manchurian railways for political and strategic ends. They suspected the Tokio statesmen of intending, by one means or another, to acquire for Japan paramount authority in Manchuria, and perhaps in still other regions under Chinese sovereignty.[1] A convention of September 4, 1909, adjusted certain disputes between the two countries;[2] but the settlement was favorable chiefly to Japan, and bad feeling in China continued.

Throughout the years when the new Chinese régime hung in the balance the government of the United States was watchful; and it lost no opportunity to bring afresh to the attention of Japan, and of the world, its strict adherence to the principles enunciated by Secretary Hay. Already, in December, 1909, Secretary Knox had submitted to China, Japan, and the four European states most interested in Oriental affairs, a proposal that the railroads of Manchuria be turned over to China and placed in the hands of a national syndicate, which should develop them for commercial rather than political purposes.[3] The suggestion was nowhere received with enthusiasm, and Japan and Russia flatly rejected it. At Tokio it was declared that the "open door" would be maintained,

[1] Coolidge, *United States as a World Power*, 367.
[2] *Am. Jour. Internat. Law*, IV., Supplement, 130–133.
[3] *Foreign Relations*, 1910, pp. 231–269.

but that Knox's proposal looked to an impossible change in the arrangements established by the Portsmouth treaty. A Russo-Japanese convention of July 4, 1910, designed to "maintain the *status quo* in Manchuria," was widely interpreted as, in effect, an answer of the two contracting powers to the attempt of the United States to deprive them of advantages which they considered to be rightfully theirs.[1]

At the outbreak of the European war in 1914 President Yuan Shih Kai issued a proclamation of neutrality and appealed to President Wilson to use his influence to prevent the spread of hostilities to Asia. But all hope of such immunity disappeared when Japan decided to enter the contest. Under the Anglo-Japanese alliance of 1902, as renewed in 1905 and 1911, Japan was bound to take up arms only if Great Britain were attacked in the Far East. There was no such attack. None the less, the Tokio government chose to present to Germany, August 15, an ultimatum demanding the immediate withdrawal of armed vessels from Japanese and Chinese waters, and the delivery to Japanese officials, not later than September 15, and "without condition or compensation," of the leased territory of Kiao-chow, "with a view to the eventual restoration of the same to China." No reply was received, and on August 23 war was declared. Four days later the siege of Tsing-tao, capital of Kiao-chow, was begun. The fortress was taken, November 7, by combined Japanese and British forces; and soon the whole of the German leased territory fell into Japanese

[1] *Am. Jour. Internat. Law*, IV., Supplement, 279.

hands, together with the German islands in the Pacific.

Japan's real motive for entering the war was to gain economic, if not also political, advantage in China, and to make good her claim to a Japanese "Monroe Doctrine" for Asia. China was potentially a fabulously rich market, and a main object of Japanese commercial policy had long been to secure the greatest possible share of the huge country's fast-growing trade. Already in 1914 seventeen per cent. had been captured, and Japanese cottons, tobaccos, drugs, matches, and other manufactures were being borne by heavily subsidized steamers to every Chinese coastal and inland port. While the European powers were occupied with the war, reasoned the Tokio statesmen, Japan could gain so great a hold on her neighbor that those powers would be obliged eventually to accept it; if they demurred, she could draw an unanswerable argument from her assistance against Germany.

To China, therefore, Japan's entry into the war boded ill. Through Premier Okuma and Ambassador Chinda, the Tokio authorities assured the United States that they had in view no action which "could give to a third party any cause of anxiety or uneasiness regarding the safety of their territories or possessions," and that they had "no thought of depriving China or any other people of anything which they now possess."[1] At Washington this avowal was taken as made in good faith, and Secretary Bryan expressed satisfaction that the integrity of China and the "open door"

[1] *Am. Year Book*, 1914, p. 99; *Independent*, LXXIX., 291.

for commerce were to be respected. Peking, however, doubted the sincerity of the statement; and when Japanese troops destined for the siege of Tsing-tao were sent across Chinese soil from the port of Lungkow, without permission being asked, and in flagrant violation of the nation's neutrality, suspicion grew to indignation.[1] Protest was unavailing, because there was no power to back it up.

The Chinese sense of impending disaster was soon proved unerring. January 18, 1915, the Japanese minister at Peking, Hioki Eki, handed to Yuan Shih Kai a document setting forth twenty-one demands made upon China by the Tokio government. To meet them meant vassalage; for they looked to thorough-going domination of the republic's political and economic affairs, and a wave of indignation swept the country. Great Britain, Russia, and other European powers were perturbed. Japan, however, was the ally of these powers, and war necessity prevented forceful protest. The United States informed both Japan and China that it would not recognize any agreement infringing its treaty rights or impairing China's territorial integrity. Assurances on these points having been obtained, no further official action was taken. Meanwhile, Chino-Japanese negotiations were entered upon; and when the Peking government hesitated to accept a revised list of demands *in toto*, it was confronted, May 7, with an ultimatum allowing only forty-eight hours for a decision on four of the five groups in which the demands were now arranged. Resistance was useless, and the

[1] Jones, *The Fall of Tsing-tao*, 45–48; *Far Eastern Rev.*, XII., 100.

authorities yielded (May 8), pathetically expressing the hope that by their action all outstanding questions would be settled, "so that the cordial relationship between the two countries may be further consolidated."[1]

Rarely has a nation realized larger gains from a successful war than Japan now achieved at the expense of China by diplomatic manœuvers, backed up with threats. For in two treaties, accompanied by thirteen exchanges of notes (signed May 25 and ratified June 9) she acquired full liberty to dispose of all German rights and privileges in the province of Shantung, and to engage in the economic exploitation of South Manchuria and Eastern Inner Mongolia; while China agreed: (1) not to cede or lease to a third power any harbor, bay, or island along her coast; (2) not to permit a foreign power to build a ship-yard, naval station, or any other military establishment on the coast of the province of Fuhkien (opposite Formosa); (3) not herself to undertake such construction with foreign capital. The leases of Port Arthur and Tairen (Dalny) and of the South Manchurian Railway, acquired by Japan from Russia in 1905, were extended from 1923 to 1997 and from 1938 to 2002, respectively.[2]

After the settlement, Japan did not cease to insist that she had no purpose to end Chinese independence, to infringe the "open door," or to interfere with the

---

[1] *Chinese Official History of the Recent Sino-Japanese Treaties*, 18; Text and correspondence in *Am. Jour. Internat. Law*, X., Supplement, 1–18. Cf. North, "The Negotiations between Japan and China in 1915," *ibid.*, X., 222–237.

[2] Iyenaga, "The Chino-Japanese Treaties," *Review of Reviews*, LII., 338–342; Rae, *Analysis of the Chino-Japanese Treaties* (1915).

rights of any other power. But her protestations were of little effect. China was bitterly resentful; Great Britain developed a perceptible coolness; the United States found increased difficulty in restraining the anti-Japanese sentiment already aroused by the Pacific coast controversies. Fresh demands upon the Peking government in 1916, concerning the affairs of Eastern Inner Mongolia, intensified the general apprehension.

Early in 1917 China broke with Germany, and threatened to take some part in the world war. The decision was momentous, for it meant that China would be entitled to a place at the council-board where the conditions of peace should be worked out; Japan was not to be allowed to speak for her. From this vantage-point she could hope to secure a full review of the Oriental situation, and to obtain relief from some of the intolerable obstacles to her progress as a modernized nation, especially the Boxer indemnity, extraterritoriality, and the Japanese menace.[1] The step was taken largely at the instance of the United States, which thus assumed an obligation to do everything within reason to see that the results were favorable to China.

Meanwhile Japan's position was strengthened by a new Russo-Japanese treaty (July 3, 1915), setting up a defensive alliance between these two powers.[2] Each pledged itself not to be a party to any "arrangement or political combination" directed against the other; and the two agreed to act in concert in the event that the

[1] *Nation*, Vol. 104, p. 453.

[2] *Japan Times*, July 9, 1916; *Am. Jour. Internat. Law*, X., Supplement, 239-241.

reorganized "territorial rights or special interests" of
either in the Far East should be menaced. This alliance, which was received enthusiastically in Japan,
was perhaps hastened by the co-operation of the two
nations in the war against the central powers of Europe.
But it was the logical culmination of a *rapprochement*
which began not long after the war of 1904–1905; and
the treaty of July 4, 1910, for the maintenance of the
status quo in Manchuria, was a step toward it.[1] It
realized the dream of Prince Ito, who conceived the
idea of a Russo-Japanese alliance even before the Anglo-
Japanese alliance of 1902, and it looked to friendliness
with Russia as the guiding factor in Japanese diplomacy for decades to come.

On its face, the new arrangement did not affect
American interests. Assurances were given by both
of the contracting powers that it was in no wise designed to interfere with the "open door" in China. In
so far as it might react unfavorably on any western
nation, that nation was expected to be Great Britain.
The alliance, however, made it doubly sure that any
American investment or other enterprise in Manchuria would have to recognize the preponderating
interests of Japan and Russia in that region.[2] More
than that, it indicated that Japan's grip on Chinese
affairs would be harder to break than had been expected, and that America's Japanese problem lay in
China, not California.

[1] *Foreign Relations*, 1910, p. 835.
[2] Kawakami, "The Far East after the War," *Review of Reviews*, LV.,
176–179.

CHAPTER XVIII

NEUTRAL RIGHTS

(1914–1916)

THE storm of general war broke in 1914 upon a world which, in the face of tremendous forces of misunderstanding and hate, was struggling toward universal and permanent peace; and the shock was the more severe because many people had fondly supposed that the goal was not far off. In point of fact, the generation that saw all Europe fly to arms was already steeped in warfare. Ignoring local and petty contests, the two decades from 1894 to 1914 witnessed not fewer than ten great wars, involving twenty-three important states and affecting every quarter of the globe. The nations, furthermore, were in these years piling up armaments on a grander scale than ever before, and keen observers could not shake off the apprehension that Europe, if not the entire world, was approaching a cataclysm.

Along with this resurgence of belligerency, and springing largely from protest against it, was a steady growth of international-mindedness, and of the ideas and agencies that make for peace. Proposals to disarm or to restrict armaments proved unavailing; although Great Britain went so far in 1913 as to suggest to the nations generally, and to Germany in particular, a cessation of naval construction for a year. Yet there were positive gains, in two main directions: an improved understanding among the nations as to the principles and rules of international law, and increased emphasis on international arbitration. Both of these developments were greatly aided by the Hague peace conferences of 1899 and 1907.[1]

In the peace movement the United States took a prominent part. It was ably represented in both of the Hague conferences, where its influence was strong; the second conference, indeed, was called at the instigation of President Roosevelt. Andrew Carnegie, Edwin Ginn, and other wealthy Americans furnished large sums for "foundations" to investigate and urge forward the interests of peace. Lectureships were established; local and national societies were formed or revived; peace literature was given wide circulation. Of largest practical importance was the willingness of the country to submit its difficulties with other nations to arbitration, and to take the lead in fortifying and extending the arbitration principle.

At the first Hague conference the United States and Great Britain secured a convention under which was set up the Hague Tribunal, not strictly a court, but a panel or list of judges (each signatory appointing from one to four) from which courts might be formed, by agreement of the nations concerned, to hear cases as they arose. The first cause argued before the new tribunal—the Pious Fund Case, in 1902[2]—was car-

[1] Latané, *America as a World Power* (*Am. Nation*, XXV.), 242–254.
[2] *Senate Docs.*, 57 Cong., 2 Sess., No. 28.

ried there by the United States; and of the twelve
cases decided prior to 1912, three involved controversies
to which the United States was a party. The most
notable was the North Atlantic Fisheries Case, decided
in 1910. Besides providing an arbitration tribunal,
the first Hague conference drew up a model arbitration
treaty which the nations were encouraged to put into
operation, and in 1908–1909 the United States became
a party to some twenty-five agreements of the kind.[1]

William J. Bryan brought to the office of secretary
of state in 1913 deep convictions on the subject
of international peace. His main idea was that
under modern conditions of communication the chief
danger of war arises from precipitateness; and the
remedy seemed to lie in some guarantee of delay, so
as to give a chance for deliberation and for attempts
at amicable settlement. The existing arbitration
treaties were only partial safeguards, and President
Wilson readily concurred in Bryan's plan to supplement them with a new set of agreements.

The means selected as most likely to keep fire from
the powder-barrel was the commission of inquiry, a
device favorably regarded by the first Hague conference, warmly advocated by Bryan and others at a
meeting of the Interparliamentary Union at London
in 1906, and formulated in the conventions adopted at
The Hague in 1907. On April 24, 1913, the President
submitted to all governments having diplomatic repre-

[1] Texts in *Am. Jour. Internat. Law*, II., Supplement, 330-337, and
in *U. S. Statutes at Large*, XXXV., passim. Cf. Taft, *The United
States and Peace*, chap. iii.

sentatives at Washington a proposal that each should enter into agreement with the United States to submit, upon the failure of diplomatic efforts, "all questions of whatever character and nature in dispute between them" for investigation and report to an international commission, and should bind themselves not to declare war or begin hostilities until the report should have been presented, although reserving the right to act independently thereafter. A memorandum of the Secretary of State suggested that the period allowed for the investigation should be one year; that during this interval neither contracting state should alter its military or naval program unless threatened with attack by a third power; and that the commission should consist of five members, two chosen by each contracting country (one from its own citizens and one from abroad) and the fifth selected by the governments concurrently.

The plan was so well received that by the close of the year thirty-one nations, including all of the principal powers of the world, signified a willingness to accept. The first treaty on these lines was concluded with the little republic of Salvador, August 7, 1913.[1] Within a few months a score of such treaties were signed, and until interrupted by the outbreak of the European war in 1914 the work proceeded rapidly.[2]

Although long on the way, the war of 1914 plunged Europe into destruction and death with amazing quickness. On July 23 peace was apparently as secure as

[1] Myers, "The Commission of Inquiry: the Wilson-Bryan Peace Plan," World Peace Foundation, *Pamphlet Series*, III., No. xi.
[2] *Am. Jour. Internat. Law*, X., Supplement, 263–309.

in many years.   Ten days later, six nations were drawing the sword, as many more were at the brink of
hostilities, and terror was spread throughout the world.
Passion ran too swiftly to brook delay; the Hague
conferences and all their works were forgotten or
ignored.   The people of America were stunned.   At
their distance, they had failed to perceive the under-
current of belligerency which of late had disturbed the
chancelleries of Europe.[1]   But they were swift to see
that the conflict brought them into a new position and
thrust upon them alarming problems and tasks.

Some persons urged from the start that the cause
of democracy and of civilization was so closely bound
up with the fortunes of the Entente nations that it
was the moral duty of the United States to join these
powers in arms.   But the country as a whole saw no
possible course save neutrality, a policy dictated alike
by present interest and by a century and a quarter of
consistent practice.   August 4, when five nations had
entered the war, President Wilson issued a formal
proclamation of neutrality, which was repeated as
successive states entered the contest;[2]   and two weeks
later he made a special appeal to his fellow-citizens
to be neutral in word and act.[3]

No less could have been asked.   Yet the demand
made upon the national powers of self-restraint was
very great.   The United States was in large part an

[1] Turner, "Causes of the Great War," *Am. Polit. Sci. Rev.*, IX.,
16–35.
[2] *U. S. Statutes at Large*, XXXVIII., pt. ii., pp. 1999–2002; *Am.
Jour. Internat. Law.*, IX., Supplement, 110–114.
[3] *U. S. Statutes at Large*, XXXVIII., pt. ii., pp. 2011–2015.

immigrant nation. Of the hundred million people in the country at the outbreak of the war, one-third were foreign-born or born of foreign parentage. These newer elements were mainly German, Irish, Slavic, Jewish, and Italian; fully one-fourth were German. The mass of the older elements, on the other hand, were of English descent or fairly assimilated to an American amalgam which was predominantly English.

The sympathies which the conflict aroused everywhere were intensified in the United States by passionate feelings born of racial kinships, family relationships, and rekindled patriotisms. To the mass of the people, especially in the eastern sections of the country, the cause of the Entente nations made powerful appeal. Germany's violation of Belgian neutrality was denounced; her harsh methods of warfare were abhorred; the Teutonic powers were considered to be the aggressors, and their interests and aims to be those of autocracy and militarism; acts of violence in the United States, traceable to pro-German propaganda, were resented; the man in the street felt instinctively that a triumphant Germany would be a menace to the United States. Individuals, societies, the press, the pulpit, did not hesitate to avow sympathy with the Entente cause and to denounce the Teutonic warfare as iniquitous. Equally outspoken, and even readier to overstep the bounds of neutral conduct in the opposite direction, were partisans of the Teutonic powers, found chiefly among the German-American population.

Majority sentiment supported the government in its efforts to curb German aggressions, and urged a more vigorous anti-German policy; a less extensive but more noisy sentiment applauded every protest against British aggressions, and demanded a directly anti-British policy. At all stages of the contest to 1917—although in diminishing degree as months passed—the public mind was divided on lines of foreign policy in a fashion reminiscent of the days of Washington and the elder Adams.

Under these conditions the enforcement of a strict neutrality became very difficult. The chief problems arose from the pro-German demand for an embargo on munitions, and from a series of acts of violence intended to frustrate the government's well-reasoned policy of permitting the exportation of munitions under the usual rules of international law. As matters stood, the Entente powers were reaping from their control of the seas the tremendous advantage of being able, as their opponents were not, to import munitions from America in unlimited quantities; and it is not surprising that all of the resources of Teutonic argument, organization, and diplomacy were brought to bear to overcome the handicap. It was passionately urged that by permitting the munitions trade the United States was taking a moral responsibility for prolonging the struggle; and no effort was spared to capitalize American resentment of British trade restrictions. The argument chiefly employed, however, was that while the sale of munitions to belligerents by citizens of a neutral state is fully sanctioned by international law, exportation from America under existing circumstances worked to the benefit of the combatants on only one

22

side, and was therefore unneutral. In notes of April 4 and June 29, 1915, the Berlin and Vienna governments pressed this point with all possible ingenuity.[1]

Sound objections could be brought against the trade in munitions, but the contention that it was unneutral failed to carry conviction. It was easy to point out that the American munitions markets were open to the Central Powers on precisely the same terms as to the Entente Allies; that it was not the fault of the United States that those nations were unable to avail themselves of their privileges; that in the Boer, Russo-Japanese, and Balkan wars Germany had followed the course against which she now protested; that the United States could not reasonably be expected in time of war to arrogate the power to alter well-established international usage. As was explained by Secretary Lansing in his reply to the Austrian protest, August 12, 1915, the United States, accustomed to rely on small defensive forces and on the right and power to purchase arms and ammunition from neutral nations in case of foreign attack, was the last nation in the world that could afford to establish a precedent of the kind that was asked.[2]

The refusal of the government to modify its attitude was followed by a campaign of violence, intended to check by direct action the manufacture and exportation

[1] World Peace Foundation, *Pamphlet Series*, V., No. 4, pt. iii., 131–133, 136–139.
[2] *Ibid.*, 139–145; Morey, "The Sale of Munitions of War," *Am. Jour. Internat. Law*, X., 467–491; Gregory, "Neutrality and the Sale of Arms," *ibid.*, 543–555.

of munitions. Incendiary fires destroyed or damaged munitions plants; bombs were concealed aboard British, French, and Italian merchant-vessels, and several ships were damaged or sunk; strikes were fomented among seamen and employees of arms and ammunition factories. Responsibility for these acts was often impossible to fix; but several German and Austrian conspirators were convicted; and in 1915 the Austro-Hungarian ambassador, Dr. Dumba, was dismissed, on admission that he had been concerned in a plan to cripple munitions factories, and especially the Bethlehem Steel Company's works, by a general strike. Similar activities led to the forced recall of the German military and naval *attachés* at Washington, Captain Franz von Papen and Captain Karl Boy-Ed.[1]

The most stupendous task imposed upon the government by the war was the defense of the rights of the country and of its citizens as neutrals. The portions of the world with which the nation had most to do were divided into two great camps, each bent on reducing the other to powerlessness, and not at all scrupulous about the interests of the bystander. The situation was therefore much like that during the era of Napoleon. But the present struggle was more desperate, its methods were more deadly, and the more extended ramification of business and other connections which had grown up during the hundred years enmeshed neutrals more completely. The chief difficulties related to commerce and to the safety of American citizens on the high seas; and the belligerents who

[1] *Am. Jour. Internat. Law*, X., Supplement (special no.), 361–366.

were responsible for them were mainly Great Britain
and Germany.

Great Britain's first object in the war was to sweep
German shipping from the seas. This accomplished,
the next purpose was to starve out the Central Powers
by cutting them off from all connection with the outside world. This was less easy; for while direct trade
could be prevented, indirect trade could readily be carried on through the Baltic countries and other neutral
territories adjacent to the Teutonic states. The trade
of the United States and other neutrals with these border countries rapidly mounted; large quantities of the
goods imported were undoubtedly trans-shipped, over-
land or across waters under Teutonic control, to Germany and Austria.

To meet this situation the British government took
drastic measures. The first was to put pressure on
the neutrals contiguous to the enemy, to secure from
them embargoes on shipments of munitions, foodstuffs,
and other supplies to Germany and Austria. A second
was to enlarge, by successive orders in council, the
contraband schedules authorized by the Declaration
of London of 1911.[1] Cotton, copper, and scores of
other articles were placed on the list, and finally foodstuffs, on the theory (which was not well founded) that
all foodstuffs in Germany had been brought under
government control, and therefore "militarized." A
third expedient was the extension of the doctrine of
"continuous voyage" to conditional contraband, to-

[1] World Peace Foundation, *Pamphlet Series*, V., No. 3, pt. ii., Ap-
pendix I.

gether with a widening of the grounds for presumption of hostile destination.

Under the accepted usages of war, the end sought in these measures was legitimate. The measures themselves, however, were arbitrary, novel, and from the neutral point of view indefensible. The inconveniences and losses suffered by neutral trade were serious, and on December 26, 1914, the United States lodged formal protest.[1] The tortuous diplomacy that followed cannot here be traced. After a conciliatory preliminary reply, the British Foreign Minister, Sir Edward Grey, submitted, February 10, 1915, a detailed argument to the effect that British naval operations were not the cause of any falling-off in the volume of American exports, and that the British policy and practice were fully consistent with the rules of international law and with a due regard for the interests of the United States and other neutrals.[2]

Hope of relaxation of British restrictive policy was diminished by a fresh turn of events. Stirred to unbounded indignation by the measures taken against her, Germany resolved upon a bold course of retaliation, and on February 4, 1915, proclaimed the waters around the British Isles to be a "war zone," in which, after February 18, enemy merchant-vessels would be destroyed at sight and neutral vessels would be exposed to grave dangers.[3] The avowed purpose was

[1] World Peace Foundation, *Pamphlet Series*, V., No. 4, pt. ii., 87–91; *Am. Jour. Internat. Law*, IX., Supplement (special no.), 1–22.

[2] World Peace Foundation, *Pamphlet Series*, V., No. 4, pt. ii., 98–115; *Am. Jour. Internat. Law*, IX., Supplement (special no.), 65–83.

[3] World Peace Foundation, *Pamphlet* Series, V., No. 4, pt. i., 32.

a submarine campaign which would cut off the British, even as the British were seeking to cut off the Germans, from foreign supplies of munitions and foodstuffs.

The neutral world received the announcement with apprehension; a warfare of commercial decrees, like that of Napoleonic times, was clearly foreshadowed. An American note of February 10 warned Germany that should her submarine commanders destroy on the high seas an American vessel or the lives of American citizens, she would be held to "strict accountability."[1] The reply, February 16, was polite, but it affirmed that the Empire was "obliged to answer Great Britain's murderous method of naval warfare with sharp countermeasures"; and all responsibility for "accidents" to neutral vessels in the war zone was again disclaimed.[2]

Still hopeful of averting disaster, Secretary Bryan addressed to the German and British governments, February 20, identic notes suggesting a compromise: Germany was to abandon her submarine campaign, and Great Britain to remit her restrictions on the importation of foodstuffs for the consumption of the German civilian population.[3] In a note of March 1 Germany gave a qualified acceptance. Great Britain, however, refused,[4] and on March 11 advanced another stage in her restrictive policy by issuing a series of regulations tantamount to a general blockade of the German Empire, and carrying the doctrine of continuous voyage so far as to impose on the shippers of

[1] World Peace Foundation, *Pamphlet Series*, V., No. 4, pt.i., 38–40; *Am. Jour. Internat. Law*, IX., Supplement (special no.), 86–88.
[2] *Ibid.*, 90–96.   [3] *Ibid.*, 97–99.
[4] World Peace Foundation, *Pamphlet Series*, V., No. 4, pt. i., 55–59.

all goods to Holland and the Scandinavian countries the burden of proving, on peril of confiscation, that the goods were not destined for Germany. On account of the control of the Baltic by Germany, the so-called blockade could not be made applicable to the Baltic ports directly. Hence it was devised and enforced on novel lines, and in such manner as to embrace many neutral ports and coasts capable of serving as approaches to the German seats of trade.

Throughout the summer of 1915 the American government confined its attention largely to negotiations with Germany on the injuries suffered from the submarine campaign. But on October 21 Secretary Lansing despatched to London a lengthy and carefully prepared reply to the British notes of preceding months, registering fresh protest against infringements on the neutral commercial rights of American citizens. The British blockade was held to be "ineffectual, illegal, and indefensible," and a protest was made against a recent ruling under which American shipowners were compelled to seek redress in British prize courts rather than through diplomatic channels. The British authorities refused to shift their ground, and during the remainder of the war the American government was obliged to content itself as best it might with the knowledge that its carefully drawn protests would form a basis for reclamation at the return of peace.

The issue with Great Britain involved only property; that with Germany involved both property and life. The use of the submarine in war was a novelty. Some delegates at the first Hague conference, in 1899, suggested that it be prohibited. Action was not taken; but no one expected the new type of craft to be used save against enemy war-vessels. Under her war-zone decree, however, Germany now turned her numerous and unexcelled submersible craft against enemy merchant shipping. The new policy became at once a source of hardly less concern to the United States than to the Entente belligerents.

In the first place, vessels were attacked without due regard for their nationality. One of the earliest victims was an oil-steamer, the *Gulflight*, which flew the American flag; and of the sixty-three merchant ships torpedoed during the first ten weeks, many were of neutral status. No less serious was the loss of American life caused by the destruction of belligerent ships. Most belligerent vessels carried Americans, whether as passengers or as members of crews, or both; and the first important British ship torpedoed, the *Falaba*, sunk in St. George's Channel, March 28, bore to his death an American engineer. The crowning defiance of human rights was the sinking of the Cunard liner *Lusitania* off the Irish coast, May 7, 1915. Of 1,917 souls on board, 1,153 were lost; and among them were 114 American men, women, and children. This event stunned the world; and scattered voices raised by pro-German enthusiasts in the United States in defense of the act were drowned in a mighty outpouring of indignation.[1]

The submarine campaign was intended to put Great Britain, in effect, in a state of blockade. This it failed to do. The number of sub-sea craft was not sufficient;

---

[1] *N. Y. Times Current History*, II., 413–447.

and despite a loss of two million tons of shipping in
the first two years of the war, the volume of British
foreign trade was not appreciably diminished. The
whole policy had small effect save to arouse in the Eng-
lishman a grimmer determination and to bring down
upon Germany the wrath of the neutral world, and
eventually the open hostility of the United States.
Notwithstanding all protests and failures, the campaign was not abandoned, save temporarily and to
meet the purposes of German military convenience.

With the sinking of the *Lusitania*, the diplomatic situation arising from submarine warfare became critical.
Outraged American feeling demanded instant and complete redress. But the German government, buoyed
by national exultation over a signal triumph of naval strategy, was not in a repentant mood, and much
caution was required to avert an open rupture. Until
now the United States had urged that submarines
should be employed against shipping only in so far
as they could be made to act under the rules of international law relating to cruisers. Thus they might be
used to enforce the right of visit and search, but not
to capture and destroy vessels without giving warning,
or without providing opportunity for crew and passengers to escape.[1] But in the first of a series of notes
on the *Lusitania* affair (May 13) President Wilson declared, through Secretary Bryan, that it was "a practical impossibility" to use submarines *in any way* in
the destruction of commerce without disregarding

---

[1] Note of February 20, 1915. *Am. Jour. Internat. Law*, IX., Supplement (special no.), 97.

"rules of fairness, reason, justice, and humanity which all modern opinion regards as imperative. He called upon the German government to disavow the acts of its submarine commanders by which American lives had been placed in jeopardy, to make all possible reparation, and to take immediate steps to prevent their recurrence. The American government, he added, would not be expected "to omit any word or any act necessary to the performance of its sacred duty of maintaining the rights of the United States and its citizens and of safeguarding their free exercise and enjoyment."[1]

The German reply was unsatisfactory. It expressed regret for the loss of American life; but on various grounds—chiefly the fact that the submarine was the only weapon which the Imperial government was in a position to use in the destruction of munitions destined for the enemy—most of the acts complained of were justified as being necessary to self-defense.[2] Reparation for the mistaken attack on the *Gulflight* was promised; on the larger issue of the *Lusitania* no satisfaction was forthcoming.

A second note, drafted by President Wilson, June 9, set forth the American demands anew. It was courteous and statesmanlike, but rather than despatch it Secretary Bryan resigned the portfolio of state.[3] It was received with evasions and fair words.[4] A third and final note, July 21, pronounced the German replies "very unsatisfactory," characterized the sinking of the

---

[1] *Am. Jour. Internat. Law*, IX., Supplement (special no.), 129-133.
[2] *Ibid.*, 133-136.   [3] *Ibid.*, 138-141.   [4] *Ibid.*, 149-153.

Lusitania as "a needless destruction of human life by an illegal act," and asserted that repetition of such acts must be regarded by the United States, when affecting American citizens, as "deliberately unfriendly."[1] To these representations no response was made. In deference, however, to a growing feeling that the friendship of the United States should not be wholly sacrificed, the German government issued to commanders instructions not to sink liners without warning. Accordingly, when, August 19, the British steamer *Arabic* was sunk unwarned, with the loss of two American lives, the act was disavowed and apology offered.[2]

Cessation of submarine activities in British waters in the autumn of 1915 raised hopes that the controversies between the American and German governments would promptly be settled, and that no fresh ones would arise. This hope, however, was dashed by three developments in the early months of 1916: (1) the failure of the later *Lusitania* negotiations; (2) the German-Austrian decision to treat armed merchantmen as war-vessels; (3) the renewal of submarine warfare, marked by the sinking of the French Channel steamer *Sussex*. In the negotiations on the *Lusitania* affair, carried on by Secretary Lansing and the German ambassador, Count von Bernstorff, the United States demanded three things: (1) disavowal of the sinking of the vessel, or admission that the act was illegal; (2) payment of indemnity, and reparation for the loss of American lives and property; (3) a promise that no

[1] *Am. Jour. Internat. Law*, IX., Supplement (special no.), 155–157.
[2] *Ibid.*, X., Supplement (special no.), 172–173.

further attacks of the kind would be made. At one
stage, the Berlin government was ready to meet the
last two points. But on the first it could not be won
over; and the interchange of views dragged through
the year without result. When, in April, 1917, war
was declared between the two nations, a settlement
was as far off as ever.

The government of the United States tried to induce
the Entente Allies to give up their practice of arming
merchant-vessels, on condition that the Teutonic powers
would agree to adhere strictly to the rules of international law concerning unarmed merchant craft.[1]
The effort failed. Great Britain insisted that her merchant ships were armed only for defense and that they
were "merely peaceful traders" and would never make
attacks.[2] Germany, however, stood for the theory
that a merchant vessel, by being armed, "assumes a
warlike character," and charged that the British ships
actually carried on offensive operations.[3] On this
ground she sought to justify the announcement of
February 10 that after February 29 all armed merchantmen of the enemy would be dealt with as war-
vessels. This meant that they would be subject to
attack and destruction anywhere on the high seas,
and without warning, and that American sailors and
travellers were exposed to fresh dangers.

The sinking of the unarmed Channel packet *Sussex*,
March 24, without warning, and with the loss of sev-

---

[1] Identic notes of January 18, 1916. *Am. Jour. Internat. Law*, X.,
Supplement (special no.), 310–313.

[2] *Ibid.*, 336–338.   [3] *Ibid.*, 314–336.

eral American lives, revived the main issue in all of
its seriousness.　After preliminary inquiries, the President read to Congress and despatched to Berlin (April
18) a note which pronounced the attack on the *Sussex*
"manifestly indefensible," and declared the United
States to have been "very patient," and concluded with
a ringing ultimatum that unless the Imperial German
government should "now immediately declare and
effect an abandonment of its present methods of submarine warfare against passenger- and freight-carrying
vessels, the government of the United States can
have no choice but to sever diplomatic relations with
the German Empire altogether."[1]

The German reply, May 4, shelved rather than settled the controversy by pledging enforcement of orders
already given to submarine commanders not to sink
merchant vessels "without warning and without saving
human lives, unless these ships attempt to escape or
offer resistance."[2]　The communication also said that
these orders would be revoked if the United States did
not force Great Britain to mitigate her blockade; and
the Imperial Chancellor was later reported as intimat-
ing that the offer was made only because Germany
was not yet ready to enlarge her submarine warfare.
President Wilson's reply, May 8, artfully assumed
Germany's complete acceptance of the American demand; and for some months further trouble was
averted.

[1] *Am. Jour. Internat. Law*, X., Supplement (special no.), 186–195.
[2] *Ibid.*, 195–199.

CHAPTER XIX

ECONOMIC PROBLEMS AND POLICIES IN WAR TIME

(1914–1917)

FOR a hundred years prior to 1914 no European or other foreign war greatly disturbed the course of events in the United States. But the Great War recast the nation's lines and forms of trade, revolutionized its industries, disrupted its revenues, set it forward on the tortuous path of government ownership, gave it an entirely new position in the world of finance, aroused heated debate on questions of military preparedness, drew from it the hugest naval appropriation ever voted by a nation at peace, dispelled its comfortable illusion of isolation, involved it in a diplomatic break with one of the major belligerents, and ended by drawing it into the maelstrom of hostilities. No better illustration can be found of the way in which nations, under modern conditions, are played upon by forces over which they have little or no control.

The effects of the conflict on the American national spirit can be measured only by posterity, but the changes that took place in the country's economic status are already on record. The first reactions were bound to be unfavorable. The delicate mechanism of international finance collapsed; markets (especially in Germany and Russia) which annually absorbed millions of dollars' worth of American goods, were closed; demand for many kinds of products in remaining markets was curtailed, and the means of transporting commodities to these markets were cut in half; confidence was destroyed, business unnerved.

But recovery soon set in. Great Britain gained control of the seas and invested neutral commerce with a reasonable degree of security. Heroic efforts of government and banking agencies on both sides of the Atlantic revived business confidence. The withdrawal of millions of farmers and artisans from the fields and factories of England and France created a rapidly rising demand for foreign foodstuffs and clothing. In the spring of 1915 the Entente powers began placing in the United States huge orders for arms, ammunition, chemicals, horses and mules, and other military equipment. Buyers from Great Britain, France, and Russia —with unlimited credit behind them, and prepared to pay fabulous prices—eagerly competed for supplies. By March, stocks were soaring; by April, all signs of depression were fading; by midsummer, the country was nearing the zenith of prosperity.

Speaking broadly, agriculture, manufacturing, and commerce alike received stimulus. The iron and steel trades, ship-building, and the manufacture of explosives, chemicals, automobiles, and machinery leaped forward; new branches of industry opened the way to a fuller utilization of the country's resources, and started or extended American manufacture from American raw materials of many articles until then supplied wholly or largely by importation. The interruption of German and other foreign trade opened unexampled opportunities in Asian, African, and South American markets. The experience of nations indicated that after the restoration of peace the country's producers and traders would have to fight for every inch of ground that they had gained. Yet analogy also indicated that the shifts of emphasis and direction in industry and trade would never be wholly undone, and that the economic life of the nation would always bear the impress of the war period.[1]

In this opinion observers were confirmed by the novel position to which the country was brought in international finance. Like all newer and rapidly developing lands, the United States had stood in need of larger amounts of capital than it could itself supply, and great sums were obtained from investors of Great Britain, France, Germany, and other nations. Twenty years of prosperity brought about a considerable reduction in the proportion of foreign to domestic capital; thus but ten to thirty per cent. of the stock of the larger railroads was owned abroad in 1914, as against forty to sixty per cent. in 1895. Nevertheless, the total of foreign holdings of American stocks and bonds when the war broke out was between four and five billion

[1] Sorrell, "Dislocations in the Foreign Trade of the United States resulting from the War," *Jour. Polit. Econ.*, XXIV., 25–75; Huebner, "Probable Effects of the War on the Foreign Trade of the United States," Acad. Polit. Sci., *Proceedings*, VI., 174–184; Johnson, "Probable Changes in the Foreign Trade of the United States resulting from the European War," *Am. Econ. Rev.*, VI., Supplement, 17–25.

dollars. Eventually they proved assets of the greatest importance to the Entente nations.

Under the changed conditions, the United States quickly became the world's great exporting country. Prior to the war, the largest recorded excess of exports over imports in any calendar year was $691,000,000, in 1913. In 1915 the figure rose to $1,768,000,000, and in the first ten months of 1916 to $2,490,800,000. Most of the increase was accounted for by the heavy export and diminished import trade with the Entente nations, chiefly Great Britain; and the effect was to set up a commercial balance highly unfavorable to those powers. European-owned American securities were sent to be resold to American investors, to a value aggregating, in 1915–1916, two billion dollars; gold was exported to the New York banks to the amount of nine hundred millions; and when these steps were inadequate, loans were floated in the United States aggregating another two billions.

These loans were a novelty in the history of American finance. Never before had the American market raised for any foreign government more than two or three hundred millions; and no government at war had borrowed in the United States prior to 1915, except Great Britain in 1900–1901 and Japan in 1904–1905. The new loans had the further curious aspect that the money raised from them was not actually sent abroad. In a sense, no money was raised at all. Without exception, the credits obtained were employed in the United States in payment for supplies; payment taking the form of two- to five-year notes or bonds,

23

which were sold by the banks to American investors at attractive prices.

The result of these various expedients was a migration of capital of such proportions as to transform the whole aspect of world trade and finance. It was precisely in this manner, although mainly in time of peace, that Great Britain built up in the nineteenth century the foreign-investment power which made her, before the Great War, the central money market of the world. Already in 1916 American capitalists were placing considerable sums in Argentina, Brazil, Sweden, Holland, and Russia; while Canada had become absolutely dependent upon her southern neighbor for the capital formerly obtained in Europe. In two years the United States was converted from a debtor to a creditor nation; "dollar exchange," long the dream of the American international banker, became an easy possibility.[1]

At the beginning of the war ninety-two per cent. of the four-billion-dollar overseas trade of the United States was carried by vessels of foreign ownership and registry; of the scores of merchant-steamships plying across the Atlantic, only six flew the American flag. Floods of argument on ways and means of rebuilding the country's once flourishing merchant marine had

[1] Noyes, "Our Loans to Europe," *Scribner's Magazine*, LXI., 131 ff; Atwood, "Paying Off the Mortgage on the United States," *World's Work*, XXXIII., 243–250, 399–403; Reynolds, "Effect of the European War on American Credits," *Jour. Polit. Econ.*, XXII., 925–936; Willis, "American Finance and the European War," *ibid.*, XXI., 144–165. Cf. a group of papers, "America's Changing Investment Market," in Am. Acad. Polit. and Soc. Sci., *Annals*, LXVIII. (1916).

failed to yield results, mainly for the reason that both
capital and labor continued to find better opportunities
for investment than those offered by the carrying trade.
In the first weeks of the war all German shipping was
driven to cover. Available British tonnage was much
reduced by captures, by the use of merchant-craft for
transport and other belligerent duty, and after a time
by destruction by the enemy's submarines. French
shipping was similarly impaired. Norwegian, Danish,
Dutch, Spanish, and other neutral tonnage was not
large.

From this situation arose a serious problem for the
United States. Surplus products were piled mountain high and the demand for them abroad, at fabulous
prices, was unprecedented; but they could not readily
be got to market. The transfer of larger coastwise
vessels to transoceanic service helped a little, as did
an act of September 2, 1914, establishing a system of
war-risk insurance. But a ship registry act of August
18 amending the Panama Canal Act of August 24, 1912,
by admitting to American registry foreign-built vessels
without regard to age, if owned by American citizens
or by a corporation whose president and managing
directors were Americans, proved a failure.[1] The Administration now proposed that the government should
itself establish, own, and operate steamship lines; and
a bill to this end was introduced in the House of Representatives August 24, 1914. Fear of foreign compli-
cations and dislike of government ownership restrained
Congress from action for a period of two years; but

[1] *U. S. Statutes at Large*, XXXVIII., pt. i., pp. 698–699.

a ship-purchase law received the President's signature September 7, 1916.[1]

This act created a Shipping Board of five members, charged with encouraging and developing a merchant marine and a naval auxiliary, and regulating water carriers engaged in interstate commerce. The Board was empowered (1) to form one or more corporations for the purchase, lease, and operation of merchant-vessels, with a maximum capital of fifty million dollars, of which at least fifty-one per cent. should be subscribed by the Board, acting for the government; (2) to acquire vessels, "suitable, as far as commercial requirements may permit, for use as naval auxiliaries," and not including craft under the registry or flag of any country at war; (3) to cancel or modify any agreement among carriers by water in foreign and interstate commerce which might be found unfair as between carriers or exporters or detrimental to the commercial interests of the country; (4) to enforce reasonable maximum rates among water carriers engaged in interstate commerce, and to correct unjust discriminations in rates among such carriers engaged in foreign trade. Government ownership was limited to five years after the war, but the regulation of interstate and foreign carriers by water was to be permanent; and the Shipping Board was given a place in the federal administrative system on a footing with the Interstate Commerce Commission and the Federal Trade Commission.[2]

[1] *U. S. Statutes at Large*, XXXIX., pt. i., pp. 728–738.

[2] Secretary of Commerce, *Annual Report*, 1916, pp. 222–235. An important group of papers on the American mercantile marine is printed in Acad. Polit. Sci., *Proceedings*, VI., No. 1 (1915).

War costs money, and the expense falls by no means wholly on the belligerents. If the European conflict brought the United States industrial prosperity, it also imposed—even in the years of neutrality—a heavy fiscal burden. On the one hand, the army, the navy, the merchant marine, and other services called for increased outlays; on the other, diminished imports cut off customs receipts. Customs revenue in the fiscal year 1915 was but $209,268,107, which was less by eighty-three millions than during the first year of the operation of the Underwood tariff, and the smallest yield in any year since 1899. At the outbreak of hostilities the nation was facing a probable deficit; a few weeks of war showed that there must be an extensive financial readjustment.

Relief might have been found, under existing laws, in issues of Panama Canal bonds, or the sale of one-year three per cent. certificates of indebtedness. But either procedure would have been only a temporary solution, and in a special message to Congress, September 4, 1914, President Wilson urged that both borrowing and use of the Treasury surplus be avoided by increased taxation.[1] After six weeks' debate, Congress passed (October 22) a War Revenue Act, for a single year, to produce fifty-four million dollars.[2] The excise duties on liquors were increased; license taxes were imposed on bankers, brokers, theatres and other amusement enterprises, and tobacco dealers and manufacturers; and stamp taxes were laid on promissory notes,

[1] *Senate Jour.*, 63 Cong., 2 Sess., 498.
[2] *U. S. Statutes at Large*, XXXVIII., pt. i., pp. 745–764.

insurance policies, bills of lading, telegraph and telephone messages, and a long list of other papers and instruments. The new taxes yielded almost up to expectation and for the moment closed the gap.

In 1915 the Administration committed itself to a program involving huge outlays on national defense, and it became evident that the revenues would have to be permanently increased. The act of 1914 was extended another year by joint resolution approved December 17, 1915,[1] and in the meantime Congress was asked to adopt revenue proposals looking to the raising of $205,000,000. A new revenue measure became law September 8, 1916.[2]

The normal rate of the income tax on both individuals and corporations was doubled, and the surtaxes on incomes exceeding $40,000 were increased on a graduated scale rising to thirteen per cent. (previously six per cent.) on incomes of $2,000,000 or more. An estate tax, or "death duty," was laid on inherited estates, on a scale ranging from one per cent. on amounts in excess of $50,000 to ten per cent. on amounts in excess of $5,000,000. An excise tax of 12½ per cent. per annum was laid on the entire net profits of manufacturers of explosives, firearms, and other munitions of war. This munitions tax, which was similar to excises used in the various belligerent countries, was limited to one year after the restoration of peace in Europe. All of these imposts accelerated the trend in American federal taxation from "consumption" taxes,

---

[1] U. S. Statutes at Large, XXXIX., pt. i., p. 2.
[2] Ibid., 756–801.

which impose their weight on the general public, to levies that take their toll from wealth, from unusual profits, from unearned increment, and from luxuries and diversions. These new taxes were successful; yet at the opening of 1917 the country was running behind at the rate of two millions a day.[1]

A prime factor in the history of the United States after 1905 was the growing political power of organized labor. One illustration was the position forced on the Democratic party as to injunctions in labor disputes. Another was the provisions of the Clayton Act of 1914 exempting labor unions from the operation of the anti-trust laws, thus withdrawing some of the legal remedies for alleged injuries to business and public well-being as against collective labor. Convincing evidence was furnished by the Adamson eight-hour law of September, 1916, pertaining to certain branches of labor on railways. Few measures in a score of years so aroused public feeling; none was more warmly contested.

The Adamson law sprang from a concerted demand of the four great brotherhoods of railway employees engaged in the freight service—engineers, firemen, conductors, and trainmen—for a basic day of eight hours, with pay at the rate of time and a half for overtime. This plan was brought forward by sectional organizations about 1909. For seven years it broadened and deepened, until early in 1914 it reached the railroad operators with the united support of 325,000 men,

[1] Speare, "The New Taxes," *Review of Reviews*, LIV., 395–398; Blakey, "The New Revenue Act," *Am. Econ. Rev.*, VI., 837–850.

and backed by threat of a strike that would tie up every railroad from Maine to California and cause an insufferable paralysis of industry and trade. The demand was not for a working-day restricted to eight hours; employees were ready to agree with operators that in the railroad business such a regulation would not be feasible. The thing that was wanted was an eight-hour standard of pay.

As matters stood, employees were paid a day's wages for running one hundred miles or working ten hours, whichever was accomplished first. If on any day they ran more than one hundred miles or worked more than ten hours, they were paid overtime *pro rata;* and if a man worked at all, even but a single hour, he received a full day's wages. In the passenger service, hundred-mile runs were normally completed within eight hours, as a rule within five or six; and while in the present controversy the passenger men finally voted to strike to enforce the demands of the freight men, no grievance of theirs was involved. On account of congestion of traffic and efforts to economize by running heavier trains, the freight service had been for years slowing up, and employees were finding their actual working day to be regularly the full ten hours, or even eleven and twelve. What they now demanded was that the bonus formerly arising from ten hours' pay for fewer hours' work be in effect revived by an arrangement under which they should be paid their present daily wage for the first eight hours, with an hour and a half's pay for each hour of work overtime. It was not intended that the conditions of employment should otherwise be altered; the question was one of wages, not hours.

The brotherhoods' demand was presented in March, 1916, and was promptly rejected by the operators, who said that to accept it would increase their wage-rolls by one hundred million dollars. This burden, it was frankly stated, would have to be unloaded on the public, and there was doubt whether the public would bear it. In June the operators offered arbitration; but the labor chiefs, feeling their strength, refused. Instead, they took a poll of their organizations and obtained authority to call a strike unless their terms were met. During the summer the situation grew more tense, and it became apparent that a crisis, long feared by railroad experts, was at hand. Publicity bureaus flooded the country with literature on both sides; while the uncompromising attitude of the brotherhoods defeated every effort to invoke mediation or arbitration under the Newlands Act. In the old days labor, being weak, had urged arbitration, and capital, being strong, had refused it. Then had followed a period in which the two were about equally powerful and arbitrations were numerous. Now it had come about that labor held the whip hand and was unwilling to delegate to any middle authority the settlement of disputes in which it was interested.

In August, when a rupture seemed imminent, President Wilson intervened. He called from conference in New York the brotherhood chairmen and the railroad managers, and heard the arguments of both sides; whereupon he proposed that the railroads meet the request of the men for ten hours' pay for the first eight hours, and that the question of the rate for overtime be submitted to arbitration. These suggestions were acceptable to neither side; and on August 28 six hundred and forty brotherhood representatives left Washington for their homes, bearing sealed orders for a strike to begin at 7 A.M., September 4.

After a final ineffectual appeal to the four brotherhood chiefs, who had remained at the capital, the President carried the matter to Congress. In an address to the two houses, August 29, he reviewed the whole controversy, criticized the managers for refusing to grant the eight-hour day, announced the failure of his independent efforts, pictured the tragical consequences which the strike would entail for the entire country, avowed the conviction that "the whole spirit of the time and the preponderant evidence of recent economic experience" speak for the eight-hour day," and proposed for immediate adoption a program of legislation of such comprehensiveness that months, and even years, might well have been consumed in its discussion.[1] There were six main items: (1) enlargement and reorganization of the Interstate Commerce Commission; (2) establishment of the eight-hour day as the legal basis of work and wages for men operating trains; (3) appointment of a commission to study and report upon the effect of the wage increase; (4) congressional support of increased freight rates, if the Interstate Commerce Commission should find reason for such increase; (5) prohibition—on the lines of the

[1] *Senate Jour.*, 64 Cong., 1 Sess., 634-635.

Canadian Industrial Disputes Investigation Act of 1907—of railway strikes and lockouts pending public investigation; (6) authorization of the President, in case of military necessity, to seize and operate railroads and to draft trainmen and other railway employees into military service. Bills were at once introduced and hearings held; and within exactly one hundred hours from the President's appearance at the Capitol a measure, piloted by Chairman Adamson of the House Committee on Interstate Commerce, was ready for the Executive's approval. In the House, 168 Democrats voted for it and 54 against it; 145 members did not vote at all.[1] In the Senate the vote, 43 to 28, followed party lines more closely.[2]

Unlike the Erdman and Newlands acts, which provided general systems of mediation and arbitration, the Adamson law was a simple measure of intervention applying to a single dispute;[3] all portions of the President's program which looked to methods of dealing with future controversies were left for later consideration. The main provision was that from January 1, 1917, employees engaged in train operation on interstate steam railroads exceeding one hundred miles in length should be paid their present daily wage for the first eight hours, and should be given pay for overtime, although *pro rata* rather than on the basis of time and a half as demanded. A commission of three was to be appointed by the President to study the

[1] *House Jour.*, 64 Cong., 1 Sess., 1006–1007.
[2] *Senate Jour.*, 64 Cong., 1 Sess., 642.
[3] *U. S. Statutes at Large*, XXXIX., pt. i., pp. 721–722.

effects of the wage increase and to report to Congress
within ten months after January 1. The wage scale
set up by the law was to continue for thirty days after
the commission's report (at the latest, to November 1,
1917), when a permanent settlement would be in
order.[1]

The immediate object of the measure was realized.
The brotherhood chiefs called off the strike, and railway business went on uninterruptedly. The settlement was a relief; but it was not a source of real
satisfaction. In the first place, the act on which it
rested was passed under duress. There was some show
of deliberation, but both the President and Congress
were driven along an unwelcome course by the threats
of the employees' organizations. Small, well-organ-
ized groups had bent the government to their purposes
before, although usually through combinations of capital rather than of labor. But it was not right that
any single group or interest should have such power.
The present action was the more displeasing because
it came during a presidential campaign and was tainted
with politics.

Another weighty objection was that the ultimate
interests of the general public were not given due consideration; over against the 325,000 employees should
have been set not only the million holders of railroad
stocks and bonds, but also the ninety million people

[1] Clapp, "The Adamson Law," *Yale Rev.*, VI., 258–275; Ripley,
"The Eight-Hour Law for Railroad Men," *Review of Reviews*, LIV.,
389–393; Carter, Trumbull, and Colby, "The Adamson Act," Acad.
Polit. Sci., *Proceedings*, VII., 170–188; Robbins, "The Trainmen's
Eight-Hour Day," *Polit. Sci. Quart.*, XXXI., 541–557.

who, without being either employees or stockholders, derived benefit or disadvantage from the conditions of railroad service. Furthermore, the four brotherhoods included less than one-fifth of the 1,700,000 men employed in railway service in the country; their members were already better paid than their fellow-employees;[1] there was no good reason why they should be singled out to receive a wage increase, especially since the effect would probably be to hold back other and larger groups from like advantages.

Finally, the argument that the law had to be passed in order to save the country from a strike was unconvincing. The President judged the case on slender evidence, and he did not exhaust his influence in behalf of arbitration. Had he let it be known that in the event of a strike he would use all of the power of the government to keep the railroads in operation, there probably would have been no strike. President Roosevelt stood firmly for arbitration against the arrogance of capital during the anthracite coal strike of 1902, and carried his point. President Wilson lost an opportunity similarly to advance the cause of industrial arbitration in 1916 by meeting the arrogance of labor with the high-minded censure which it deserved.[2]

The motives and policies underlying the Adamson law formed an important issue in the later stages of the campaign of 1916.[2] Among railway employees the

[1] Bureau of Railway Economics, *Railway Trainmen's Earnings*, 1916, Misc. Series, No. 28.
[2] Van Hise, "The Railroad Hours of Labor Law," Am. Acad. Polit. and Soc. Sci., *Annals*, LXIX., 256–264.
[3] See p. 378.

Democrats gained strength from the measure; but the labor vote at large was not visibly affected. After the election, the railway operators announced their intention to contest the constitutionality of the law in the courts. Suit was brought in the United States circuit court at Kansas City, and with a view to bringing the question immediately before the Supreme Court, Judge Hook, on November 22, 1916, pronounced the law unconstitutional, and therefore not enforceable. The Supreme Court gave the case an advanced position on its docket, and on January 10, 1917, argument was closed. The main grounds on which the attorneys for the railroads attacked the law were: (1) it was contrary to public interest and entirely for private interest; (2) it proposed to take property without due process of law; (3) it interfered with freedom of contract; (4) Congress had no power to enact railroad wage legislation.

Meanwhile President Wilson pressed afresh upon Congress those portions of his original railroad program which were designed to afford relief for the roads and to provide better means of averting strikes. Action was not forthcoming. On the contrary, the restiveness of the brotherhoods under the suspension of the Adamson law brought another period of tension, which culminated in a threat of a general strike March 17. Diplomatic relations with Germany had then been severed and war was impending. A strike at such a juncture would be doubly ruinous, and public feeling ran high. A mediating committee appointed by the President labored with representatives of the two sides, and finally got from the operators a promise of some concessions and from the brotherhood chiefs a brief postponement of the strike. March 19, the situation was saved by announcement of the Supreme Court's decision on the Adamson law.[1]

To the surprise of the legal profession, the Court declared the law constitutional and enforceable in every feature. The decision, however, was by the narrowest possible margin: Chief Justice White and four associates—including two new members of somewhat radical temperament, Justices Brandeis and Clarke—joined in it; the other four associates dissented. The majority opinion, written by the Chief Justice, stressed four main points: (1) the public interest begets a public right of regulation "to the full extent necessary to secure and protect it"; (2) carriers and their employees are engaged in a business vested with a public interest; (3) the right of Congress to regulate interstate commerce involves the right to arbitrate disputes compulsorily by fixing wages, hours, and other conditions of the business; (4) Congress is clothed with full power to keep open the channels of interstate trade.

It had long been the fashion among radicals to rail at the Supreme Court as a bulwark of Wall Street and an enemy of progress. This practice was of the very essence of Bryanism. But in the eight-hour-law decision the tribunal took a forward step that alarmed many of the most progressive thinkers. It sustained Congress in the first attempt of that body to fix wages

[1] Wilson *vs.* New, 243 U. S., 332; Powell, "The Supreme Court and the Adamson Law," *Univ. of Pa. Law Rev.*, LXV., 3–27.

of private employees; it opened the way for Congress to legislate wages downward as well as upward, to compel men to work whether they wanted to or not, and to make arbitration compulsory. It practically said that Congress could pass any measure affecting the operation of the railroads which public necessity should be deemed to require.

The decision seemed a great triumph for organized labor. Yet it was a two-edged sword. To keep the trains running, Congress might meet labor's demands with increased wages, but it had the alternative of meeting them with measures to compel arbitration, and thus to take from railway labor its most powerful weapon, the strike. Shrewd labor leaders saw from the beginning that the Adamson Act had an awkward bearing; most of them would have felt little regret if it had been held unconstitutional.

Other momentous questions thrust themselves into the foreground. To what extent should the operators' demands for increases of rates be met? If the wages of members of the brotherhoods could be thus regulated by federal authority, why not the wages of other groups of employees of interstate carriers? Must the wages prescribed or sanctioned be "just and reasonable," as railway rates are required to be? Should there be set up a special investigative and administrative agency—a wages commission—with powers over wages similar to the powers of the Interstate Commerce Commission over rates and services? Would the new federal jurisdiction pave the way for government ownership and operation?

The country's sense of relief at the passing of one more of the swiftly recurring crises in the railway world was tempered by the realization that these and other questions would demand answer, and that the transportation problem was steadily growing more complex.

24

CHAPTER XX

THE ELECTION OF 1916

(1913–1916)

THREE questions claimed the attention of observers of American party politics after the heated presidential contest of 1912. Could the Democratic party, whose successful candidate had received the support of only forty per cent. of the electorate, win such increased confidence as to become a majority party? Would the Progressive party strike root and prove a steady contender for the control of the nation's affairs? What steps would be taken by the Republican party to regain the esteem of the progressive-minded people of the country and win back the millions of voters who had turned from it? The events of the first three and a half years of Wilson's presidency threw much light on these uncertainties, yet without wholly clearing them up.

While, in 1913, the Democrats set about the task of ruling the nation, the defeated parties turned their thought to the recovery of strength for future contests. Within six weeks after the election, Progressive leaders and workers held many sectional conferences; and on December 10 and 11 a national conference at Chicago brought together fifteen hundred members of the

party, representing every state in the Union. It was
the sense of this meeting that the party should hold
strictly to its program, and plans were developed for
nation-wide organization and propaganda. In a magazine article explaining the Progressive position Roosevelt affirmed that the new party was "sundered from
the men who now control and manage the Republican
party by the gulf of their actual practices," and he
contended that the Progressives alone gave real power
to the rank and file, as distinguished from the bosses.[1]

The Republicans were prompted to heart-searching.
President Taft drew consolation from the fact, as he
viewed it, that the party had been "victorious" in
saving the country from "an Administration whose
policy involved the sapping of the foundations of
democratic, constitutional, representative government."[2] But most leaders found it difficult to be so
optimistic; radicals felt that the situation demanded
a complete reorganization of the party; while many
persons who had been classed with the reactionaries
were frank to admit that large concessions would have
to be made.[3] An informal conference of representatives from eleven states was held at Chicago May
11, 1913. It was announced as a first step toward
reuniting the party and reconstructing it "on progressive lines," and it recommended to the National
Committee that a special national convention be held

[1] *Century Magazine*, LXXXVI., 826–836.
[2] Speech before the Union League Clubs of New York and Philadelphia, Jan. 4, 1913. *Am. Year Book*, 1913, p. 60.
[3] Butler, *What is Progress in Politics; an Address Delivered in Chicago*,
Dec. 14, 1912.

during the year to provide for increased popular control over the party machinery, and especially "to consider the expediency of changing the basis of representation in future conventions so that the delegates shall proportionally represent Republican voters and not general population." The suggestion was seconded, September 23, by the Republican convention of the state of New York.[1]

To consider the proposed changes, the National Committee met at Washington December 16, 1913. A special convention was felt to be inexpedient; but the Committee voted to submit for approval by the state conventions a reapportionment of delegates in the national nominating convention, so as to give to each state four delegates at large (with one additional for each congressman at large), one from each congressional district, and one additional from each district in which the Republican vote for presidential electors in 1908, or for the Republican candidate for Congress in 1914, should have been not less than 7,500. Under this arrangement the convention would be more truly representative, although the distribution of votes would still be very different from the distribution of party strength throughout the country. The Chicago convention of 1916 was made up on the new plan; the number of delegates was reduced from 1,078 to 985, the southern states losing a total of 82. This mild reconstruction of convention machinery touched a deep grievance of the progressive elements remaining in the Republican party, but it by no means

[1] *Am. Year Book*, 1913, p. 61.

covered the case, and the seceders were not deeply impressed.

The few state and special congressional elections of 1913 were favorable to the Democrats, but in 1914 the party suffered a reverse more serious than that of an ordinary off-year. Two seats were gained in the Senate, but the House majority was cut from 147 to 29. The Progressives also fared badly. Though Roosevelt took part in the campaign, and several Progressive leaders were before the people as candidates, the party's popular vote fell to 1,800,000 (less than one-half of that of 1912), and the Progressive group in the House was reduced from fifteen to seven. Joseph G. Cannon and many other Republican "standpatters" regained their seats; the collapse of Progressivism was freely predicted.

At the dawn of the presidential year 1916 the political situation was confused. The country was very prosperous, and the people were in a money-getting, rather than a heroic, mood. The Administration was fortified by a brilliant record of reform. Never had platform pledges been redeemed so faithfully; never had such a mass of constructive legislation been put on the statute book in a period so brief. Foreign relations, however, had not been so well handled; and in the differences of opinion on foreign policy, and on internal questions whose roots ran back into the foreign situation, lay the basis of a stirring contest. "Watchful waiting" in Mexico invited discussion; on the government's attitude toward Germany and other European belligerents opinion was already deeply di-

vided; in the background lowered the problem of
national "preparedness." Still, there was much reason
for supposing that the unhealed breach in the Republican party would give the Democrats another easy,
perhaps inglorious, victory.

As the national conventions approached, it became
more certain that the campaign would turn on questions of foreign policy. The attack of Villa's bandits
on Columbus, New Mexico, March 9, gave the Mexican
situation a serious turn; the position of the United
States as a neutral in the world war offered fresh difficulties and humiliations; the mobilization of the
National Guard on the Rio Grande border disclosed
the nation's inability to meet such emergencies; the
President's belated conversion to preparedness yielded
legislation which many well-informed people judged
inadequate. In articles in the *Metropolitan Magazine*,
and in addresses, Roosevelt belabored the Administration for inconsistency and timidity; in a powerful speech before an unofficial convention of New
York Republicans, February 15, ex-Secretary Root contributed to the ground swell of public dissatisfaction.[1]

The Republican convention assembled at Chicago
June 7; and by decision of the Progressive National
Committee in January, the Progressive convention
met in the same city on the same day. These arrangements were planned to make it easy for the two groups
of delegates to work to a common end. But when the
time for the conventions came, fusion seemed unlikely.

[1] Bacon and Scott [eds.], *Addresses of Elihu Root on International Subjects*, 427–447. Cf. *Review of Reviews*, LIII., 298–303.

The rank and file of the Progressive party demanded the nomination of Roosevelt; such sentiment as had developed in favor of preparedness pointed in the same direction; and the Progressive delegates arrived in Chicago bent on putting the ex-President formally in the race. This meant two nominees; for while Roosevelt had adherents in the Republican gathering, it was plain that the men who dominated the convention would not accept him on any terms; the revolt of 1912 was too fresh in the party memory. Committees appointed by the two conventions conferred in good spirit, but no common basis of action could be discovered, and each convention carried through its program independently.

Though the future of the decimated Republican party was at stake, the proceedings in the Coliseum were tame. Contests for seats produced no such excitement as in 1912; there were no secessions, stampedes, or record-breaking demonstrations; the oratory was flat; inspiring leadership and moral force were lacking; conservatives still controlled, and few of them gave evidence of being chastened by defeat. The party was called on, none the less, to pick a leader from a field more open than at any time since 1896, and interest in the nominations could not fail to be keen. The pre-convention campaign brought to light a strong preference of the voters for Charles E. Hughes, former governor of New York, and now an associate justice of the federal Supreme Court; although he refused to permit his name to be used in the primaries and declined to state his views on current questions.

Root had a large following; Roosevelt had supporters;
and there were many "favorite sons," including Theodore E. Burton of Ohio, Charles W. Fairbanks of
Indiana, Albert B. Cummins of Iowa, Lawrence Y.
Sherman of Illinois, and John W. Weeks of Massachusetts. On the first ballot Hughes received 253
votes, Weeks 105, Root 103, Cummins 87, Burton 82,
Fairbanks 72, Roosevelt 67, and Sherman 63. On the
third ballot Hughes was nominated with 949½ votes.[1]
The vice-presidential nomination went to Fairbanks,
who had held the office during the second Roosevelt
administration.

The platform, which was exceptionally brief, dealt
most pointedly with foreign relations. It affirmed
that the Administration had totally failed to protect
American citizens in their fundamental rights, and by
its "phrase-making and shifty expedients" had "destroyed our influence abroad and humiliated us in our
own eyes." It denounced Wilson's "indefensible
methods of interference" in the internal affairs of
Mexico, and pledged aid in the restoration of order,
together with adequate protection of American interests. It advocated military and naval preparedness, although in terms so general as to be meaningless;
and it approved the Monroe Doctrine, without attempt-
ing to say what the phrase meant. It pronounced the
Underwood tariff a failure, both because of the decline
of revenue and because the cost of living had not been
curbed; and it stamped the President's plan for

[1] Sixteenth Republican National Convention, *Official Report of Proceedings*, 202.

government-owned merchant - vessels as futile and dangerous.[1]

The Progressives carried on their deliberations with an enthusiasm reminiscent of 1912; and when it became certain that Roosevelt would not be accepted by the Republicans, they put their favorite formally in nomination, chose John M. Parker of Louisiana as their vice-presidential candidate, adopted a platform, and adjourned. The platform criticized the Wilson Administration less sharply than did the Republican. It solemnly reaffirmed the declarations of 1912 on social justice; it made definite recommendations on military and naval preparedness.

The question instantly arose whether Roosevelt would accept the nomination or whether he would try to throw the Progressive support, at once or later, to the Republican candidate. For a decision the country had not long to wait. A conditional declination was forwarded before the convention adjourned;[2] and in a subsequent letter to the National Committee, in whose hands had been left the determination of the course to be pursued, the reasons for a final refusal to run were given at length. These reasons were, in a word, that the nation's welfare demanded the defeat of Wilson, and that the Republican nominee was worthy of the support of all progressive-minded and patriotic men.[3] This turn of events sorely disappointed

---

[1] Sixteenth Republican National Convention, *Official Report of Proceedings*, 88–95; *Republican Campaign Text-Book*, 1916, pp. 48–52; Stanwood, *The Presidency*, II., 340–346.

[2] *Am. Year Book*, 1916, p. 30.

[3] *Republican Campaign Text-Book*, 1916, pp. 31–39.

many Progressives, and the vice-presidential candidate,
Parker, refused to give up the race. The majority
supported the National Committee in its decision to
take no further steps to place a third ticket in the field;
and overtures from Hughes helped to assuage discontent.[1] But efforts to deliver the influence of the
National Committee and the votes of the party members were only partially successful.

The Democratic convention met at St. Louis, June
14. Unlike its Baltimore predecessor, it was free
from schism, and its prearranged program was carried through without mishap. The platform of 1912
pledged the party's candidate to a single term. This
clause was adopted, however, at the behest of Bryan,
and Wilson early made it known that on the question
of a second term he would be controlled, not by the
platform declaration, but by public opinion.[2] His
candidacy was avowed many months before the convention of 1916; there was no opposition, and his
renomination took place by acclamation.[3] The vice-
presidential nomination was mildly contested, but went
to the incumbent, Thomas R. Marshall of Indiana.
With little real work on its hands, the convention resolved itself into a party love feast, and floods of
oratory were loosed in laudation of the President and
his co-workers.

The Administration, appealing to the country for

---

[1] Hughes to the Progressive Committee, June 26. *Republican Campaign Text-Book*, 1916, pp. 39–40.

[2] *Am. Year Book*, 1916, p. 34.

[3] Democratic National Convention of 1916, *Official Report of Proceedings*, 107.

a vote of confidence and a fresh lease of power, was in
reality its own platform. Yet lengthy and fulsome
resolutions set forth the legislative achievements of the
past three years; and by declaring for a multitude of
further economic and social reforms the convention
threw out tentacles toward numerous groups of voters,
especially the Progressives. The platform denied that
the interests of American citizens had been neglected,
commended the refusal of the Administration to intervene in Mexico, and praised the diplomatic victories of
the President in his dealings with the belligerent states
of Europe. The note of Americanism was sounded in
a thinly veiled thrust at the German-American elements
which were opposing the President's course; and increases of the army and navy were advocated in a
manner novel in a Democratic platform.[1]

The minor parties which placed tickets in the field
were the same as in 1912. In a convention at New
York, April 23, the Socialist Labor party nominated its
candidate of 1912, Arthur Reimer of Massachusetts.
The Socialist party held no convention, but nominated
its candidates — Allan L. Benson of New York and
George R. Kirkpatrick of New Jersey—and adopted
its elaborate platform by mail referendum. The Prohibitionists met at St. Paul and nominated ex-Governor
Frank J. Hanly of Indiana and Ira D. Landrith of
Massachusetts.[2]

The one question in which from the outset the

---

[1] *Democratic Campaign Text-Book*, 1916, pp. 3–26; Stanwood, *History of the Presidency*, II., 350–360.

[2] *Ibid.*, 339–340, 360–372.

voters were really interested was whether, in the existing state of the country and of world affairs, Wilson
or Hughes would make the better president.   Platform
declarations were ignored or openly flouted; each of
the candidates quickly became his own platform.
Certain clear advantages lay with Wilson.   The first
was the strategical superiority that usually falls to
the party in power, in being able to "make the news"
and shift the issues at will.   A second was the fact—
of exceptional importance in the present juncture—
that the Democratic candidate was experienced in the
duties of the presidency, while his opponent was not.
A third was the Administration's record of legislation,
spread before the country afresh, and in masterful
fashion, in Wilson's acceptance speech of September 2.[1]

A fourth factor was the President's virile leadership
of a united party.   The politicians did not like him;
but, apart from negligible elements who were alienated
by his foreign policy, the rank and file were for him.
Indeed, he was recognized to be stronger than his
party, and it was assumed that he would draw heavily
from the Progressives and from the independent vote.
Starting with a somewhat archaic Jeffersonian equipment of political principles, and under the suspicion
of being a cloistered doctrinaire and amateur, he had
proved himself a practical and adroit politician, an
adept at divining the trend of public opinion, and a
statesman capable of infusing the radical democratic
impulses of Bryan into the less idealistic program of
the nationalist school.

[1] *Democratic Campaign Text-Book*, 1916, pp. 29–40.

The two candidates had much in common. Both were sons of clergymen; both were of Celtic descent, Wilson being Scotch-Irish and Hughes Welsh; both were of exceptional intellectual caliber and lofty personal character; both had been university professors; both had made their political reputations as reforming state governors, showing the same traits and fighting for the same things; both had been chosen to harmonize discordant elements in their parties; both had a passion for issues and principles rather than personalities.[1] Wilson was keener, cleverer, more imaginative, of nimbler wit, and probably a better manager of men; Hughes was of tougher intellectual fiber and more inclined to move straight to his objective.

Although Hughes was pictured by his opponents as a "sphinx" and a "man of mystery," the country found him no less simple, affable, and human than the President. His nomination was by no means agreeable to the old-line politicians of his party. Many of them he had flayed and humiliated during his insurance investigations and his subsequent governorship in New York. But his total abstention from politics during his six years on the supreme bench had kept him clear of both the factional strife in his party and the more recent controversies arising from the varying attitudes of the people toward the war in Europe. He was "available," and on that account, as well as because of his high character and proved ability, his nomination was demanded by the voters. At the

[1] Hendrick, "The Recall of Justice Hughes," *World's Work*, XXXII., 397–410.

opening of the campaign it seemed that no better choice could have been made.

For manager of his campaign Hughes chose a close friend, William R. Wilcox of New York. The Democratic manager was Vance McCormick of Pennsylvania. From the outset all elements realized that Wilson was a minority president, and that he could not be re-elected in a dual contest unless supported by many voters who were not normally Democratic. Democratic effort was directed, therefore, to the capture of the Progressive and independent votes; and the arguments chiefly used were drawn from the progressive legislation of the past three and a half years. Wilson made no campaign tours. But at his summer home, Shadow Lawn, at Long Branch, New Jersey, he addressed numerous delegations, always laying stress on the progressiveness of his party; and in a speech of September 30 he paid a glowing tribute to the Progressive party of 1912 as "a group in our politics" which "has the real red blood of human sympathy in its veins." [1]

Beyond appealing to their legislative record, the Democrats gave attention chiefly to answering the charges brought against their conduct of foreign affairs. They freely admitted that Mexican relations were in an unsatisfactory state; but they argued that a firmer course would have meant war and probable annexation, which the people did not want. They asserted that, without making unreasonable concessions to the belligerents of Europe, the country had been

[1] *Am. Year Book*, 1916, p. 41.

saved from the disaster of war with any one of them.[1]
Votes were made by a sharp rebuke which the President, near the close of the campaign, administered
to an anti-British agitator, Jeremiah O'Leary, who
sent to the White House an offensive letter. "I would
feel deeply mortified," ran the caustic reply, "to have
you or anybody like you vote for me. Since you have
access to many disloyal Americans and I have not, I
will ask you to convey this message to them."[2]

The prospect of Republican victory was worth little
except in so far as the party candidates and managers
could do two things: win the Progressives to genuine
co-operation, and discover a great issue on which the
Administration could be taken at a disadvantage.
In both tasks there was only moderate success. Following the example of Roosevelt, the mass of former
Progressives supported Hughes. But large numbers refused to do so, and in some states, notably California,
lack of consideration for Progressive feelings caused a
defection which turned the scale.

In the matter of issues the party did not rise to its
opportunity. At the outset, Hughes's acceptance
speech, delivered in Carnegie Hall, New York, July 31,
proved disappointing. Notwithstanding some inspiring passages, it was given up mainly to scattered and
petty criticism of the Administration. In speech-making tours which reached every important section
of the country except the far South, the candidate
failed to develop any constructive program of domes-

---

[1] Creel, *Wilson and the Issues*, chaps. ii.–v.
[2] *Am. Year Book*, 1916, p. 41.

tic and foreign policy to which the party could summon
the country on lofty lines.   At all stages much stress
was placed on the failure of the Administration to protect American life and property in Mexico and on the
high seas; and it was asserted that the Republicans
were more in earnest about the improvement of the
national defenses than the Democrats had shown themselves to be.   But when pressed to say what they, if
in power, would have done that the Democrats had
left undone, the Republican leaders made no clear
answer.   The simple truth was that the country did
not want war, nor even the risk of war, and was quite
content with the policies of the Administration.   This
was especially true of the Middle West.

As the contest entered its final stages the lack of a
vital Republican issue was partially met by the sudden
enactment of the Adamson railroad law.[1]   The President's wavering before the opposed demands of the
railway brotherhoods and the railway operators made
an unfavorable impression, and the passage of a far-
reaching statute on a subject in deep controversy, at
the behest of the labor leaders, and without due investigation, aroused widespread dissatisfaction.   The
measure was supported by many Republican members;
but it was the work of a Democratic congress, acting
under the spur of a Democratic president, and the
odium of it fell properly on the President's party.   The
new issue was seized by Hughes and his fellow-cam-
paigners; and while the argument that Wilson had
saved the country from a ruinous strike was added to

[1] See pp. 353-363.

the contention that he had kept the country out of war, the Administration's submission on the railroad question cost it great numbers of votes. In fact, it came near causing defeat.

November 7, more than eighteen and a half million voters, almost one-fourth of them women, registered their choice at the polls. On the strength of early returns from eastern and some middle western states, the press on election night proclaimed, and the Democratic management conceded, a victory for Hughes. The country awoke the following morning to discover, however, that results in the far West were unexpectedly favorable to the President, and that there was still a chance of his election. Hours of uncertainty lengthened into days, while public interest rose to heights untouched during the campaign. In several states the vote was so close that a recount was necessary; and finally the situation so resolved itself that Wilson could win by carrying either of two of the closest states, Minnesota and California. In the Minnesota recount Hughes kept his original lead, and the state's twelve electoral votes fell to him on an official popular plurality of 396; but California's thirteen electoral votes went into the Democratic column by a margin almost as narrow, and decided the contest. The total number of electoral votes was 531, with 266 required to elect. Wilson received 277, Hughes 254. No presidential contest had been won by an equally narrow margin in the electoral college since 1876. The popular vote was: Wilson, 9,128,837; Hughes, 8,536,380; Benson, 590,415; Hanly, 221,196; and Reimer, 13,922.

25

Parker, running on a headless Progressive ticket, received 42,836 votes for the vice-presidency.

Wilson thus became the first Democratic president to succeed himself since Jackson; also the first, except Cleveland, to serve two terms. He received two million votes more than any other Democratic candidate in the history of the country, and from his re-election the Democrats drew deep satisfaction. Yet, study of the vote tempered elation. After all, the election had been saved by a margin of one-third of one per cent. of the votes cast in a single state; outside the "solid south," where a presidential election involves no real contest, Hughes had a decided plurality; senatorial elections in thirty-two states showed a Progressive-Republican trend and reduced the Democratic majority in the upper branch of Congress from sixteen to ten; and the largest Democratic vote on record failed to retain for the party an assured control of the House of Representatives. Democrats and Republicans each won 214 seats, and the balance of power fell to a handful of independents. In the state elections the honors were about even, although in five states that were carried by Wilson Republican governors were elected. All in all, enthusiastic Republicans had some reason for declaring that while their party had lost the presidency it had virtually regained national ascendancy.

The presidency was lost by the Republicans because Wilson everywhere proved stronger than his party; in most states Hughes ran far behind the local Republican candidates. This does not mean that Hughes

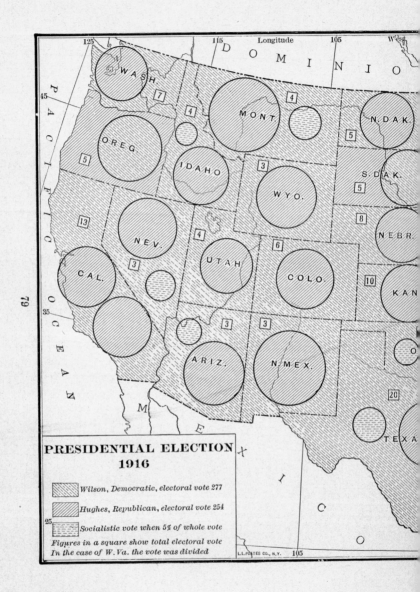

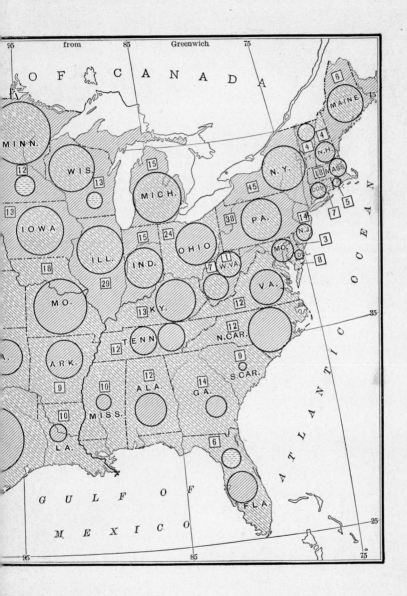

was a weak candidate, or that any other man could
have made a better showing. It indicates simply that
the amalgamation of the Republican and Progressive
forces was incomplete, and that, as the Democrats had
confidently expected, large numbers of Progressives
either voted for Wilson or did not vote at all.

The President proved very strong in those sections
of the country in which Roosevelt's popularity was
formerly greatest. The election, indeed, turned to a
considerable degree on sectional and occupational interests. In general, Hughes carried the East and
Middle West; Wilson the South and far West. The
Adamson law failed to capture the labor vote for the
Democrats, and in all important industrial communities except Ohio Hughes was victorious; but in the
rural and agricultural regions the swing was strongly
toward the President.[1]

Broadly, the alignment was town against country,
agriculture against industry; and the Democrats were
saved from complete defeat only by their inroads on
Republican strength among the farming populations
of the newer states. These inroads were easy to make,
for the reason that these people regarded the President
as a genuine progressive, and because they thoroughly
approved his pacific foreign policy; Hughes they considered to be the candidate of a party dominated by
reactionaries and jingoes. The much-feared "hyphen"
vote, *i. e.*, the vote of the German-American elements
which disliked the President's dealings with Germany,

[1] Dodd, "The Social and Economic Background of Woodrow Wilson," *Jour. Polit. Econ.*, May, 1917.

did not materialize. Of seven states containing the largest numbers of German-Americans, the Democrats carried three.

The part played by women and by the woman's suffrage issue was notable. Women voted for president and vice-president in a fourth of the states, and both of the leading parties declared for the enfranchisement of women by state action. Soon after his nomination, Hughes put himself on record for nation-wide enfranchisement by constitutional amendment; and all the presidential candidates except Wilson eventually took this position.[1] A Woman's Party now made its appearance; and in view of the Republican candidate's pronouncement, it threw its weight into the scale against the Democratic nominee, though without perceptible effect.

In Illinois, the only state in which the votes cast by men and women were tabulated separately, the two sets were divided in almost exactly the same ratio, indicating that the political psychology of one sex is not unlike that of the other. There was no reason to suppose that the results in other states were different. Illinois was carried by the Republicans; but all of the remaining eleven woman-suffrage states, except Oregon, went Democratic. Special interest attached to the election, in Montana, of the first female member of Congress, Miss Jeannette Rankin.[2]

The general results of the election gave no clear indication of the political future of the country. Some

[1] See p. 155.
[2] Keller, "Women in the Campaign," *Yale Rev.*, VI., 233-243.

observers proclaimed a new sectional alignment, in which South, West, and Pacific coast were set off against North and East. The returns showed, however, that in many states and communities insignificant changes of the votes would tip the scale, and that therefore the new political map was not printed in fast colors. The one fact unmistakably established was that the Republican-Progressive breach of 1912 had not been healed. Of more than four million Progressives who voted for Roosevelt in 1912, half went back into the Republican party in 1914; of the remaining two million, from a third to a half voted in 1916 for Wilson, many voted for Hughes under protest, and only a handful supported the Republican candidate gladly. The extraordinary position of the country when, on March 4, 1917, President Wilson entered on his second term threw party alignments into the background and made political prophecy more than usually futile.

CHAPTER XXI

PREPAREDNESS AND THE APPROACH OF WAR
(1914–1917)

THE cataclysm beyond the Atlantic turned the thought of Americans to the ability of their own country to give a good account of itself if drawn into this, or some future, conflict. Expert testimony was hardly needed to establish the fact that the nation was unprepared for war with a great power; experience soon showed that it was not even prepared for a military demonstration against Mexico.[1] The country was rich in the elements of military and naval strength: increasing wealth, unlimited capacity for food production, vast ship-yards and munitions plants, thousands of engineers and other trained men ready in time of need to place their skill at the public service, millions of citizens jealous of the nation's honor and capable of any sacrifice in its behalf. But these resources were not organized; and only a small military force was available for instant use.

For many decades it had been assumed that geo-

---

[1] Secretary of War, *Annual Report*, 1916, pp. 8–21; Executive Committee of the Mayor's Committee on National Defense, *The Mobilization of the National Guard, 1916; its Economic and Military Aspects*, (New York, 1917).

graphical and political isolation made the nation immune from foreign aggression. Later, as the country was drawn into closer relations with the outside world, the idea grew that measures of defense were desirable, especially such as looked to power on the sea. Beginning in the first Cleveland administration, a "new navy" was built up, which, after the Spanish war proved its usefulness, was brought into third place among the admiralties of the world. But the army was neglected. On the eve of the war with Spain, the regular troops numbered only 26,000; and while in 1901 the military establishment was reorganized on the basis of 100,000 officers and men, the number actually in service was for several years only about 60,000. In 1914 it was 92,000, including 19,000 persons belonging to the non-combative administrative and educational branches. Belgium, with only seven million people, had a larger armed force when invaded by Germany.

The chance that the United States would be drawn into the conflict seemed in 1914 very slender; yet it suggested precaution. A National Security League and a Navy League were organized by persons who saw the danger, and suggestions for strengthening the army and navy multiplied. On naval increase there was little difference of opinion. The contest between Great Britain and Germany was expected to show that a nation's greatest asset in war is sea-power. Accordingly, in August, 1915, Congress adopted a three-year naval program which called for an expenditure of six hundred million dollars on ships alone. The intention was to put the United States by 1920 approximately where Great Britain stood in 1914; and thus it fell to the Democrats, the party traditionally opposed to a large navy, to carry the heaviest naval appropriation ever voted by a nation at peace.

On the increase of land forces the nation made up its mind more slowly. To most persons it was unthinkable that the country should ever need a great army for use on foreign soil; and defense against invasion by a European or Asiatic power was to be the task of the navy. The American people were of peaceful convictions and intentions; they followed the startling events of Europe with interest and curiosity, but not with apprehension; whatever their sympathies, they felt themselves to be only distant onlookers, safe in their detachment. Public men shared the delusion. Secretary Bryan declared that in case of need "the United States could raise a million men between sunrise and sunset." President Wilson said to Congress (December 8, 1914) that provision for voluntary military training should be extended, and that the organized militia of the states should be "developed and strengthened"; but he asserted that the nation must continue to depend, in time of peril, "not upon a standing army, nor yet upon a reserve army, but upon a citizenry trained and accustomed to arms."[1]

A year passed with no action, although the prolongation of the war and the controversies between the United States and the belligerents gave point to the

[1] *Senate Jour.*, 63 Cong., 3 Sess., 13.

discussion. December 8, 1915, the President recommended to Congress a standing army of 142,000 and a
reserve of 400,000 "disciplined citizens"; and in a
speaking tour of the Middle West, undertaken to sound
out public opinion, he surprised his hearers by painting
the nation's dangers in strong colors and declaring
that in the work of preparing for self-vindication and
defense there was "not a day to be lost." The Administration's program met a cool reception from both
Congress and the country, and the President acted
with less than his customary decision. The Secretary
of War, Garrison, felt a lack of support and resigned,
being succeeded by Newton D. Baker, a lawyer of
Cleveland. Congress floundered in pointless discussion, and finally passed the Hay bill (June 3, 1916),
which was permeated with politics and fell far short of
the demands of the situation.

This National Defense Act[1] provided for an increase of the normal peace strength of the regular
army, by five annual accessions, to 175,000 officers and
men; although in case of need the period of increase
might be shortened; and, by executive order, the number of officers and men might be raised to 220,000.
The measure also undertook to make of the militia
a more effective second line of defense. The reported
strength in 1915 (125,000) was to be increased, by five
one-year stages, until each state should have a peace
strength of eight hundred officers and men for every
senator and representative, giving a grand total of
about 425,000. Enlisted men were required to take

[1] *U. S. Statutes at Large*, XXXIX., pt. i., pp. 166–217.

oath to the federal government, as well as to their
state; the President was empowered to fix the units in
any state or territory, with a view to co-ordination on
a national scale; organization, equipment, and discipline were to be the same as in the regular army;
in addition to heavy increases of existing subsidies for
equipment and training, federal pay was provided for
both officers and men.[1]

Military experts viewed the new law with disfavor.
They felt that what the country needed (besides a
larger standing army) was not more amateur soldiers,
but a body of trained reserves, under full control of
the national government. They pointed out that
earlier acts had failed to unify the militia, and argued
that the Hay law, while carrying federalization so far
that some of its provisions were of doubtful constitutionality, would not give better results. The
country's second line of defense still consisted of forty-
eight little armies under the control of forty-eight
different authorities; the cost of the new system was
excessive; and a few months' experience fulfilled the
prediction that the Guard units could not be recruited
to their full strength. With war lowering on the
horizon, the nation found itself at the opening of 1917
with its problem of military organization still unsolved.

Another current of agitation was directed to ending
war altogether. Existing guarantees of peace—inter-

[1] Smith, "Army Reorganization in the Sixty-fourth Congress," Acad.
Polit. Sci., *Proceedings*, VI., No. 4, pp. 79–87; "The National Guard;
its Status and Defects," *Review of Reviews*, LIV., 163–167; Marvin,
"Millions for Defense, but Not One Cent for Tribute," *World's Work*,
XXXII., 173–178.

national law, improved means of international understanding, arbitration treaties, the Hague International Commission of Inquiry, the Hague Court of Arbitration—were obviously insufficient; the national and international peace societies had aroused interest, but had failed in their main object; the theory that industry, trade, and finance were too highly developed to permit war had broken down; the notion that modern engines of destruction had made war impossible was shown to be well founded only to the extent that the methods of carrying on war were totally changed.

Still there was hope that the present conflict would be the "war that would end war." Opinions as to the way to reach this result differed; and several peace associations brought new programs into view. One was the Society to Eliminate the Economic Causes of War; another was the World's Court League;[1] a third, founded at The Hague, was the Central Organization for a Durable Peace. Of largest promise was the League to Enforce Peace, organized at a conference in Independence Hall, Philadelphia, June 17, 1915.

Discarding the world-state idea as impracticable, the League to Enforce Peace looked to a voluntary group of nations, bound together by engagements which, while not making war impossible, would prevent hostilities from being entered upon lightly and arbitrarily. The program contained four essential points: (1) justiciable questions arising between the signatory powers, not settled by negotiation, should be submitted to a judicial tribunal for hearing and judgment;

[1] *World Almanac and Encyclopædia*, 1917, p. 461.

(2) other questions, not settled by negotiation, should be submitted to a council of conciliation for "hearing, consideration, and recommendation"; (3) the signatories should jointly "use forthwith" both their economic and military forces against any one of their number going to war, or committing acts of hostility, against another of the signatories before the matter in dispute should have been duly submitted; (4) conferences of the signatory powers should be held from time to time to formulate and codify rules of international law.

The plan thus provided a machinery of international police, to restrain a nation from war until causes and motives could be stated and examined. It struck a reasonable balance between irresponsible nationalism and sentimental internationalism; and it won wide favor. Europeans of distinction pledged support, and there seemed a chance to make the American organization, in course of time, a branch of a great international society.[1]

During most of 1916 the European war went on with no clear advantage on either side. Then came, in early winter, the collapse of Roumania before the armies of Mackensen and Falkenhayn, followed by a move which took the world completely by surprise. On December 12—six days after the fall of Bucharest—the German Imperial government, with the assent of its allies, sent notes to the Entente powers suggest-

[1] Dickinson, "The Foundations of a League of Peace," World Peace Foundation, *Pamphlet Series*, V., No. 2; Anon., "Historical Light on the League to Enforce Peace," *ibid.*, VI., No. 6; Lowell, "A League to Enforce Peace," *Atlantic Monthly*, Vol. 116, pp. 392–400.

ing negotiations for peace, though mentioning no terms.[1]

The Entente nations were a unit in receiving the proposal unfavorably. They wanted peace; but they knew that the war had not yet been won. Germany was manifestly not "on her knees"; the very indefiniteness of her offer indicated that she was prepared to make no large concessions. Furthermore, Hohenzollern autocracy was still in the saddle, and peace made with William II. was felt to be merely a truce with another Napoleon. Far from courting peace, the Entente nations were bracing themselves for efforts on a grander scale. They were mobilizing their whole populations, reconstructing their industries, reorganizing their governments. After two years of "muddling," Great Britain, in particular, was just becoming an efficient fighting nation.

Upon the outbreak of war in 1914, President Wilson tendered his good offices in behalf of peace, but obtained only formal acknowledgments. Again, after the German retreat from the Marne, he sounded the Berlin government, without avail. Many times in later months he was urged to renew offers of mediation, to call a conference of neutral states, and to take other steps looking toward a pacification; and he talked much of the part he hoped to make the United States play in restoring peace. But no suitable opportunity came until the German government itself proposed negotiations.

[1] Am. Assoc. for Internat. Conciliation, *Official Documents looking toward Peace*, Ser. I., 11–12.

This suggested an attempt to induce the two groups of belligerents to define more precisely the purposes for which they were carrying on the war; and to that end the President sent an identic note, December 18, to all of the fourteen warring nations, saying that the United States was "as vitally and as directly interested" as the belligerents in the measures to be taken to secure the future peace of the world, and suggesting that the present confused situation would be much cleared and the possibility of peace increased if the parties to the conflict would forthwith publish "such an avowal of their respective views as to the terms upon which the war might be concluded . . . as would make it possible to compare them."[1]

At the moment, the President's action was criticized, in both the United States and the Entente countries, as meddling and as playing into the hands of the Teutonic governments. The Senate, none the less, finally indorsed it by resolution; American sentiment shifted; and resentment in Europe gave place to cordial appreciation. Aside from putting the nation on record in an honorable way, the note accomplished nothing. Germany's reply, December 26, parried the main question and suggested simply that delegates of the belligerent states should meet "at a neutral place" for an exchange of views. The Entente response to the Berlin overtures was issued from Paris four days later. It proved a flat refusal to consider peace until Germany should openly offer "complete restitution, full repara-

[1] Am. Assoc. for Internat. Conciliation, *Official Documents looking toward Peace*, Ser. II., 3–6.

tion, and effectual guarantees." January 11, 1917, a note to the American government indicated, on general lines, the things for which the Entente nations considered themselves bound to fight to the end.[1]

The net result of the peace proposals was to intensify feeling and stir both sides to fresh exertions; and out of this came an unexpected crisis for the United States. January 31, Count von Bernstorff, German ambassador at Washington, submitted a memorandum from his government saying that the Teutonic powers would now be compelled to fight for existence with all the weapons at their disposal, and announcing that after February 1 neutral and belligerent ships found in zones of the high seas encircling the Entente countries would be sunk on sight by submarines. American passenger vessels were to be immune only if they sailed at the rate of one a week, took a prescribed course, painted their sides in red and white stripes, arrived on Sunday, and departed on Wednesday. This was an utter abrogation of international law, an announcement of a policy of sheer "frightfulness."

The note had the effect of a clear challenge to the United States. In April, 1916, President Wilson, when protesting against the sinking of the Channel steamer *Sussex*, had threatened severance of diplomatic relations unless Germany should abandon her warfare against merchant craft. The Berlin government gave conditional reassurances; and for nine months there had been little cause for complaint.[2] Now the whole issue was reopened, and in uglier form than before.

[1] *Review of Reviews*, LV., 120. [2] See p. 343.

Nothing remained but to carry out the threat of April, 1916; and this was instantly done. February 3, diplomatic relations between the two countries were severed; and on the following day President Wilson suggested to other neutral nations that they could aid in the pacification of the world by taking similar action.

The problem of the government was now to find some means of protecting American commerce and American lives on the high seas; and after a delay that tried the patience of many people, the President appeared before Congress, February 26, and asked a grant of power to this end. March 1, the House passed an Armed Ships bill, by a vote of 403 to 13, giving the President authority to supply merchant ships of American registry with defensive arms and ammunition.[1] A bill of similar purport, but adding a blanket grant of power, was held up in the Senate by eleven members styled by the President "a group of willful men"; and the session closed, March 4, without action. March 8, the new Senate, in special session, adopted by a vote of 76 to 3 a clôture amendment bringing to an end the chamber's time-honored rule of unlimited debate.[2]

Backed by high legal authority, the President came to the conclusion that he already had most of the power which he desired. Accordingly, the announcement was made that guns would be mounted on American merchant ships bound for European waters, and that expert gunners would be supplied by the navy.

[1] *House Jour.*, 64 Cong., 2 Sess., 311.

[2] *Senate Jour.*, Special Sess., reported in 64 Cong., 2 Sess., 234.

The decision brought war perceptibly nearer; for the arrangements were almost certain to lead to encounters with submarines, and such encounters would be difficult to view in any light other than as hostile acts. Further action by Congress was plainly needed. Hence a special session was called for April 16; and lowering clouds caused the date to be set back to April 2.

During the interval the country drifted rapidly toward war. American vessels were sunk without warning and with loss of life; on the day on which Congress assembled the *Aztec* was sent to the bottom off the coast of France; from Berlin came no indication of a change of heart. The Sixty-fifth Congress met at the appointed time. Under normal circumstances, the almost evenly matched party strength in the House would have been likely to produce a contest over organization; but everything now gave way to the foreign danger, and Speaker Clark was easily re-elected over the Republican candidate, James R. Mann, by a vote of 217 to 205. On the same day the two houses were brought together to hear the President's message.

The country knew that the burden of the message was to be war. The President went to the Capitol under double guard, and the crowded floors and galleries were breathless when he rose to speak. In measured tones he called upon Congress to "declare the recent course of the Imperial German government to be in fact nothing less than war against the government and people of the United States," and recommended an immediate addition of half a million men

26

to the army, selected on the principle of universal
liability to service, with subsequent increments of
equal size. In both houses a war resolution was introduced, as follows: "Whereas the German Imperial
government has committed repeated acts of war against
the government and the people of the United States
of America; Therefore be it resolved. . . . that the
state of war between the United States and the Imperial German government which has thus been thrust
upon the United States is hereby formally declared."
The full resources of the country were pledged to bring
the conflict to a successful end. The Senate passed this
resolution, April 4, by a vote of 82 to 6; the House at
3 A.M. April 6, by a vote of 373 to 50; and thus the
United States became a party to the greatest armed
conflict in history.

The decision was the result of a profound change of
view and policy. For two years the notion had prevailed that the war was simply a contest of rival
European states for territory, trade, and other practical
advantages. The menace to American rights was supposed to be temporary; American institutions were not
thought of as endangered. The country had the
President's word for it that "with the causes and objects of this great war" it was "not concerned." On
this basis, the government acted with great caution
and forbearance. It tried to preserve neutrality "in
thought and action"; it drew the ill-will of spirited
citizens by its mildness toward the violators of American rights; it clung to the view that the greatest service the United States could render civilization was to

keep out of the conflict, so as to maintain some part of the world where the processes of peace would continue; it promised itself and the American people that the country would play a glorious part as a peace-maker, achieving great ends for civilization by mediation. Still standing by this program, the President went before the nation in the campaign of 1916; and the people, rallying to the cry "He kept us out of war," gave it the stamp of their approval.

Then came a rude awakening. The peace plan collapsed; Germany's submarine campaign was renewed with ungovernable fury; neutral rights vanished; an intercepted letter showed that the Berlin government was encouraging Carranza to make war on the United States for the conquest of the Southwest.[1] These were grim actualities, from which there was no escape. They gave point to two main criticisms brought against the government's whole course in the war.

One of these criticisms was that a firmer course from the beginning would have inspired greater respect for neutral rights and might have prevented a large part of the difficulties between the United States and the belligerents.[2] The other was that the Administration misconceived the war's true character. Long before the peace moves of 1916, many Americans felt, as did the peoples of the Entente countries, that the war had become a great moral contest between democracy and autocracy; that if Germany won, democracy the

---

[1] *Review of Reviews*, LV., 355.
[2] Smith, "American Diplomacy in the European War," *Polit. Sci. Quart.*, XXXI., 481–518.

world over would suffer a staggering blow; that the United States was directly concerned and ought to cast her weight into the scale to make certain the overthrow of the Prussian autocratic ideal. A belief that Wilson did not see the conflict in this light caused coolness toward the United States in the Entente countries, and led to vigorous protest in the English and French press against his "peace without victory" note of December 18, 1916.[1]

The German government officially disclaimed desire for war against the United States, and said that it would not be held responsible at the bar of history. Its argument was: (1) the Entente powers had spurned the German offer of peace; (2) Germany now faced a struggle for sheer existence; (3) the United States, having failed to compel Great Britain to abandon the blockade of the German coasts, was essentially unneutral; (4) this blockade must be met with the only effective weapon at hand, the submarine. The Kaiser's government knew that America was totally unprepared for war on a grand scale; and it believed that the submarine would bring the Entente nations to their knees before the new enemy could get into action.

The United States had ample cause for war in the attacks upon her lawful commerce, the slaughter of more than two hundred of her citizens upon the high seas, and the intrigues against her neutrality and her security, carried on both within the country and elsewhere. Yet the nation went into the conflict on account of no one of these things, nor all of them to-

[1] *World's Work*, XXXII., 350.

gether, but rather to combat the spirit of autocracy and ruthlessness that lay behind them. The conflict had so shaped itself as to have become America's no less than Europe's: America's ideals were derided; her institutions were threatened; her rights as a nation among nations were ignored; the system of international law and comity which the United States had helped to build was trampled under foot; the physical safety of the people was menaced; nothing could be plainer than that this country would soon be forced to grapple single-handed with German imperialism should the Teutonic powers emerge from the present conflict victorious.

With stout heart and high hope, the nation girded itself for its part in the supreme task of making the world "safe for democracy."

CHAPTER XXII

CRITICAL ESSAY ON AUTHORITIES

THERE is no lack of printed materials on most subjects dealt with in this volume. For obvious reasons, memoirs and biographies are few, and general histories hardly exist. But no earlier decade produced such quantities of books treating of current affairs; newspaper and magazine discussion attained new standards of quality as well as of quantity; government publications steadily increased in bulk and value. The following lists aim to call attention to the best literature in the field, with emphasis on documents and other sources.

BIBLIOGRAPHIES

There is no bibliography which covers the entire ground. Among important reference lists published by the Library of Congress, and compiled by A. P. C. Griffin or H. H. B. Meyer, successive Chief Bibliographers, may be mentioned: *List of Books, with References to Periodicals, relating to Railroads in their Relation to the Government and the Public* (1907); *Select List of References on Corrupt Practices in Elections* (1908); *List of Works relating to the Supreme Court of the U. S.* (1909); *Select List of References on the Valuation and Capitalization of Railroads* (1909); *Select List of References on the Cost of Living and Prices* (1910); *List of References on Reciprocity* (1910); *Select List of References on Parcel Post* (1911); *Select List of References on Employers'*

Liability and Workmen's Compensation (1911); *Select List of References on Boycotts and Injunctions in Labor Disputes* (1911); *Select List of References on the Initiative, Referendum, and Recall* (1912); *Select List of References on the Conservation of Natural Resources in the U. S.* (1912); *Select List of References on the Monetary Question* (1913); *Select List of References on Federal Control of Commerce and Corporations* (1914); *List of References on Water Rights and the Control of Waters* (1914); *List of References on Child Labor* (1916); *List of References on Embargoes* (1917); *The United States at War; Organizations and Literature* (1917).

Good book reviews and lists of new books and of magazine articles are to be found in the *American Historical Review* (1895—), *American Economic Review* (1911—), *American Political Science Review* (1907—), *Political Science Quarterly* (1886—), *Quarterly Journal of Economics* (1886—), *Journal of Political Economy* (1893—), *American Labor Legislation Review* (1911—), *American Journal of International Law* (1907—), *Annals of the American Academy of Political and Social Science* (1890—), *American Journal of Sociology* (1895—), *Nation* (1865—), and *Yale Review* (1892—). Brief book lists are printed also in the *American Year Book* (1910—). For detailed lists of magazine articles see the *Readers' Guide to Periodical Literature* (1910—).

Other bibliographies of a special character include E. Channing, A. B. Hart, and F. J. Turner, *Guide to the Study and Reading of American History* (revised edition, Boston, 1914); F. J. Turner, *List of References on the History of the West* (Cambridge, 1913); A. B. Hart, *Manual of American History, Diplomacy, and Government* (new edition, Cambridge, 1908); P. H. Goldsmith, *Brief Bibliography of Books in English, Spanish, and Portuguese relating to the Republics commonly called Latin America, with Comments* (New York, 1915).

An indispensable guide to current government publications is the *Monthly Catalogue of United States Public Documents*, issued by the Superintendent of Documents at Washington. A publication which aims to be a clearinghouse of information on public affairs is the *Bulletin of the Public Affairs Information Service* (1915—).

COMPENDIUMS AND PERIODICALS

Two annuals which are convenient for general reference are the *American Year Book* (1910—) and the *New International Year Book* (1907—). Of several yearly compendiums published by, or in connection with, newspapers, the most serviceable is the *World Almanac and Encyclopedia* (1905—). Periodicals which contain articles and other materials of large value for the study of current affairs are named on p. 401. Others of more popular nature include the *Review of Reviews, World's Work, North American Review, Atlantic Monthly, Outlook, Independent, Forum, Literary Digest, New Republic.* Associated Press despatches and despatches of Washington correspondents in the metropolitan and other dailies give full, and as a rule reliable, information on current affairs. The most important personal organs are Bryan's *Commoner* and La Follette's *Weekly*. A. C. McLaughlin and A. B. Hart [eds.], *Cyclopædia of American Government* (3 vols., New York, 1915), contains many articles on the public affairs of the decade.

MEMOIRS AND BIOGRAPHIES

The period lies too close at hand to have yielded much literature of this kind. *Theodore Roosevelt; an Autobiography* (New York, 1913), although written under a sense of restraint, is of decided value. R. M. La Follette, *Autobiography; a Personal Narrative of Political Experiences* (Madison, 1913), is a vivid human document. More formal memoirs are: J. B. Foraker, *Notes of a Busy Life* (2 vols., Cincinnati, 1916), and S. M. Cullom, *Fifty Years of Public Service* (Chicago, 1911). The career and personality of Roosevelt are dealt with in laudatory vein in F. E. Leupp, *The Man Roosevelt; a Portrait Sketch* (New York, 1904); J. A. Riis, *Theodore Roosevelt, the Citizen* (New York, 1904); J. L. Street, *The Most Interesting American* (New York, 1915); C. G. Washburn, *Theodore Roosevelt; the Logic of his Career* (Boston, 1916). The best account of President Wilson is H. J. Ford, *Woodrow Wilson; the Man and his Work* (New York, 1916), written by a colleague and close friend, yet in a judicious spirit. A popular biography is W. B. Hale, *Woodrow Wilson; the Story of his Life* (New York, 1912), and an English estimate of the man, and of American politics in his day, is H. W. Harris, *President Wilson from an English Point of View* (New York, 1917). In lieu of a substantial biography, a useful source of information on the Republican presidential candidate of 1916 is W. L. Ransom, *Charles E. Hughes, the Statesman as Shown in the Opinions of the Jurist* (New York, 1916). A biography which is really a popular party history is W. D. Orcutt, *Burrows of Michigan and the Republican Party* (2 vols., New York, 1917). J. G. Pyle, *The Life of James J. Hill* (2 vols., New York, 1917), is indispensable to the student of economic history.

TARIFF

The tariff was a leading issue throughout most of the period, and was the subject of many official investigations and reports. For voluminous hearings leading up to the Payne-Aldrich Act of 1909 see *House Documents*, 60 Cong., 2 Sess., Nos. 1502 and 1505; on the Taft program of reciprocity with Canada, *Senate Documents*, 61 Cong., 3 Sess., No. 787, and *Senate Documents*, 62 Cong., 1 Sess., Nos. 56 and 89. The report of Taft's Tariff Board on Schedule K [wool and woolens] is in *House Documents*, 62 Cong., 2 Sess., No. 342; on Schedule I [cotton manufactures], *ibid.*, No. 643. Hearings and reports preliminary to the Underwood Act of 1913 are in *House Documents*, 62 Cong., 3 Sess., No. 1447, and 63 Cong., 1 Sess., No. 5. The tariff measures of the period are described in F. W. Taussig, *The Tariff History of the United States* (6th edition, New York, 1914). The same author's *Some Aspects of the Tariff Question* (Cambridge, 1915) discusses in pointed fashion the effects of the American tariff system on the sugar, iron and steel, and textile industries. I. M. Tarbell, *The Tariff in Our Times* (New York, 1911), narrates the tariff history of the country since the Civil War, from the point of view of a keen anti-protectionist. The relation of the tariff to certain industries is further brought out in R. G. Blakey, *The United States*

Beet-Sugar Industry and the Tariff (New York, 1912); M. T. Copeland, *The Cotton Manufacturing Industry in the United States* (Cambridge, 1913); and P. T. Cherington, *The Wool Industry* (New York, 1916).

PUBLIC FINANCE

A monumental collection of materials is the publications of the National Monetary Commission, *Senate Documents*, 61 Cong., 2–3 Sess., and 62 Cong., 2 Sess., serial numbers 5605–5640, 5642, 5859–5861, 6146. The banking and currency problems of the country are fully set forth in *Senate Documents*, 63 Cong., 1 Sess., No. 232. The annual reports of the Secretary of the Treasury contain much information. Thoughtful discussions of the banking question include O. M. W. Sprague, *Banking Reforms in the United States* (Cambridge, 1911); C. N. Fowler, *Seventeen Talks on the Banking Question* (Elizabeth, N. J., 1913); L. Bendix, *The Aldrich Plan in the Light of Modern Banking* (New York, 1912); P. M. Warburg [ed.], *Essays on Banking Reform in the United States* (New York, 1914). Satisfactory expositions of the new banking and currency system of 1913 are H. P. Willis, *The Federal Reserve* (New York, 1915), and T. Conway and E. M. Patterson, *The Operation of the New Bank Act* (Philadelphia, 1914).

RAILROAD REGULATION

The best general treatise on American railroads is E. R. Johnson and G. G. Huebner, *Railroad Traffic and Rates* (2 vols., New York, 1911); the best exposition of railway organization is W. Z. Ripley, *Railroads: Finance and Organization* (New York, 1915). A useful collection of facts is *Statistics of Railways, 1905–1915*, published by the Bureau of Railway Economics (Washington, 1916). Important books dealing with the power of the federal government to regulate commerce, and with the Interstate Commerce Act and its amendments, are T. H. Calvert, *The Regulation of Commerce under the Federal Constitution* (Northport, 1907); E. P. Prentice, *The Federal Power over Carriers and Corpora-*

tions (New York, 1907); F. N. Judson, *The Law of Interstate Commerce and its Federal Regulation* (Chicago, 1906); J. H. Beale, *Railroad Rate Regulation, with Special Reference to the Powers of the Interstate Commerce Commission under the Acts to Regulate Commerce* (2d edition, rewritten by B. Wyman, New York, 1915); H. B. Fuller, *The Act to Regulate Commerce, construed by the Supreme Court* (Washington, 1915); T. L. Kibler, *The Commodities Clause of the Hepburn Act* (Washington, 1916); F. Frankfurter, *Selection of Cases under the Interstate Commerce Act* (Cambridge, 1915).

The most systematic and authoritative discussion of the problems and methods of railroad regulation is W. Z. Ripley, *Railroads: Rates and Regulation* (New York, 1912). An excellent analysis of tendencies in the United States is H. S. Haines, *Problems in Railway Regulation* (New York, 1911). Other useful books on the subject include H. S. Haines, *Restrictive Railway Legislation* (New York, 1905); A. N. Merritt, *Federal Regulation of Railway Rates* (Boston, 1907); R. J. McFall, *Railway Monopoly and Rate Regulation* (New York, 1916); S. O. Dunn, *The American Transportation Question* (New York, 1912); H. Elliott, *The Truth about the Railroads* (Boston, 1913); G. A. Rankin, *An American Transportation System* (New York, 1909); E. Hungerford, *The Railroad Problem* (Chicago, 1917). An important monograph on a subject of increasing importance is H. B. Vanderblue, *Railroad Valuation* (Boston, 1917).

CORPORATIONS AND TRUSTS

A useful compendium is *The Federal Anti-Trust Laws, with Amendments* (Govt. Printing Office, 1916), containing a list of cases instituted and citations of cases decided. An indispensable volume is *Trust Laws and Unfair Competition* (Govt. Printing Office, 1916), compiled under the direction of J. E. Davies, and describing the legislation and judicial decisions affecting trusts in the United States and the principal foreign countries. For a compilation of federal anti-trust decisions see also *Senate Documents*, 62 Cong., 1 Sess., No. 111. A serviceable history of the growth of "big business" is E. T. B. Perine, *The Story of the Trust*

Companies (New York, 1916); of somewhat similar character is C. N. Fay, *Big Business and Government* (New York, 1912); and J. Moody, *The Truth about the Trusts*, is a well-informed analysis of the conditions that have made trusts inevitable. The principal work on the Standard Oil Company is I. M. Tarbell, *History of the Standard Oil Company* (2 vols., New York, 1904). A briefer account is G. H. Montague, *Rise and Progress of the Standard Oil Company* (New York, 1903); and there is a well-informed sketch by C. M. Keyes in *World's Work*, XVI.–XVII. (1908–1909). A. Cotter, *Authentic History of the United States Steel Corporation* (New York, 1916), is popular but reliable.

The legislative history of the trust question is well presented in O. W. Knauth, *The Policy of the United States towards Industrial Monopoly* (New York, 1914); the first great trust decision of the century is discussed in B. H. Meyer, *History of the Northern Securities Case* (Madison, 1906); and an able argument that the trust decisions of the Supreme Court between 1909 and 1914 made the Sherman law an adequate regulatory measure is contained in W. H. Taft, *The Anti-Trust Act and the Supreme Court* (New York, 1914). Important constructive studies are C. R. Van Hise, *Concentration and Control: a Solution of the Trust Problem in the United States* (New York, 1912), and E. D. Durand, *The Trust Problem* (Cambridge, 1915). W. H. S. Stevens, *Unfair Competition* (Chicago, 1917), breaks some new ground. Useful collections of articles, court decisions, and other illustrative materials are to be found in W. Z. Ripley [ed.], *Trusts, Pools, and Corporations* (revised edition, Boston, 1916), and W. S. Stevens [ed.], *Industrial Combinations and Trusts* (New York, 1913).

LABOR

Extensive information on conditions of employment in the iron and steel industries is presented in *Senate Documents*, 62 Cong., 1 Sess., No. 110. Hearings before the Employers' Liability and Workmen's Compensation Commission are reported in *Senate Documents*, 62 Cong., 1 Sess., No. 90. and

2 Sess., No. 338; and the workmen's compensation laws of
the United States and foreign countries are printed in *Senate
Documents*, 63 Cong., 2 Sess., No. 336, and in Bulletin of
United States Bureau of Labor Statistics, Whole No. 203
(1917).   A voluminous report on the condition of woman
and child wage-earners is in *Senate Documents*, 61 Cong.,
2 Sess., No. 645; and a report of the United States Board
of Mediation and Conciliation on the effects of arbitration
proceedings on the rates of pay and working conditions of
railroad employees is in *Senate Documents*, 64 Cong., 1 Sess.,
No. 493.   Much useful information is contained in the
annual reports of the Commissioner of Labor, and in the
American Labor Year Book (1916—).   The results of extensive investigations are presented in W. J. Lauck and E.
Sydenstricker, *Conditions of Labor in American Industries*
(New York, 1917). S. Gompers, *Labor in Europe and America*
(New York, 1910), contains personal observations of work-
ingmen's conditions by the President of the American
Federation of Labor.   The essentials of American trade
union organization are set forth in T. W. Glocker, *The
Government of American Trade Unions* (Baltimore, 1913).

Most phases of industrial disputes are dealt with in H. W.
Laidler, *Boycotts and the Labor Struggle* (New York, 1913);
L. Wolman, *The Boycott in American Trade Unions* (Baltimore, 1916); A. E. Suffern, *Conciliation and Arbitration in
the Coal Industry of America* (Boston, 1915); G. E. Barnett
and D. A. McCabe, *Mediation, Investigation, and Arbitration
in Industrial Disputes* (New York, 1916); C. H. Mote, *Industrial Arbitration* (Indianapolis, 1916); G. G. Groat, *The
Attitude of American Courts in Labor Cases* (New York, 1911).
An important group of papers is "The Present Labor Situation; Compulsory Investigation and Arbitration," Am.
Acad. Polit. and Soc. Sci., *Annals*, LXIX. (1917).   A tren-
chant discussion of labor's entrance into politics is R. Hunter,
Labor in Politics (Chicago, 1915), and a thorough account
of the tendencies of organized labor in the United States
toward violence is J. G. Brooks, *American Syndicalism: the
I. W. W.* (New York, 1913).   J. R. Commons and J. B.
Andrews, *Principles of Labor Legislation* (New York, 1916),
is the best work of its kind.   F. R. Jones, *Digest of Work-*

men's Compensation Laws in the United States and Territories (4th edition, New York, 1915), is a convenient guide.

CONSERVATION AND RECLAMATION

The most important official publication is the report of the National Conservation Commission, 1909, printed as *Senate Documents*, 60 Cong., 2 Sess., No. 676. The proceedings of the White House conference of May, 1908, are printed in *House Documents*, 60 Cong., 2 Sess., No. 1425. The extensive materials relating to the Ballinger-Pinchot controversy appear in *Senate Documents*, 61 Cong., 3 Sess., No. 719; and the final report of the National Waterways Commission is in *Senate Documents*, 62 Cong., 2 Sess., No. 469. The best general exposition of conservation problems and policies is C. R. Van Hise, *The Conservation of Natural Resources in the United States* (New York, 1910). The conservation of water resources is discussed scientifically in G. F. Swain, *The Conservation of Water by Storage* (New Haven, 1915), and popularly in J. L. Mathews, *Conservation of Water* (Boston, 1910). The relation of rail to water transportation is set forth in H. G. Moulton, *Waterways versus Railways* (Boston, 1912). A well-written treatise on the reclamation of arid lands is R. P. Teele, *Irrigation in the United States; a Discussion of its Legal, Economic, and Financial Aspects* (New York, 1915).

IMMIGRATION

The monumental collection of materials on this subject is the report of the Immigration Commission, with evidence, etc., in forty-two volumes, published in *Senate Documents*, 61 Cong., 2 and 3 Sess., various numbers. Abstracts of the Commission's report are printed in *Senate Documents*, 61 Cong., 3 Sess., No. 747. J. W. Jenks and W. J. Lauck, *The Immigration Problem*, (3d edition, New York, 1913), by a member of the Commission and an expert in charge of its industrial studies, embodies the results of the Commission's investigations. The most illuminating book that has been written on immigration in its larger aspects is H. P. Fairchild, *Immigration; a World Movement and its*

American Significance (New York, 1913). The economic aspects of the subject are stressed in I. A. Hourwich, *Immigration and Labor* (New York, 1912), and F. J. Warne, *The Immigrant Invasion* (New York, 1913); the sociological aspects in E. A. Ross, *The Old World in the New* (New York, 1914), and A. McClure, *Leadership of the New America* (New York, 1917); the personal and picturesque aspects in P. Roberts, *The New Immigration* (New York, 1912), and E. A. Steiner, *On the Trail of the Immigrant* (New York, 1906), and *Nationalizing America* (New York, 1916). Among numerous studies of the immigration of special peoples are H. P. Fairchild, *Greek Immigration to the United States* (New Haven, 1911); S. Joseph, *Jewish Immigration to the United States from 1881 to 1910* (New York, 1914); E. G. Balch, *Our Slavic Fellow Citizens* (New York, 1910); S. C. Johnson, *History of Emigration from the United Kingdom to North America, 1763-1912* (London, 1913); K. C. Babcock, *The Scandinavian Element in the United States* (Urbana, 1914). A valuable legal work is C. L. Bouvé, *Treatise on the Laws governing the Exclusion and Expulsion of Aliens in the United States* (Washington, 1912). M. C. Coolidge, *Chinese Immigration* (New York, 1909), argues against the exclusionist policy. Japanese immigration is dealt with in several of the works mentioned under Oriental Relations (p. 415).

THE DEPENDENCIES

A compilation of acts of Congress, treaties, proclamations, and judicial decisions relating to the non-contiguous territories of the United States in the period 1898-1908 is in *Senate Documents*, 61 Cong., 1 Sess., No. 47. For the revised statutes and codes of Porto Rico, to 1911, see *Senate Documents*, 61 Cong., 3 Sess., No. 813. The report of the Alaska Railroad Commission is in *House Documents*, 62 Cong., 3 Sess., No. 1346. The annual reports of the governors of the several territories contain much information on current events and conditions. Three important works on American administration in the Philippines are D. C. Worcester, *The Philippines, Past and Present* (2 vols., new edition, New York, 1914); J. A. LeRoy, *The Americans in the Philippines* (2 vols., Boston, 1914); and C. B. Elliott, *The Philippines* (Indianapolis, 1917). A popular account of the work of the United States in the islands is C. Crow, *America and the Philippines* (New York, 1914), and an able plea for Philippine independence by a native writer is M. M. Kalaw, *The Case for the Filipinos* (New York, 1916). On Porto Rico, L. S. Rowe, *The United States and Porto Rico* (New York, 1904), remains the best book; but a useful supplement is M. Bloomfield, *Study of Certain Social, Educational, and Industrial Problems in Porto Rico* (Boston, 1912). Much information on Alaska is contained in A. W. Greeley, *Handbook of Alaska* (New York, 1914), and on Hawaii in W. R. Castle, *Hawaii Past and Present* (New York, 1917). On the most recently acquired insular possessions, see W. Westergaard, *The Danish West Indies* (New York, 1917). A useful popular book is W. D. Boyce, *United States Colonies and Dependencies* (Chicago, 1914).

STRUCTURE AND METHODS OF GOVERNMENT

Political science made great strides during the period, and the literature of the subject became very extensive. The most important government publications in the field owed their origin to President Taft's Economy and Efficiency Commission, created in 1910. The President's message on economy and efficiency, with accompanying papers, is in *House Documents*, 62 Cong., 2 Sess., No. 458, and the Commission's reports are in 62 Cong., 2 Sess., Nos. 670, 732, 854, and 3 Sess., Nos. 1110 and 1252.

The office of president is discussed at first hand in W. H. Taft, *Our Chief Magistrate and his Powers* (New York, 1916). On the development of the executive departments the best works are M. L. Hinsdale, *History of the President's Cabinet* (Ann Arbor, 1911), and H. B. Learned, *The President's Cabinet* (New Haven, 1912). G. Hunt, *The Department of State* (New Haven, 1914), is an excellent book, and it is unfortunate that there are not volumes of similar character on the other federal departments. The diplomatic service is described in F. Van Dyne, *Our Foreign Service* (Rochester, 1909), and J. W. Foster, *The Practice of Diplomacy as Illus-*

trated in the Foreign Relations of the United States (Boston, 1906). A serviceable book on the navy is R. W. Neeser, *Our Many-Sided Navy* (New Haven, 1917). D. S. Alexander, *History and Procedure of the House of Representatives* (Boston, 1916), meets a long-felt need; and S. W. McCall, *The Business of Congress* (New York, 1911), is a useful account by a former member of the House. H. B. Fuller, *The Speakers of the House* (Boston, 1909), deals in popular style with the personal side. The weakness of the federal fiscal system is laid bare in H. J. Ford, *The Cost of our National Government; a Study in Political Pathology* (New York, 1910).

Materials on the principles of "direct government" are presented in W. B. Munro [ed.], *The Initiative, Referendum, and Recall* (New York, 1912), and C. A. Beard and B. E. Schultz [eds.], *Documents on the State-Wide Initiative, Referendum, and Recall* (New York, 1912). The subject is discussed on general lines in E. P. Oberholtzer, *The Referendum, Initiative, and Recall in America* (new edition, New York, 1911); D. F. Wilcox, *Government by All the People* (New York, 1912); and a group of papers, "The Initiative, Referendum, and Recall," in Am. Acad. Polit. and Soc. Sci., *Annals*, XLIII. (1912). The workings of direct government in the state which has carried the system farthest are described briefly in A. H. Eaton, *The Oregon System* (Chicago, 1912), and to better effect in J. D. Barnett, *Operation of the Initiative, Referendum, and Recall in Oregon* (New York, 1915). See also Commission to Prepare Information for the Massachusetts Constitutional Convention, *Initiative and Referendum* (Boston, 1915).

The doctrine of judicial review is discussed in E. S. Corwin, *The Doctrine of Judicial Review; its Legal and Historical Basis* (Princeton, 1914); C. G. Haines, *The American Doctrine of Judicial Supremacy* (New York, 1914); and H. A. Davis, *The Judicial Veto* (Boston, 1914). Important general discussions are W. H. Taft, *Popular Government; its Essence, its Permanence, and its Perils* (New Haven, 1913), and N. M. Butler, *Why Should We Change Our Form of Government?* (New York, 1912).

Two valuable books on the neglected subject of state government were published at the close of the period: A. N. Holcombe, *State Government in the United States* (New

27

York, 1917), and J. M. Mathews, *Principles of American State Administration* (New York, 1917). Among many good treatises on municipal government, mention can be made of only W. B. Munro, *Government of American Cities* (revised edition, New York, 1916), and *Principles of Municipal Administration* (New York, 1916).

The main treatise on the short ballot is R. S. Childs, *Short Ballot Principles* (Boston, 1911). H. L. Sumner, *Equal Suffrage* (New York, 1909), is an impartial study of the operation of woman's suffrage in Colorado.

PARTIES AND POLITICAL MOVEMENTS

Important collections of speeches and other papers include: W. H. Taft, *Presidential Addresses and State Papers* (New York, 1910); T. Roosevelt, *The New Nationalism* (New York, 1911), comprising mainly speeches made during a western tour in 1910, and *Progressive Principles* (New York, 1913), containing speeches during the campaign of 1912; *Speeches of William Jennings Bryan, Revised and Arranged by Himself* (2 vols., New York, 1911); W. Wilson, *The New Freedom* (New York, 1913), consisting chiefly of speeches delivered during the campaign of 1912; J. G. Schurman [ed.], *Addresses of Charles Evans Hughes, 1906–1916* (revised edition, New York, 1916). E. Stanwood, *History of the Presidency* (2 vols., Boston, 1916), brings this standard work to the presidency of Wilson.

The period was notable for political unrest and party change; and many books were written—as a rule, by young men sympathetic with progressivism—to interpret public conditions and tendencies. F. C. Howe, *Privilege and Democracy in America* (New York, 1910), is suggestive, but not uniformly judicious. W. E. Weyl, *The New Democracy* (New York, 1912), is a thoughtful study. W. E. Walling, *Progressivism—and After* (New York, 1914), deals with tendencies in many nations, though chiefly the United States. A powerful argument for a new nationalism is H. Croly, *The Promise of American Life* (New York, 1909), and a keen historical analysis of American political and economic tendencies is the same author's *Progressive Democracy* (New York, 1914).

FOREIGN RELATIONS TO 1914

Much of the diplomatic correspondence prior to 1911 will be found in the annual volumes of *Foreign Relations.* The official collection of international agreements is W. M. Malloy [compiler], *Treaties, Conventions, International Acts, Protocols, and Agreements Between the United States of America and Other Powers, 1776–1909, Senate Documents,* 61 Cong., 2 Sess., No. 357. A Supplement (*Senate Documents,* 62 Cong., 3 Sess., No. 1063), compiled by G. Charles, brings the collection to March 4, 1913. The proceedings in the North Atlantic coast fisheries arbitration of 1910 are in *Senate Documents,* 61 Cong., 3 Sess., No. 870. The best general survey of the foreign relations of the United States is C. R. Fish, *American Diplomacy* (New York, 1915); although the subject is treated in greater detail in W. F. Johnson, *America's Foreign Relations* (2 vols., New York, 1915). The completion of a hundred years of continuous peace with Great Britain gave timeliness to H. C. Lodge, *One Hundred Years of Peace* (New York, 1913), and W. A. Dunning, *The British Empire and the United States* (New York, 1915). A forward-looking book is G. L. Beer, *The English-Speaking Peoples* (New York, 1917). W. E. Weyl, *American World Politics* (New York, 1917), contains a well-considered review of the country's foreign policies. R. Bacon and J. B. Scott [eds.], *Addresses of Elihu Root on International Subjects* (Cambridge, 1916), is a useful volume. See also titles under Latin American Relations below and Oriental Relations (p. 415).

LATIN AMERICAN RELATIONS

For correspondence and other materials relating to the diplomatic history of the Panama Canal from 1901 to 1910, see *Senate Documents,* 63 Cong., 2 Sess., No. 474. Committee hearings on the Canal in 1912 are reported in *House Documents,* 62 Cong., 2 Sess., No. 680. E. R. Johnson's report on Canal traffic and tolls is in *Senate Documents,* 62 Cong., 2 Sess., No. 575; on relations of the Canal to the railways, in *Senate Documents,* 63 Cong., 2 Sess., No. 875.

The diplomacy of the Canal project is accurately narrated in M. W. Williams, *Anglo-American Isthmian Diplomacy, 1815–1915* (Washington, 1916), and from the English point of view in L. Oppenheim, *The Panama Canal Conflict between Great Britain and the United States of America* (Cambridge, 1913). The commercial uses of the Canal are discussed in L. Hutchinson, *The Panama Canal and International Trade Competition* (New York, 1915), and E. R. Johnson, *The Panama Canal and Commerce* (New York, 1916).

The best work on the dealings of the United States with the countries around the Caribbean is C. Lloyd Jones, *The Caribbean Interests of the United States* (New York, 1916). Two other informing books on conditions in these countries are S. Bonsal, *The American Mediterranean* (New York, 1912), and F. Palmer, *Central America and its Problems* (New York, 1910).

Mexico under Diaz is well described in P. F. Martin, *Mexico of the Twentieth Century* (2 vols., London, 1907), and C. R. Enoch, *Mexico* (London, 1909). R. J. McHugh, *Modern Mexico* (London, 1914), is a satisfactory work of more recent date. Popular accounts of the country's condition after 1911 include J. K. Turner, *Barbarous Mexico* (4th edition, Chicago, 1914), and R. W. Smith, *Benighted Mexico* (New York, 1916). C. W. Barron, *The Mexican Problem* (New York, 1917), is a good survey of economic conditions. Mrs. E. L. O'Shaughnessy, *A Diplomat's Wife in Mexico* (New York, 1916), is an interesting collection of letters written from the American embassy in 1913–1914; and R. Batchelder, *Watching and Waiting on the Border* (Boston, 1917), is a vivid description of the work of frontier patrol. A serviceable biography is D. Hannay, *Porfirio Diaz* (New York, 1917).

The fullest and best discussion of the Monroe Doctrine is A. B. Hart, *The Monroe Doctrine; an Interpretation* (Boston, 1916); but of interest are H. Bingham, *The Monroe Doctrine; an Obsolete Shibboleth* (New Haven, 1913), and C. H. Sherrill, *Modernizing the Monroe Doctrine* (Boston, 1916). Mention should be made of A. C. Coolidge, *The United States as a World Power* (New York, 1908).

Commercial relations are dealt with in E. B. Filsinger, *Exporting to Latin America* (New York, 1916). An important collection of papers is G. H. Blakeslee [ed.], *Latin America* (New York, 1914). E. Root, *Latin America and the United States*, edited by R. Bacon and J. B. Scott (Cambridge, 1917), is a convenient volume of speeches and state papers. Latin American affairs as viewed by an English scholar and statesman are described in J. Bryce, *South America, Observations and Impressions* (New York, 1912); as seen by a French publicist, in G. Clemençeau, *South America of Today* (New York, 1912); and as observed by a young Peruvian diplomat, in F. G. Calderon, *Latin America: its Rise and Progress*, translated by B. Miall (New York, 1913).

ORIENTAL RELATIONS

The Far Eastern problems of the United States are fully surveyed, with an anti-Japanese slant, in T. F. Millard, *America and the Far Eastern Question* (New York, 1909), and the same author's *Our Eastern Question* (New York, 1916). American-Japanese tension provoked much discussion. Among useful books on the subject are C. Crow, *Japan and America; a Contrast* (New York, 1916); J. A. B. Scherer, *The Japanese Crisis* (New York, 1916); H. A. Millis, *The Japanese Problem in the United States* (New York, 1915); J. F. Abbot, *Japanese Expansion and American Policies* (2d edition, New York, 1916); J. F. Steiner, *The Japanese Invasion* (Chicago, 1917); M. Flowers, *The Japanese Conquest of American Opinion* (New York, 1916); and G. H. Blakeslee [ed.], *Japan and Japanese-American Relations* (New York, 1912). A well-considered plea for a more liberal attitude toward Japan is S. L. Gulick, *The American-Japanese Problem* (New York, 1914). The best discussions from the Japanese point of view are K. K. Kawakami, *American-Japanese Relations* (London, 1912), *Asia at the Door* (New York, 1914), and *Japan in World Politics* (New York, 1917). A useful survey of recent Oriental history is S. K. Hornbeck, *Contemporary Politics in the Far East* (New York, 1916). Among books which seek to interpret Far Eastern peoples and affairs to Americans, the best are P. S. Reinsch, *Intellectual and Political Currents in the Far East* (Boston, 1911); E. A. Ross, *The Changing Chinese* (New York, 1911); and A. B. Hart, *The Obvious Orient* (New York, 1911). An excellent introduction to Chinese history is K. S. Latourette, *The Development of China* (Boston, 1917). Chinese affairs in the twentieth century are well discussed in J. O. P. Bland, *Recent Events and Policies in China* (London, 1912), and A. R. Colquhoun, *China in Transformation* (revised edition, New York, 1912); and a detailed account of the Chinese revolution is given in F. McCormick, *The Flowery Republic* (New York, 1913). A book of solid worth is H. B. Morse, *The International Relations of the Chinese Empire* (New York, 1910). For current events in the Orient see *Japan Year-Book; China Year-Book; Far Eastern Review* (1904—); and *Asia*, succeeding the *Journal of the American Asiatic Association* (1898–1917).

THE PEACE MOVEMENT

There are several editions of the documents drawn up and adopted at the two Hague conferences. One is J. B. Scott, *The Hague Peace Conferences of 1899 and 1907* (2 vols., Baltimore, 1909). Another is A. P. Higgins, *The Hague Peace Conferences and Other International Conferences concerning the Laws and Usages of War* (Cambridge, 1909). The most convenient is *The Hague Conventions and Declarations of 1899 and 1907* (New York, 1915), published for the Carnegie Endowment for International Peace. The work of the conferences is discussed in the first of Scott's volumes, and more briefly in W. I. Hull, *The Two Hague Conferences and their Contributions to International Law* (Boston, 1908), and J. H. Choate, *The Two Hague Conferences* (Princeton, 1913). Another important publication of the Carnegie Endowment is J. B. Scott, *The Status of the International Court of Justice* (New York, 1916), accompanied by a volume of documents. The influence of the United States for peace is described in W. H. Taft, *The United States and Peace* (New York, 1914), and W. I. Hull, *The New Peace Movement* (Boston, 1912). An argument for the judicial

settlement of international disputes is presented in N. M.
Butler, *The International Mind* (New York, 1913), and a
promising movement prompted by the Great War is ex-
plained in R. Goldsmith, *A League to Enforce Peace* (New
York, 1917).   A work of large vision is T. Veblen, *An Inquiry into the Nature of Peace and the Terms of its Preservation* (New York, 1917).   The literature of the subject
grows rapidly through the publications of the World Peace
Foundation, the American Association for International
Conciliation, and the American Society for the Judicial
Settlement of International Disputes.   The activities of the
Carnegie Endowment for International Peace are described
in its *Year Book* (1911—).

THE GREAT WAR

The international conflict which began in 1914 led to an
unprecedented outpouring of documents, pamphlets, and
books.   Much was published in haste, and only a small
portion of this earlier output will prove of lasting worth.
Desiring to justify their actions before the world, the various
belligerent governments made public an unusual quantity
of diplomatic correspondence and other official papers.
This material—brought forth in "red books," "white books,"
etc.—is of large value.   Yet historians will probably have
long to wait for the numberless important documents that
have not been disclosed.   A convenient edition of the materials first made available is J. B. Scott [ed.], *Diplomatic
Documents relating to the Outbreak of the European War*
(2 vols., New York, 1916), published for the Carnegie Endowment for International Peace.   A monumental collection of
source materials is the *Times* [London], *Documentary History
of the War*, to be completed in several volumes (London,
1917—).

A general history of the war, including numerous documents, is the *European War* (New York Times Current History, 12 vols. to 1917).   On diplomatic antecedents of the war
see C. Seymour, *The Diplomatic Background of the War, 1870–
1914* (New Haven, 1916), and A. Bullard (pseud.), *The Diplomacy of the Great War* (New York, 1916).   M. P. Price, *The*

Diplomatic History of the War (revised edition, London, 1915), brings together the best available documents, and E. C. Stowell, *The Diplomacy of the Great War of 1914; the Beginnings of the War* (Boston, 1915), is the first volume of a carefully written diplomatic history, with documents.

Among books intended primarily to acquaint Americans with the causes and conditions of the war are A. B. Hart, *The War in Europe* (New York, 1914); F. H. Simonds, *The Great War; the First Phase* (New York, 1914), and *The Great War; the Second Phase* (New York, 1915); E. F. Baldwin, *The World War* (New York, 1914). The German view is set forth in H. Münsterburg, *The War and America* (New York, 1914), and E. von Mach, *What Germany Wants* (Boston, 1914), and *Germany's Point of View* (Chicago, 1915). The English view is well stated in R. Muir, *Britain's Case against Germany* (Manchester, 1914); the French, in Y. Guyot, *Causes and Consequences of the War*, translated by F. A. Holt (London, 1916). The conflicting testimony is weighed in J. M. Beck, *The Evidence in the Case* (New York, 1914), with results unfavorable to Germany.

Bibliographies of the subject include the following: G. H. Blakeslee, *List of Books* (Worcester, 1917). A. B. Hart, *America at War* (New York, 1917)—references, analyses, sources.

THE UNITED STATES AND THE GREAT WAR

Portions of the diplomatic correspondence between the United States and the belligerent governments concerning neutral rights are printed in the *American Journal of International Law*, IX., special supp. (July, 1915). Important groups of papers are G. H. Blakeslee [ed.], *The Problems and Lessons of the War* (New York, 1916); A. B. Hart *et al.*, *Problems of Readjustment after the War* (New York, 1915); "International Relations of the United States," in Am. Acad. Polit. and Soc. Sci., *Annals*, LIV. (1914); "America's Interests as Affected by the European War," *ibid.*, LX. (1915); "America's Interests after the European War," *ibid.*, LXI. (1915); "America's Relation to the World Conflict," *ibid.*, LXXII. (1917); "The Foreign Relations of the

419] CRITICAL ESSAY ON AUTHORITIES   419

United States," in Acad. Polit. Sci., *Proceedings* VII., (1917).
H. C. Lodge, *War Addresses* (Boston, 1917), is a useful collection of speeches by a leading member of the Senate. The
position of the United States is discussed in P. M. Brown,
International Realities (New York, 1916), and a plea for American leadership in international affairs is made in Norman
Angell (pseud.), *America and the New World State* (New York,
1915).   C. G. Fenwick, *The Neutrality Laws of the United
States* (Washington, 1913), is an authoritative work. The
war's economic bearings are considered in E. J. Clapp,
Economic Aspects of the War (New Haven, 1915); J. C.
Brown, *The Tariff and the Coming Trade War* (New York,
1916); and T. J. Hughes, *State Socialism after the War*
(New York, 1916). The experiences of the American ambassador at the German Imperial Court from 1913 to 1917
are related in J. W. Gerard, *My Four Years in Germany*
(New York, 1917).

The history of the American land forces from colonial
times to 1915 is fully presented in F. L. Huidekoper, *The
Military Unpreparedness of the United States* (New York,
1915). Increased preparedness is urged in H. D. Wheeler,
Are We Ready? (Boston, 1915); F. V. Greene, *The Present
Military Situation in the United States* (New York, 1915);
T. Roosevelt, *America and the World War* (New York, 1915),
and *Fear God and Take Your Own Part* (New York, 1916).
A group of papers of uneven value is "Preparedness and
America's International Problem," in Am. Acad. Polit. and
Soc. Sci., *Annals*, LXVI. (1916).

A condensed list of books on the war is A. B. Hart and A.
O. Lovejoy, *Handbook of the War for Public Speakers* (New
York, 1917); and an extended classified bibliography is given
in A. B. Hart, *America: References, Outline, Sources* (New
York, 1917).

INDEX

424 INDEX

ened by United States with severance of diplomatic relations, 343; proposes negotiations for peace (1916), 390–391; announces extension of submarine warfare, 393; United States severs diplomatic relations with, 394; at war with United States, 395–396; defense of her course, 398.

Gomez, J. M., elected president of Cuba, 249; starts revolution in 1916, 251.

Gompers, S., support of Bryan in 1908, 14; influence in American Federation of Labor, 77; views on the character of labor, 81.

Great Britain, protests against exemption of American coastwise shipping from Panama tolls, 271–274; yields to Mexican policy of United States, 292; proposes "naval holiday," 325–326; restricts neutral trade by orders in council, 334–335; extends rules of blockade and contraband, 336–337; replies to American protests, 337; purchases in United States, 345–347; refuses to negotiate with Germany (1916), 392–393.

Great War, suddenness of outbreak, 328–329; American neutrality proclaimed, 329; divided opinion in United States, 330–331; British restrictions on neutral trade, 334–335; Germany inaugurates submarine campaign, 335–336; the *Lusitania* crisis, 338–342; United States threatens severance of diplomatic relations with Germany, 343; effect on American financial status, 347–348; causes United States to increase shipping, 349–350; effects on taxation in United States, 351–353; stimulates military preparations in United States, 385–388; Germany proposes peace negotiations, 390–391; Wilson requests statement

of European war aims, 392; Entente powers refuse to negotiate, 392–393; Germany announces extension of submarine warfare, 393; United States severs diplomatic relations with Germany, 394; United States declares a state of war with Germany, 395–396; development of American attitude toward, 396–399; bibliography, 417–419.

Grey, E., defends British restrictions on neutral trade, 335.

Haiti, becomes protectorate of United States, 259–260.

Harlan, J., opinion in Standard Oil case, 70–71.

Harriman, E. H., railroad power, 41–42.

Harrison, F. B., appointed governor-general of Philippines, 237.

Hearst, W. R., and the Independence League, 5.

Hill, J. J., railroad interests, 41–42.

Hitchcock, F. H., Republican campaign manager in 1908, 11.

House of Representatives, power of Speaker, 171–172; question of reorganization in special session of 1909, 173; committees reconstituted, 179–180.

Huerta, V., becomes provisional president of Mexico, 288; Wilson administration withholds recognition, 289–291; question of salute to American flag, 293; resigns, 294.

Hughes, C. E., nominated for the presidency (1916), 369–370; overtures to Progressives, 372; strength as a candidate, 375–376; campaign activities, 377–378; defeat, 379–383.

Immigration, increase after 1900, 122; relation to alien departures, 123; economic and political effects, 123–124; earlier regulation, 125; investigated by fed-